COGNITIVE ANALYTIC THERAPY

COGNITIVE ANALYTIC THERAPY

Developments in Theory and Practice

Edited by

Anthony Ryle

UMDS at Guy's Hospital, Munro Clinic, London, UK

JOHN WILEY & SONS

Chichester · New York · Brisbane · Toronto · Singapore

Other Wiley Editorial Offices

John Wiley & Sons, Inc., 605 Third Avenue,
New York, NY 10158-0012, USA

Jacaranda Wiley Ltd, 33 Park Road, Milton,
Queensland 4064, Australia

John Wiley & Sons (Canada) Ltd, 22 Worcester Road,
Rexdale, Ontario M9W 1L1, Canada

John Wiley & Sons (SEA) Pte Ltd, 37 Jalan Pemimpin #05-04,
Block B, Union Industrail Building, Singapore 129809

Library of Congress Cataloging-in-Publication Data
Cognitive analytic therapy : developments in theory and practice /
    edited by Anthony Ryle.
        p.   cm. — (Wiley series in psychotherapy and counselling)
    Includes bibliographical references and index.
    ISBN 0-471-95602-3 (cased). — ISBN 0-471-94355-X (pbk.)
    1. Cognitive-analytic therapy.   I. Ryle, Anthony.   II. Series:
Wiley series on psychotherapy and counselling.
    [DNLM: 1. Cognitive Therapy.   WM 425 C6752 1995]
    RC489.C6C64   1995
    616.89′ 142—dc20
    DNLM/DLC
    for Library of Congress   94-45112
                                                                        CIP
British Library Cataloguing in Publication Data

A catalogue record for this book is available from the British Library

ISBN 0-471-95602-3 (cased)
ISBN 0-471-94355-X (paper)

Typeset in 10/12 Times by Vision Typesetting, Manchester, UK
Printed and bound in Great Britain by Biddles Ltd, Guildford and King's Lynn

This book is printed on acid-free paper responsibly manufactured from
sustainable forestation, for which at least two trees are planted for each
one used for paper production.

Contents

About the Editor

Anthony Ryle, *CAT office, Munro Clinic, Guy's Hospital, London SE1 9RT, UK*

Anthony Ryle qualified in medicine in 1949 and was until 1964 in general practice where his interest in neuroses and therapy began and where his first research was carried out. He was Director of the University Health Service at the University of Sussex and then Consultant Psychotherapist at St Thomas's Hospital, London until his retirement in 1992. He is now Senior Research Fellow and Honorary Consultant Psychotherapist at UMDS at Guy's Hospital, London. Dr Ryle is the author of five previous books and of over 70 papers and chapters in the field of psychotherapy research and theory, and has been involved in the initiation and development of Cognitive Analytic Therapy, research and theory, since the late 1970s.

Contributors

Gillian Butler, *Departments of Psychology and Psychiatry, Warneford Hospital, Oxford OX3 7JX, UK*

Gillian Butler is a consultant clinical psychologist in the Department of Psychology and University Department of Psychiatry at Warneford Hospital. She is interested in CBT, in particular for complex, longstanding problems. Having done research into the treatment of anxiety states, she is now focusing on worry and social anxiety.

Pauline Cowmeadow, *York Clinic, Guy's Hospital, St Thomas's Street, London SE1 1NP, UK*

Pauline Cowmeadow is a consultant psychotherapist at Guy's Hospital. She has trained in CAT and in long-term psychotherapy. Her special interests include work with patients in medical settings, and developing psychotherapy within the National Health Service.

Francesca Denman, *Psychotherapy Department, Casell Hospital, 1 Ham Common, Richmond, Surrey TW10 7JF, UK*

Chess Denman trained at Guy's Hospital and at the Cassell Hospital. She is now Consultant Psychotherapist at Addenbrookes Hospital, Cambridge. Her special interests include audit and research in psychotherapy.

Tim Leighton, *Clouds House, East Knoyle, Salisbury, Wiltshire, SP3 6BE, UK*

Tim Leighton is director of training and research at Clouds House addiction treatment centre. He now teaches and supervises CAT.

Mikael Leiman, *Department of Psychology, University of Joensuu, PO Box 111, 80101 Joensuu, Finland*

Mikael Leiman is a psychologist at the University of Jeonsuu. He has played a major part in the theoretical development of CAT and has established a training programme in Finland.

Norma Maple, *25 Burlington Avenue, Kew, Richmond, Surrey TW9 4DF, UK*

Norma Maple is a CAT therapist and group analyst. She trained at the Institute of Group Analysis and in CAT at Guy's Hospital, where she continues to have a clinical and teaching role.

John Marzillier, *24 Norham Road, Oxford OX2 6SF, UK*

John Marzillier is a clinical psychologist and psychotherapist in private practice. He is interested in teaching and research into integration of cognitive and psychodynamic therapies, and on ethical dilemmas in the practice of psychotherapy.

Ian Simpson, *Department of Psychotherapy, St Thomas's Hospital, London SE1 7EH, UK*

Ian Simpson trained at the Institute of Group Analysis and works as a groupwork supervisor in the Department of Psychotherapy at St Thomas's Hospital

Preface

This book offers an account of the evolution and features of Cognitive Analytic Therapy (CAT) and a review of the main developments of the past five years. As regards practice, the core features of the model are firmly established; Chapter 2 summarises my idea of the current 'state of the art' and is as near to manualisation as I would wish to go. Clinical work with three difficult groups of patients is described in Chapter 1, with regard to borderline personality disorder; in Chapter 3, where Pauline Cowmeadow describes work with deliberate self-harmers; and in Chapter 4, where Francesca Denman considers the problems of working with subjects with eating disorders.

Theoretical developments have, up to now, depended largely on my own writing and that of Mikael Leiman, and the latter takes this further in Chapter 6, in which he proposes a key role in human psychology for sign mediation. Despite the fact that most CAT therapists have prior training in other models and in many cases continue to work in them, there has been relatively little discussion of the contradictions and confusions this may engender. For this reason no attempt has been made to impose a uniform voice on the other contributors. For example, in their authoritative review of developments in cognitive therapy, John Marzillier and Gillian Butler describe many convergences with CAT but, to my mind, offer a version of CAT which concedes too much to both psychoanalytic and cognitive theories and which raises many of the issues discussed critically by Leiman. Clearly, further debate is called for here. Other issues are addressed more directly in Tim Leighton's discussion, with me, of CAT's right to call itself analytic, and in Chapter 5 where Norma Maple and Ian Simpson consider the compatibility of CAT and group analysis.

CAT developed from a research orientation, and has (too slowly) accumulated a body of research, summarised in Chapter 10. This chapter and the discussion of audit in Chapter 9, represent a willingness to assess the model and will, it is to be hoped, be a stimulus to an increasing volume of empirical work.

The last five years have seen the establishment of basic training in many places in the UK and abroad, the graduation of the first UKCP-recognised psychotherapists from the advanced training, and the establishment of the Association of Cognitive Analytic Therapists. The work of the contributors to this book rests upon the teachers, supervisors, organisers and therapists who have borne the strains of a rapidly expanding enterprise, and thanks are due to all these people. Particular thanks are due to Mark Dunn and the overworked, under-resourced office staff at the Munro Clinic, to Professor J.P. Watson for maintaining and developing the links between ACAT and the medical school (UMDS) at Guy's hospital (I believe to our mutual advantage) and, finally, to Michael Coombs, Wendy Hudlass and others at John Wiley & Sons, who have always been helpful, straightforward and efficient in their dealings with me.

Anthony Ryle
February 1995

1 Cognitive Analytic Therapy: history and recent developments

Anthony Ryle

Cognitive Analytic Therapy (CAT) is a time-limited, integrated psychotherapy. Its features and development have been described in two previous books (Ryle, 1982, 1990) and in numerous papers, but both the theory and the practice continue to evolve and will, it is to be hoped, continue to do so. This book is therefore an account of work in progress, and is addressed both to new readers and to the increasing number of workers who are involved in the practice of CAT. It is also a reflection of the contributions of many of the latter in practice, theory and research,

This first chapter offers a summary of the evolution of CAT, with, in particular, a review of the main developments of the past five years. In the second chapter an up-to-date description of CAT clinical practice will be presented, in a form which aims to define what CAT is without becoming a therapy cookbook. In the remaining chapters a number of authors will consider clinical and theoretical issues within CAT and related fields.

The pre-history of CAT

The origins of CAT may be traced back to my extensive use of repertory grid techniques (Kelly, 1955) to study the characteristics of psychotherapy patients and to investigate the nature of change brought about by therapy; this work was summarised in Ryle (1975). The experience of applying this cognitive approach to therapies carried out on psychodynamic lines and contact with

Cognitive Analytic Therapy: Developments in Theory and Practice, Edited by A. Ryle
© 1995 John Wiley & Sons Ltd

personal construct theory generated a search for a 'common language' for the psychotherapies (Ryle, 1978). At the same time the continuing use of grid techniques to measure change, and the mobilisation of patients' reflective capacities in the course of administering and feeding back grid tests, contributed to the development of new ways of describing core neurotic problems in terms of three patterns, labelled dilemmas, traps and snags (Ryle, 1979). These descriptions, in turn, opened a new way to measure individual change in therapy. It was from these sources that the 'cognitive' concerns and collaborative style of CAT emerged.

Dilemmas, traps and snags are described in the 'Psychotherapy File' (see Appendix 2.1 to Chapter 2). This file is given to patients at the end of the first therapy session, and those descriptions identified by patients as applying are discussed in subsequent meetings. From these discussions and from other evidence a written list of the neurotic processes which therapy will aim to modify is prepared. Neurosis, on this basis, was understood to represent the persistent use of restrictive or damaging strategies; the three identified patterns described three ways in which these strategies had, up to the present time, resisted revision. The next stage in the evolution of CAT was to locate these patterns in a general model of the organisation of intentional action, the Procedural Sequence Model.

Basic theory and practice: the Procedural Sequence Model

The Procedural Sequence Model (PSM), first presented in detail in Ryle (1982), established a theoretical model in which current behavioural and cognitive models could be accommodated, and which served also as a basis for the restatement of a number of psychoanalytic ideas, using a cognitive language. According to this model, intentional acts or the enactment of roles in relationships are maintained by repetitive sequences of mental, behavioural and environmental processes, as follows: (1) perception and (2) appraisal in terms of knowledge, values, other plans and predicted consequences; (3) the (effective or not) enactment; (4) the consequences of the enactment (notably the responses of others) are evaluated; leading to (5) the confirmation or revision of the aim and of the means. While the psychodynamic concern with conflict can be included in this description, notably at stage 2, the main emphasis is on the ways in which procedures are self-reinforcing, and, in the case of problem procedures, particularly resistant to revision. Most procedures, and the higher-order procedures whereby they are activated, operate without conscious thought, but certain aspects of enacted procedures are open to self-reflection.

The therapeutic methods which developed alongside the evolution of this model were centred on the process of reformulation. During the first three to four weeks of therapy patients are involved in self-monitoring symptoms, unwanted behaviours and mood shifts, and in reading and discussing the Psychotherapy File. This, combined with the therapist's consideration of the patient's history and current situation and of the developing therapy relationship, culminates in the identification and listing of the main Target Problems (TPs) and the underlying dilemmas, traps and snags (Target Problem Procedures, TPPs). This is discussed in detail, modified as necessary and then agreed. It forms the agenda and 'scaffolding' of the therapy. The remaining sessions, usually twelve in number, are devoted to the recognition of these TPPs through diary keeping and other forms of self-monitoring and through the noting of them as they are presented in the narratives brought to therapy and as they are enacted in the therapy relationship. Once recognition is achieved, revision may involve specific behavioural techniques, role play or other techniques, but in most cases the heightened and more accurate self-reflection, coupled with the experience of an explicit, non-collusive relationship with the therapist, allows the development of new procedures.

Developments from 1982 to 1989

The next stage of the development of CAT involved the more systematic incorporation of ideas from the object relations theories, notably as presented by Ogden (Ogden, 1983; Ryle, 1985). In this, the idea of *reciprocal role procedures* (RRPs) was emphasised. As in all procedures, the prediction of the outcome of one's acts is an important aspect of the sequence; in *role* procedures these are, above all, the responses of others. Reciprocal role procedures are seen to develop on the basis of early relationships. The infant is seen as learning to respond to or elicit the caretaker's role behaviours, but also as becoming able to enact this other role (for example, to dolls, to others, to the self). Hence each relationship is the basis on which two (reciprocal) roles are learned. The *repertoire of reciprocal roles* so acquired is the basis of relating to others (one role being played, the other elicited) and also of self management, insofar as patterns of relationships with caretakers determine how the self is cared for and controlled. The repertoire of childhood will be open to subsequent elaborations, but an individual's array acquires a certain stability early on, due largely to the way in which others are chosen or induced or seen to offer reciprocations apparently confirming the repertoire.

This model differs from the Kleinian view in that, while innate variations in the power of feelings clearly exist, it is early life experience or trauma and deprivation rather than clashes between innate instinctual forces which are seen to determine the range and quality of an individual's repertoire, and the degree to which it becomes integrated. The phenomenon of splitting (the presence of contrasted, more-or-less dissociated ways of construing self and the world) is understood in the CAT model to reflect a failure of integration, usually in the face of fairly gross deprivation, trauma or inconsistency, rather than as having a primarily defensive function against innate instinctual forces. The persistence of splitting is understood as being the result of the way in which individuals are able to elicit confirmation from others for each of their separate, split-off 'sub-personalities' or 'self-states'. Splitting both causes and is maintained by the absence of a central self-observing capacity. Projective identification is understood as a form of relating, in which pressure is put upon the other to respond in a way representing the feared or disavowed pole of a dissociated reciprocal role pattern (see Ryle (1994d) for an elaboration of this). Symptoms and defences such as repression and denial are characteristics of particular relationship and self-management procedures, shaped in ways which avoid certain feelings or aims because of their earlier feared or forbidden implications.

On the basis of this model the neurotic individual is understood in terms of the restrictions or distortions evident in his or her procedural repertoire. Some procedures may be characterised by a particular inability to reflect upon, remember, perceive or acknowledge certain situations or wishes. The problems of patients with borderline personality disorder are further compounded by the fact that their range of procedures is divided between a number of more-or-less dissociated self-states; developments in the descriptions of borderline structure are described below.

In line with these theoretical clarifications there were further elaborations in clinical methods. As part of the generally collaborative approach of CAT it had become common practice to show patients the written summaries of their assessment interviews. From this evolved a new component in the reformulation process: at the fourth session therapists summarised their understanding of the patient's situation, usually in the form of a letter, sometimes in the patient's own voice. These rehearse the history and present circumstances, proposing a different emphasis on many aspects of the story, with the aim of acknowledging personal meanings and feelings more directly and of attributing responsibility more equably. They trace how present problematic procedures are either repetitions of early harmful patterns or are (costly) attempted 'solutions' to early situations, now serving to cause difficulty or restriction. Such issues will be explored jointly in the first three sessions and, at the fourth, the therapist will offer a written summary of them for detailed discussion and, if necessary, revision. This account will conclude with a list of the problem procedures identified and will anticipate how these may influence the therapy relationship and the work of therapy. These written descriptions are usually supplemented by *sequential diagrammatic reformulation* (SDR), in which a flow diagram is constructed tracing how current procedures serve to maintain or reinforce current negative patterns.

The developments summarised above were described in the first book to present CAT as a formal psychotherapy method (Ryle, 1990). During and since that time developments in cognitive psychotherapy, in psychoanalysis and in other integrative approaches have indicated parallel or convergent tendencies. Thus within cognitive therapy interest in personality structure and in the therapy relationship has grown (e.g. Guidano, 1987; Lockwood and Young 1992; and see Chapter 7 in this volume). In psychoanalysis the relevance of observational studies has been increasingly recognised (Stern, 1985; Westen, 1990) and cognitive processes have been more attended to (Westen, 1991). Several authors, while retaining a basically psychoanalytic approach and confining interventions to interpretation, have demonstrated how interventions are normally focused on a small number of core issues, and have shown how these recur both in the patient's narratives and in their way of relating to the therapist (Horowitz and Eels, 1993; Luborsky, Barber and Diguer, 1992). In the integrative field, Wachtel's early (1977) integration of behavioural and psychoanalytic ideas and methods has led to the model of 'Cyclical Psychodynamics' (Gold and Wachtel, 1993) which, in its emphasis on self-maintaining vicious circles, in its attention to both intra- and inter-psychological processes and in its use of a range of therapeutic methods, is close to CAT. Safran's (1990a, b) linking of traditional cognitive and behavioural therapy with interpersonal theory, and his concepts of the interpersonal schema and the cognitive–interpersonal cycle and his emphasis on the use of the therapy relationship to 'disconfirm dysfunctional interpersonal schemas' is also similar in most respects. In the field of group therapy Wessler (1993) describes another CAT (Cognitive Appraisal Therapy) which shares many assumptions and methods with Cognitive Analytic Therapy.

Recent developments

During the past five years the theoretical base of CAT has been further elaborated, with ideas from object relations theories being more fully integrated and linked with those derived from the works of Vygotsky and his followers and from Bakhtin (Ryle, 1991; Leiman, 1992, 1994a). At the same time the exploration of the differences between CAT theory and psychoanalytic ideas continued (Ryle, 1992, 1993, 1994a). These developments were reflected in practice in a clearer and more theory-based approach to reformulation, especially as regards Sequential Diagrammatic Reformulation. These changes were especially influential in the development of understandings of borderline personality disorder. The research which took place during this time, reviewed in Chapter 10, also contributed to, and was shaped by, these developments. In the rest of this chapter the following topics will be considered: the Procedural Sequence Object Relations Model and the SDR; Vygotsky and Bakhtin; the continuing debate with psychoanalysis; new observational studies of child development and new understandings of borderline personality disorder.

The Procedural Sequence Object Relations Model and developments in Sequential Diagrammatic Reformulation

Reformulation based on the Procedural Sequence Model described individual procedures in terms of the aim, following the processes of thought and action involved through to the consequence and, in the case of neurosis, to non-revision. The aim was to identify general procedural patterns capable of encompassing a wide range of individual activities. Links with other procedures might be indicated, for example, at the stages in the sequence of appraisal, action planning and prediction of consequences, but in general each procedure was addressed as an individual problem. In most cases there would be three or four procedures described in a reformulation, but some of these might be alternative ways of describing the same basic phenomenon; for example, a self-destructive act might be attributed to a dilemma ('as if I must harm myself or harm others') or as a snag ('as if guilty and therefore self-punishing').

The development of the Sequential Diagrammatic Reformulation technique (Beard, Marlowe and Ryle, 1990) allowed the sequential, self-maintaining nature of procedures to be conveyed more explicitly and precisely, and also opened the way to a clearer description of how different procedures might be connected. For example, the fear or expectation of abandonment by others could be shown to generate a dilemma '*either* involved, risking abandonment, *or* avoiding closeness (abandoning the other)'. The former role could in turn generate procedures for controlling emotionally significant others. The latter could lead to compensatory symptomatic procedures such as bulimia, which could substitute for emotional emptiness.

The formal qualities of the SDR were only slowly established. Early sequences of states, acts and consequences were followed by the construction of a central core, from which the various procedures were seen to be generated. This was usually identified in terms of a single role or state, such as 'abused' or 'rejected', being based on reported early experiences and comparable to the 'chronically endured pain' identified by Mann and Goldman (1982). This practice, however, reflected or encouraged the tendency of many therapists to recognise and respond more easily to the deprived and abused aspect of their patients than to the depriving, abusing aspects. To correct this, and to reflect the focus in the emerging Procedural Sequence Object Relations Model

(PSORM) on the reciprocal role patterns derived from early experience, the practice of describing the core in terms of reciprocal roles, in particular Inner Parent–Inner Child (IP–IC) relations (such as 'powerfully rejecting inner parent to submissive and needy inner child') was adopted. Relationship procedures derived from such a core could be seen to reflect the enactment of either the IP or IC role in relation to another (playing the complementary IC or IP role). Self-management patterns could often be seen to be modelled on the same reciprocal roles. There remained, however, three problems with this approach to the SDR. Firstly, it could lead to a too simple equation of reported early experience with the role patterns, ignoring the often partial, polarised or distorted perceptions of the child. Secondly, it could lead to a neglect of other formative relationships. Thirdly, the core reciprocal role pattern could be treated as a representation of the 'inner world' of the patient, rather than as a major determinant of behaviour and the basis on which subsequent experience is patterned. I now consider it best to regard the core repertoire of reciprocal roles as an heuristic device, serving to link and explain a range of phenomena. The construction of the core will draw on a range of data, including the history, current patterns of self-management and of relating to others, the emerging transference and countertransference responses and may involve hypothesising what roles (roles being understood to include action, emotion and communication) might have been replaced by avoidant, defensive or symptomatic procedures. The presumed parent–child origins of many role patterns, which often make sense to the patient, may still be indicated as IP–IC procedures, provided that the considerations above are remembered.

The emphasis on reciprocal role patterns encompasses the concepts described in psychoanalysis in terms of identification, introjection and projection, internal objects and part objects. A particular role is not granted the quasi-autonomous status of an internal object, but such roles may be modelled on historical figures or may appear as idealised characters in dreams or fantasy. Such figures, however, need to be thought of in relation to their reciprocating roles; St George implies the dragon and the dragon implies St George. Roles which were historically untenable, through prohibitions or associated unmanageable affects, may be 'projected' (that is, induced in the other) or they may be replaced by symptomatic or avoidant procedures, or by defensive procedures in which there is restricted access to memory, feeling or wish. All such procedures, once established, will be stable due to the fact that the confirming reciprocations of the enacted role can usually be elicited from others, leaving the core repertoire unchanged. Compared with the PSM, the PSORM offers, in this way, a more general understanding of the stability of personality.

Taking account of these theoretical developments, it will be clear that the present reformulation process, described in detail in the next chapter, is a complex procedure, requiring both conceptual clarity and accurate empathy from the therapist. The complete diagrammatic and written reformulation combines the two modes of conveying knowledge and influence described by Bruner (Bruner, 1986; Ryle, 1994b). Thus the letter is an example of the 'narrative' mode whereby experience may be endowed with different meanings, while the TP and TPP descriptions and the SDR represent the 'paradigmatic' mode, offering descriptions the accuracy of which has been, and will be, tested against experience. The completion of the reformulation and the patient's participation in this task will have initiated the work of therapy and the reformulation itself will be in active use through the rest of therapy. How this may contribute to change will now be considered in the light of the ideas of Vygotsky and Bakhtin.

Vygotsky, Bakhtin and the debate with Psychoanalysis

An early influence on the development of CAT was a paper describing Bruner's development of Vygotskian ideas (Wood, Bruner and Ross, 1976). This introduced the notion of the 'scaffolding' role of the teacher in providing, but progressively handing over, the tools or concepts necessary for the ordering and execution of a task. The direct introduction of Vygotskian ideas followed my meeting with Mikael Leiman in 1983, at which he recognised similarities between the PSM and the use made of reformulation in CAT and Vygotsky's (1962, 1978) emphasis on mediation in higher mental processes and Leonjew's (referred to in Leiman, 1994b) circular and hierarchical model of higher mental functions. A comparison of 'activity theory' (derived from Vygotsky and his school) and object relations theories as presented in the PSM was presented in Ryle (1991). In this paper it was suggested that activity theory and object relations theory were complementary in many ways. The understanding of higher learning through joint activity with a more experienced other, offered by activity theory, was extended to therapy, as being at least partly analogous; it was suggested that the best approach was for the therapist (teacher) to involve the patient (pupil) in tasks for which appropriate concepts are provided and for which responsibility is progressively handed over. This understanding is in marked contrast to the idea that change requires the induction of regression.

A year later Leiman (1992) extended this integrative endeavour in a paper critically examining the limitations of Vygotsky's definition of the sign. In a consideration of Winnicott's concept of the transitional object on the one hand, and of the writings of Bakhtin on the other, he pointed out how these disparate sources converge in locating, as initially *between* people, the signs (transitional objects, words, all cultural artifacts) which, when internalised,. are the basis of the individual psyche. The earliest developmental stages, understood as joint action sequences, were further considered in Leiman (1994a).

The contribution of a theory of sign mediation to the understanding of early development is considered by Leiman in Chapter 6. This approach is an important contribution, emphasising the cultural, that is the specifically human, elements in human personality. In highlighting the role of dialogue in human thought and personality (see Holquist, 1990) these ideas can largely replace the pseudo-biological elements of psychoanalytic theory, and correct what Leiman identified as a 'cognitivist' bias in the PSM and PSORM. Our aims and our intentions, as much as the other characteristics of our procedural repertoire, are learned in interaction with others and mediated by the language and concepts of the culture we are raised in. We do not, usually, validate our acts like scientists but we can reflect upon them using our more or less adequate symbolic mediating tools, notably language. From which it follows that the extension of the capacity for self-reflection is an appropriate aim of therapy (Leiman, 1994b).

It is of interest to consider an early discussion of psychoanalysis from this viewpoint. Despite its polemical style, the critique of the philosophical assumptions underlying psychoanalysis, written in the twenties by Voloshinov (a colleague of, or pseudonym for, Bakhtin) (Voloshinov, 1987) raises many issues which are still of relevance. Voloshinov argues that Freud, while attempting and claiming a scientific psychology, was in fact trapped in the assumptions of subjective psychology, projecting into the unconscious many of the same qualities as are characteristic of the conscious. The polarisation of the conscious and unconscious, their 'mutual incomprehension and hostility' and their 'endeavour to deceive each other' suggest to Voloshinov a relation between 'two ideas, two ideological trends, two antagonistic persons', rather than opposing, essentially different, psychical forces.

However, in the object relations school of psychoanalysis, the unconscious has been increasingly described in terms compatible with Voloshinov's conflicting ideas and antagonistic persons; one could argue that, in this respect, Freud's projection of the qualities of the conscious into the unconscious turned out to have been appropriate. The dynamic unconscious can be understood as the suppressed partner in an inner relationship, of whom we are not directly aware but whose existence is declared by unbidden thoughts and omissions and, more importantly, by evidently motivated acts and in the determining of our relationships with self and others. It is no less shaped by our experiences than are those aspects we can reflect upon, and is equally formed through culturally transmitted 'signs'.

The fascination exerted by the 'discovery' of the unconscious, and with the decoding of obscure messages from it, has dominated psychoanalysis, and neither other forms of unconsciousness nor the source and form of consciousness have been attended to with the same enthusiasm. The polarisation of conscious and unconscious has obscured the common origins and shared features of the two systems. In my view, the mythic elements of psychoanalytic theory, whether expressed as the clash of dark forces or named after heroes like Oedipus, are reflections of how culture has shaped both the conscious and unconscious mind. Myths are powerful because they distil the experience of centuries. But they refer to the content, not the structure, of mind, or demonstrate how the mind's functioning is shaped both by its biological properties and by the way experience is reordered through signs which in turn determine further activity and the shaping of further experience.

The practical implications of these differences in outlook are manifest in CAT in the central role accorded to *descriptive reformulation*. Procedural descriptions do not distinguish between procedures or parts of procedures which are open to introspection and those which are not. The description of a procedure may be derived from the patient's introspection, that is to say upon the aspects of inner dialogue which he or she can report, but must also take account of a range of other observations. We enact procedures all the time without reflection and without recall of the circumstances under which they were formed. The two poles of a dilemma, the evident source of a snag, or the assumptions generating a trap, may or may not be in awareness. But whether awareness is partial or complete, and whether the formative events or situations are recalled or buried in amnesia, the shape of the procedure may still be discerned. Once this has been achieved, consciousness can intervene to block or modify the procedure.

If the classical preoccupation with conflict and defence is set aside, or retained as only one of many ways in which we may be barred from introspection, the therapeutic task becomes more general; it is to identify all those ways in which an individual's repertoire of procedures is restricted or distorted, and all those ways in which conscious awareness of these restrictions may be limited but capable of extension. Therapeutic change involves, inseparably, new *experiences*, new *behaviours* and new *understandings*, but it is through new understandings, especially new capacities for self-understanding, that the patient becomes capable of independent and continuing change. In a paper considering the place of consciousness in psychotherapy (Ryle, 1994c) I suggested the following possible sources of procedural restriction and limited capacity for self-reflection, all of which, once identified with the patient, are open to correction:

1. Restricted experience Narrow family role definitions, or culturally inappropriate ones, or family beliefs about the world (for example as excessively dangerous) may leave an individual with a small repertoire which, as always, may be maintained by the extraction of evident confirmation from the world.

2. Restricted self-reflection   Conscious self-reflection will be learned from the kind of reflection offered by others. Parents concerned with appearance, achievement or obedience may have children who display, perform or obey but who may have no awareness or concepts with which to consider their own subjective experience and who in consequence may be open to abuse and unable to seek corrective or compensatory experiences.

3. Disjointed self-reflection   This may result from inconsistent, contradictory parenting, which is often accompanied by disjointed or misleading accounts. This may make integration of the different reciprocal role procedures impossible.

4. Errors of attribution   Errors due to the child's false deductions about causality and responsibility can lead to guilt and to avoidant or symptomatic procedures. Irrational guilt for imaginary consequences of what was wished for, often reinforced by adult suggestions that desires are in themselves bad, can lead to guilt. The guilt of victims is similarly based on the belief that what happened must have been deserved.

5. Unmanageable experiences   These can overwhelm the capacity to feel, think or act and may become unthinkable. Examples include childhood abuse and bereavement, and abnormal grief reactions or post-traumatic stress disorder in adults. Other people often reinforce the tendency to put the experience out of mind and procedures are evolved for avoiding thoughts or actions likely to lead to remembering.

6. Silencing   This is an example of the above in which the perpetrator of abuse also threatens dire punishments if the event is ever mentioned.

7. Defensive anxiety reduction   Anxiety reduction in the face of critical or threatening voices from actual parents or from the internalised voices of parents can be alleviated through the forgetting of desire or of the possibility of pursuing it. This represents the classic ego defences.

These different forms of restriction, derived from both trauma and deprivation, frequently coexist, and all need to be considered. Whatever their origins, procedures tend to be self-perpetuating, and the therapist's task is to identify, describe and not reciprocate the damaging procedures.

While some problems are maintained by powerful intrapsychic forces which appear self-perpetuating, all procedures originate in interpersonal experiences, and the specific, targeted interpersonal activity of therapy can provide the basis of a changed inner dialogue.

It is for this reason that the CAT therapist is primarily concerned with *accurate description* and *non-collusion* rather than with interpretation. Interpretation can be experienced as omniscient, feeding fantasies of magical care, or as critical and intrusive, repeating patterns which can be subsumed under persecuting or abusive reciprocal role procedures. Description, on the other hand, can be discussed and modified in a direct, equal conversation; any hypothetical elements can be clearly identified as such. Persistent interpretation can induce a regressed state which further emphasises the power of the analyst and which can exclude from the work of therapy the patient's own capacity (Ryle, 1992, 1993). Whether or when such regression may be necessary or helpful, and how far the phenomena produced in the analysand are derivatives of human development rather than products of the analytic relationship, are open questions. But in CAT and other forms of brief therapy the aim is to avoid regression and to mobilise the patient's capacity for self-reflection. In this respect, experience shows that the zone of proximal development (to use Vygotsky's phrase) is extensive, even in patients who are seriously damaged.

It is perhaps worth noting that an absence of any detailed consideration of the origins of consciousness in culture and language is also characteristic of cognitive psychology. Thus Stinson and Palmer (1991), in the context of a stimulating discussion of parallel processing models, attribute consciousness to 'innate neurological influences' and of processes which 'unfold during development'. I believe that the important attempts by writers such as Horowitz and his colleagues (Horowitz, 1988, 1991) and Westen (1991) to integrate psychoanalytic and cognitive understandings would be more fruitful if these ideas were incorporated. The extension of self-awareness and self-control and self-possibility are central goals of psychotherapy. Theories which polarise conscious and unconscious mental processes and neglect the former, theories which seek to explain culture in terms of psychology rather than psychology in terms of culture, theories which fail to note the difference between biological evolution and cultural development, and theories which model the mind in terms of affectless rationality can distort the act of therapy. The historical tendency to greater human complexity and the possibility of greater freedom through consciousness is a model for the task of therapy.

Observational studies of early development and their relevance to CAT

It was always my aim to base CAT on a developmental theory which was compatible with what was reliably known from observational studies.

However, the main emphasis up to now has been on the differentiation of the theory from the object relations theories from which it was derived. This involved the rejection of aspects of those theories (notably those emphasising innate intrapsychic conflict, those equating the phenomena of regression and psychosis with early development and those proposing untenable developmental timetables) and the introduction of alternative understandings derived from the work of Vygotsky and Bakhtin, summarised above and developed in the chapter in this book by Leiman.

While these developments were taking place, the work of Stern (1985) announced a new convergence between developmental psychologists and analysts and was evidence of what has become a massive explosion of new research in the field of early development. To assimilate the full impact of this on the theory and practice of CAT will require serious attention over the next few years; in the meantime two bodies of work with clear implications for CAT will be discussed briefly.

Despite Leiman's reservations about the 'biologism' of attachment theory (Leiman, 1994a), the theory has generated an impressive volume of research on psychological phenomena. Bowlby's (1969) concept of the intergenerational transmission of 'working models of relationships' is close to what, in CAT, would be described as the creation of the individual's repertoire of reciprocal roles, implicit in which is the assumption that, as these are formed in interaction with parents, they will inevitably reflect the parents' own repertoires.

In a recent paper, Fonagy et al. (1994) review and add to research stemming from Bowlby and initiated by his colleague Ainsworth concerning this process of intergenerational transmission. Much of this work depended on the development of two research tools, the Strange Situations technique and the Adult Attachment Interview. The former, applied to infants aged 12–18 months, involves watching the child's response to a brief separation from, and reuniting with, the parent. This yields a reliable classification of children into four main attachment styles, namely securely attached, avoidant, angry/passive and disorganised. The latter, on the basis of interviewing, described early attachment experiences as generating four groups, namely the autonomous, the dismissive–detached, the preoccupied–entangled and those who have failed to mourn the loss of an important attachment figure.

Using these methods Fonagy and his colleagues demonstrated that parental attachment styles, assessed during pregnancy, were highly predictive of the attachment styles of their subsequently born children, assessed at 12 and 18 months, the association being stronger for mothers than for fathers. The child's attachment style was specific to the parent concerned, indicating that 'working models' were separately transmitted, an observation which can be seen to justify the common CAT practice in reformulation of identifying separately the reciprocal role patterns derived from each parent.

In a further important study, mothers were rated (a) on the degree of early deprivation they had experienced, and (b) on their capacity for self-reflection. Ten out of ten deprived mothers rated high on self-reflection had securely attached children, compared with only one out of seventeen similarly deprived mothers who were low on self-reflection. The capacity for self-reflection is understood to operate by allowing the mother to acknowledge and reflect upon the child's experience and mental state. A child endowed with the capacity for self-reflection is, in turn, less at the mercy of abuse or neglect. Abuse, however, is likely to be committed by an unreflective parent who is unlikely, therefore, to engender self-reflection in the child. This effect may be heightened, according to Higgitt and Fonagy (1993), by the child's defensive inhibition of the capacity to reflect upon the mental states of (hostile) caretakers; these authors see this as a major source of borderline states.

The second source which I would like to refer to is the powerfully argued book by Hobson (1993) in which the phenomena of autism are considered in the light of recent studies of normal development. Hobson argues that the organic defect underlying autism causes an impairment of the active interest in persons and relatedness which characterises normal children from birth onwards. He emphasises that the normal infant, from the beginning, is interested in persons as persons, not in bodies that later are seen to have minds. Thought and feeling develop in the perceptually anchored, intersubjective exchanges of the pre-verbal child, and only within this affectively driven connection can the child learn the difference between persons and things, between self and others and between real and pretend or reality and image. These discriminations are made prior to language and prepare the path for it. Lacking this intensity of connection, the autistic child acquires incomplete understanding of these differentiations and only a partial command of language.

Hobson is clear that symbolic functioning can only arise in the context of an interpersonal relationship in which both engage with an object or event in the world. But, despite his acknowledgement of Vygotsky's contributions, despite his rejection of cognitivist views of the 'child as scientist', and despite his specific recognition of the autistic incapacity for abstract thought, he seems to pay little attention to the role of the adult in providing the signs (contexts, objects, communications) which, internalised, become the tools of mediated thought. This recognition would in no way undermine his central argument for the inseparability of thought, affect and relationship, nor his basic thesis about autism.

These two contributions, both incidentally by psychoanalysts working on observational data, do not contradict the broadly conceived developmental account on which CAT is based, but both add considerable fine grain to that account, and both highlight the importance of the individual's intersubjectively acquired 'theory of mind'. While Hobson illuminates the way in which this is acquired by contrasting normal and autistic development, Fonagy demonstrates how such a 'theory' may be underdeveloped through the lack of reflection from caretakers and, he argues, from defensive inhibition in the face of hostility. The nature of the damage is clearly different in the two cases, but the arguments of both fully justify the emphasis placed on learning in the context of a relationship which is part of all therapies but which is given a central place (with a Vygotskian concern for mediating tools) in the practice of CAT.

Borderline personality disorder

The diagnostic features of borderline personality disorder (BPD), as summarised in the DSM-III(R) (American Psychiatric Association, 1989), include a pervasive instability of mood and self-image, self-harm and self-neglect, destructive and unstable relationship patterns, identity diffusion and impulsivity. There are frequently associated Axis 1 disorders, notably depression, alcoholism and eating disorders, and the condition is not reliably distinct from other Axis 2 diagnoses (histrionic and narcissistic personality in particular). Berelowitz and Tarnopolsky (1993), in reviewing recent research, conclude that the diagnosis, while reliably identifying a group of seriously disturbed patients, might be better regarded as 'severe personality dysfunction'.

While instability figures large in the diagnostic criteria, for example as 'stable lability' (Higgitt and Fonagy, 1993) or as 'identity diffusion' in the DSM-III(R), and while psychoanalytic ideas of structure (notably splitting) have contributed to these understandings, a useful understanding of the structures generating this unstable picture has been wanting. It is here that the CAT-derived model of multiple self states has a contribution to make.

The multiple self states model of borderline personality organisation

In the course of reformulating the problems of borderline patients receiving CAT, it became increasingly evident that it was both possible and necessary to identify and describe the various 'sub-personalities' or 'self states', the alternations of which determine the patient's confusing experiences and actions. Once these were identified, the disconcerting 'state switches' could be recognised and their provocations monitored (Marlowe, 1994). Each self state can be described in terms of mood, access to and control of emotion, and the reciprocal role repertoire generating self-management and relationship procedures. These descriptions are similar to those employed by M.J. Horowitz (1979) in his analysis of therapy transcripts in terms of 'states of mind'. The model so constructed is in line with the suggestion made by L.M. Horowitz (1994) that the DSM term 'identity diffusion' should be replaced by 'identity confusion', implying shifts between 'contrasting, even contradictory, identities'. The model has similarities with accounts of multiple personality disorder (MPD) (Ross and Gahan, 1988) but in the case of BPD most states have never been clearly identified, let alone named, by patients or by clinicians; moreover the degree of dissociation between states is seldom as absolute in BPD as in MPD.

The Self States Sequential Diagram

In order to emphasise the need to identify separate self states, I suggest that the sequential diagrams of borderline structure patients should be called 'Self States Sequential Diagrams' (SSSD). These should be constructed for diagnosed borderline patients, for those who, in the course of early sessions or assessment interviews, give clear evidence of state switches and in those who give many positive responses to the screening questions at the end of the 'Psychotherapy File'. The construction of the SSSD requires a detailed attention to the history and current relationship patterns of the patient and an alertness to state switches occurring during or between sessions, including those less dramatic ones sensed largely through countertransference changes. In addition, patients must be recruited to the task of describing their states in detail and of noting shifts between them. This task culminates in the patient systematically rating all the self states against descriptions relating to mood, access to feeling self and others, using provided descriptions with individual additions. These ratings may be processed as a repertory grid (Ryle and Marlowe, 1995). This provides an indication of how well discriminated the different states are (some may be paired or clustered) and comparison with the SSSD can ensure that the latter contains all the self states. It is quite possible to construct an SSSD without the grid analysis, provided the need to identify all states with distinct reciprocal role patterns is borne in mind; the 'broken egg' diagrams introduced into CAT several years ago (see Chapter 2), which described a split into two states, became somewhat conventionalised and led to some equally discriminable states being left out of the diagrams. It is important to identify all states, as only a full account of reciprocal role patterns can permit the prediction and recognition of transference–counter-transference changes.

The construction of the SSSD is described in Chapter 2 and research related to it and to the self states model is summarised in Chapter 10. The studies reported lend some empirical support to the model and suggest that diagrams can be constructed by patient–therapist pairs which are accurately reflective of early therapy events and stories and which are predictive of later therapy events and feelings.

The nature of borderline self states

All borderline patients have one, usually dominant, state which reflects the remembered interactions of childhood. Some procedures generated from this state may be derived from the originally child role, accepting abuse or neglect; others may represent the enactment of the original adult role (abusing and neglecting) towards others and/or the self. A second common state is the split-off idealising or the admiring–admired grandiose pattern described in the 'broken egg' diagrams. Other common patterns are: emotional blankness in relation to others seen as out of reach, hurtful and sometimes also vulnerable; out of control rage in relation to others seen as humiliating or abusive; submission to the critical demands of self or others expressed in placation, perfectionism or manic activity. These are not complete descriptions, and it should be remembered that either pole of the pattern may be enacted, elicited or replaced by symptomatic procedures. In every case it is essential to go through the process with the patient of identifying and characterising each state, for this process, apart from ensuring accuracy and comprehensiveness, plays a large part in building the working alliance and in establishing or equipping a capacity for self-observation in the patient.

The causes of borderline personality disorder

Abuse, both physical and sexual, and neglect, figure in the early histories of most borderline patients. Beyond that, the relative importance of

1. being deprived of the reflections of self-reflective caretakers
2. a defensive inhibition of thinking about the mental states of others, and
3. the disruption of self-reflection due to constant state switches

is hard to assess. In CAT the role of inadequate reflection from others in childhood in limiting the capacity for conscious self-reflection has been recognised, but the main emphasis has been on the disruption of self-awareness and the absence of an ongoing process of self-monitoring, whereby the results of ones own acts could be recognised and responsibility accurately perceived. While fully endorsing the emphasis on self-reflection and on the capacity to think about the mental states of others (capacities which probably grow from the same experiences), incapacity in these respects is not, in my experience, typical of all the states in borderline patients. Some, indeed, have an uncanny awareness of others mental states, including those of their therapists. This capacity, however, serves them but little as long as they are prone to state switches, often into states characterised by powerful one-dimensional reciprocal role patterns in which the other is essentially, and forcefully, required to do no more than reciprocate.

The different explanations are, of course, compatible with each other and may vary in importance between cases. But the experience of time-limited work centred on integration through the use of reformulation shows that in many patients surprisingly rapid extensions of self- and other-awareness and of integration can be achieved. These changes seem more understandable as the result of the new higher-order capacities for self-observation than as the result of the resolution of defensive inhibition.

Cognitive Analytic Therapy with borderlines

In a condition widely acknowledged to be difficult to treat and having a relatively poor short-term prognosis, any successful brief intervention demands some attention. Case histories describing such reasonably effective interventions have been published (Ryle, 1990; Ryle, Spencer and Yawetz, 1992; Ryle and Beard, 1993; Ryle and Low, 1993; Dunn, 1994) and will not be repeated here. As a result of clinical experience of this nature and of a small pilot study, an ongoing research programme accumulating and following up cases of BPD was started in 1992. In this, normal CAT practice is varied, patients being offered up to 24 sessions (the final number being agreed at around session 12) and medication needs being assessed and treated by psychiatrists outside the project. Therapists are mostly trainees selected for experience and ability, and supervision is provided in groups of three for one-and-a-half hours weekly, which is a better ratio than is usually possible. Patients are recruited on the basis of standard diagnostic procedures and all sessions are audiotaped.

Some early findings from this project are reported in Chapter 10, but it is too early to be able to offer hard data concerning the overall outcome of the interventions, or linking process measures with outcome. The experience of the pilot study and the early cases in this series is, however, encouraging; it seems that dropout rates are relatively low and that at the three-month follow-up about half of the patients no longer meet DSM-III(R) criteria for BPD.

The central feature of CAT in these cases is the joint creation and use of the SSSD and the avoidance of, or recovery from, collusive involvement with the patient, the explicit aim being the achievement of integration through self-awareness. The work of such therapies is very intense and demanding on both patient and therapist, but the containment offered by the reformulation makes it possible to endure the difficult times and make constructive use of whatever aspect of the patient presents.

Most authorities still recommend long-term work in borderline patients. Gunderson and Sabo (1993), for example, in reviewing the available treatments, suggest that psychoanalytic psychotherapy requires at least three sessions per week for a minimum of four years. More practicable interventions are also being reported, however, Linehan (Shearin and Linehan, 1993) describes a two-year behavioural intervention combining individual and group therapy and demonstrating a thorough and sensitive awareness of countertransference problems. Stevenson and Meares (1992) report a series of severe borderline patients treated by intensively supervised trainees in twice-weekly therapy based on a self psychology model. Therapy lasted for one year and all patients derived some help, with 30% no longer meeting borderline diagnostic criteria at the post-therapy assessment one year after treatment. The place of CAT in services treating borderline patients will, it is to be hoped, be evaluated in relation to approaches such as these.

References

American Psychiatric Association (1989). *Diagnostic and Statistical Manual of Mental Disorders* (3rd edn, revised). Washington, DC: APA.

Beard, H., Marlowe, M. and Ryle, A. (1990). The management and treatment of personality disordered patients: the use of Sequential Diagrammatic Reformulation, *British Journal of Psychiatry*, **156**, 541–545.

Berelowitz, M. and Tarnopolsky, A. (1993). The validity of borderline personality: an updated review of recent variance. In: Tyrer, P. and Stein, G. (Eds), *Personality Disorder Reviewed*. London, Gaskell.

Bruner, J. (1986). *Actual Minds, Possible Worlds*. Cambridge, Mass., Harvard University Press.

Bowlby, J. (1969). *Attachment and Loss. Vol.1: Attachment*. London, Hogarth.

Dunn, M. (1994). Variations in Cognitive Analytic Therapy technique in the treatment of a severely disturbed patient, *International Journal of Short Term Psychotherapy*, **9** (2/3), 119–134.

Fonagy, P., Steele, M., Steele, H., Higgitt, A. and Target, M. (1994). The theory and practice of resilience, *Journal of Child Psychology and Psychiatry*, **35** (2), 231–257.

Gold, J.R. and Wachtel, P.L. (1993). Cyclical psychodynamics. In: Stricker, J. and Gold, J.R. (Eds), *Comprehensive Handbook of Psychotherapy Integration*. New York, Plenum Press.

Guidano, V.F. (1987). *The Complexity of the Self: A Developmental Approach to Psychopathology and Therapy*. London, Guilford Press.

Guidano, V.F. (1991). *The Self in Process*. London, Guilford Press.

Gunderson, J. and Sabo, A.N. (1993). Treatment of borderline personality disorder: a critical review. In: Paris, J. (Ed), *Borderline Personality Disorder: Etiology and Treatment*. Washington, APA.

Higgitt, A. and Fonagy, P. (1993). Psychotherapy in borderline and narcissistic personality disorder. In: Tyrer, P. and Stein, G. (Eds), *Personality Disorder Reviewed*. London, Gaskell.

Hobson, R.P. (1993). *Autism and the Development of Mind*. Hove, Lawrence Erlbaum Associates.

Holquist, M. (1990). *Bakhtin and his World*. London, Routledge.

Horowitz, L.M. (1994). Pschemas, psychopathology and psychotherapy research, *Psychotherapy Research*, **4** (1), 1–19.

Horowitz, M.J. (1979). *States of Mind*. New York, Plenum Press.

Horowitz, M.J. (Ed) (1988). *Psychodynamics and Cognition*. Chicago, Chicago University Press.

Horowitz, M.J. (Ed) (1991). *Person Schemas and Maladaptive Interpersonal Patterns*. Chicago, Chicago University Press.

Horowitz, M.J. and Eells, T.D. (1993). Case reformulations using role-relationship model configurations: a reliability study, *Psychotherapy Research*, **3** (1), 57–68.

Kelly, G.A. (1955). *The Psychology of Personal Constructs*. New York, Norton.

Leiman, M. (1992). The concept of sign in the work of Vygotsky, Winnicott and Bakhtin: further integration of object relations theory and activity theory, *British Journal of Medical Psychology*, **65**, 209–221.

Leiman, M. (1994a). Projective identification as early joint action sequences: a Vygotskian addendum to the procedural sequence object relations model, *British Journal of Medical Psychology*, **67**, 97–106.

Leiman, M. (1994b). The development of cognitive analytic therapy, *International Journal of Short Term Psychotherapy*, **9** (2/3), 67–82.

Lockwood, G. and Young, J.E. (1992). Cognitive therapy of personality disorders, *Journal of Cognitive Psychotherapy*, **6**, 5–9.

Luborsky, L., Barber, J.P. and Diguer, L. (1992). The meanings of narratives told during psychotherapy: the fruits of a new observational unit, *Psychotherapy Research*, **2** (4), 277–290.

Mann, J. and Goldman, R. (1982). *A Casebook in Time-Limited Psychotherapy*. New York, McGraw-Hill.

Marlowe, M.J. (1994). Cognitive analytic therapy and borderline personality disorder: reciprocal role repertoires and sub-personality organisation, *International Journal of Short Term Psychotherapy*, **9** (2/3), 161–169.

Ogden, T.H. (1983). The concept of internal object relations, *International Journal of Psychoanalysis*, **64**, 227–241.

Ross, C.A. and Gahan, P. (1988). Techniques in the treatment of multiple personality disorder, *American Journal of Psychotherapy*, **40**, 40–52.

Ryle, A. (1975). *Frames and Cages*. London, Chatto and Windus.

Ryle, A. (1978). A common language for the psychotherapies, *British Journal of Psychiatry*, **132**, 585–594.

Ryle, A. (1979). The focus in brief interpretative psychotherapy: dilemmas, traps and snags as target problems, *British Journal of Psychiatry*, **135**, 46–64.

Ryle, A. (1982). *Psychotherapy: A Cognitive Integration of Theory and Practice*. London, Academic Press.

Ryle, A. (1985). Cognitive theory, object relations and the self, *British Journal of Medical Psychology*, **58**, 1–7.

Ryle, A. (1990). *Cognitive Analytic Therapy: Active Participation in Change*. Chichester, John Wiley.

Ryle, A. (1991). Object relations theory and activity theory: a proposed link by way of the procedural sequence model, *British Journal of Medical Psychology*, **64**, 307–316.

Ryle, A. (1992). Critique of a Kleinian case presentation, *British Journal of Medical Psychology*, **65**, 309–317.

Ryle, A. (1993). Addiction to the death instinct? A critical review of Joseph's paper 'Addiction to near death', *British Journal of Psychotherapy*, **10** (1), 88–92 (with response by Ann Scott, 93–96)

Ryle, A. (1994a). Psychoanalysis and cognitive analytic therapy, *British Journal of*

Psychotherapy, **10** (3), 402–404.

Ryle, A. (1994b). Persuasion or Education? *International Journal of Short Term Psychotherapy*, **9** (2/3), 111–118.

Ryle, A. (1994c). Consciousness and psychotherapy, *British Journal of Medical Psychology*, **67**, 115–124.

Ryle, A. (1994d). Projective identification: a particular form of reciprocal role procedure, *British Journal of Medical Psychology*, **67**, 107–114.

Ryle, A. and Beard, H. (1993). The integrative effect of reformulation: cognitive analytic therapy with a patient with borderline personality disorder, *British Journal of Medical Psychology*, **66**, 249–258.

Ryle, A. and Low, J. (1993). Cognitive analytic therapy. In: Stricker, G. and Gold, J.R. (Eds), *Comprehensive Handbook of Psychotherapy Integration*. New York, Plenum Press.

Ryle, A. and Marlowe, M.J. (1995). Cognitive analytic therapy of borderline personality disorders: theory and practice and the clinical and research uses of the self states sequential diagram. *International Journal of Short Term Psychotherapy*, **10** (1), in press.

Ryle, A., Spencer, J. and Yawtez, C. (1992). When less is more or at least enough, *British Journal of Psychotherapy*, **8** (4), 401–412.

Safran, J.D. (1990a). Towards a refinement of cognitive analytic therapy in the light of interpersonal theory: Theory, *Clinical Psychology Review*, **10**, 87–105.

Safran, J.D. (1990b). Towards a refinement of cognitive analytic therapy in the light of interpersonal theory: Practice, *Clinical Psychology Review*, **10**, 107–121.

Shearin, E.N. and Linehan, M.M. (1993). Dialectical behaviour therapy for borderline personality. In: Paris, J. (Ed), *Borderline Personality Disorder: Etiology and Treatment*. Washington, APA.

Stern, D.N. (1985). *The Interpersonal World of the Infant*. New York, Basic Books.

Stevenson, J. and Meares, R. (1992). An outcome study of psychotherapy for patients with borderline personality disorder, *American Journal of Psychiatry*, **149** (3), 358–362.

Stinson, C.H. and Palmer, S.E. (1991). Parallel distributed processing models of person schemas and psychopathologies. In: Horowitz, M.J. (Ed), *Person Schemas and Maladaptive Interpersonal Schemas*. Chicago, University of Chicago Press.

Voloshinov, V.N. (Tr. Titunik, I.R.) (1987). *Freudianism: A Critical Sketch*. Bloomington, Indiana University Press.

Vygotsky, L.S. (Tr. Hanfman, E. and Vakar, G.) (1962). *Thought and Language*. Cambridge, Mass., MIT Press.

Vygotsky, L.S. (1978). *Mind in Society*. Cambridge, Mass., Harvard University Press.

Wachtel, P.L. (1977). *Psychoanalysis and Behaviour Therapy*. New York, Basic Books.

Wessler, R.L. (1993). Groups. In: Stricker, G. and Gold, J.R. (Eds), *Comprehensive Handbook of Psychotherapy Integration*. New York, Plenum Press.

Westen, D. (1990). Towards a revised theory of borderline object relations: implications of observational research, *International Journal of Psycho-Analysis*, **71**, 661–693.

Westen, D. (1991). Social cognition and object relations, *Psychological Bulletin*, **109** (3), 429–455.

Wood, D., Bruner, J. and Ross, G. (1976). The role of tutoring in problem-solving, *Journal of Clinical Psychology and Psychiatry*, **17**, 89–100.

2   The practice of CAT

Anthony Ryle

Much of the theory and practice of CAT is shared with other therapies. It is not, however, an eclectic salad: whatever is done is done in relation to the underlying model of therapeutic change. This involves the creation of a human relationship between the patient and therapist, devoted to the achievement of change, involving the joint creation of descriptions of the patient's harmful procedures which serve to enhance the patient's capacity for self-observation and control and to guide the therapist in ensuring that the relationship serves its therapeutic purpose. Within the technical framework of CAT, described below, each therapist, with each patient, will work out the best way to work together.

Responsibility of therapists

Therapy must be carried out in appropriate settings, with suitable patients, in ways governed by a professional code of ethics. Therapists should belong to appropriate professional and defence organisations. In CAT particular emphasis is placed on being explicit about the reasons for the rules and conventions governing therapy; these are designed to protect patients and also to make the work of therapists manageable. Patients should be encouraged to raise any difficulties with the therapist but should be aware that formal complaints procedures exist. Therapists should be in supervision at a level determined by their experience.

Cognitive Analytic Therapy: Developments in Theory and Practice, Edited by A. Ryle
© 1995 John Wiley & Sons Ltd

Referral of patients

Cases referred for CAT will vary according to the settings. In hospital settings most will come from psychiatrists or from general practitioners. In mental health centres and other community resources, cases will usually be discussed at team meetings before being allocated. In general practice cases will be referred by, or discussed with, the patient's practitioner. In private practice some will be self-referred. Therapists need to pay particular attention to diagnosis and assessment before offering treatment where little prior consideration has been given to diagnosis and suitability for therapy.

Assessment and selection for treatment

The assessment procedure needs to answer the following questions.

1. Is the patient suffering from a problem which is appropriate for psychological treatment? A patient may be excluded because he or she is suffering from more or less normal responses to life events, in which case supportive counselling may be appropriate. Another reason for exclusion is when the patient is suffering from a condition needing medical treatment. Physical illness may present as fatigue, depression and vague somatic complaints. These symptoms should be investigated medically, and they should only be explained psychologically where there is positive evidence for a link with the patient's procedures. Where full investigation has shown no organic cause for symptoms but the patient presents only somatic symptoms, treatment can only proceed if the patient agrees to accept the possibility of a psychological cause and cooperates with self-monitoring etc. A third reason for exclusion is when the patient is suffering from a mental illness requiring pharmacological treatment. Uncommon examples would be an undetected paranoid illness or early schizophrenia and in case of doubt psychiatric advice should be sought. The most common condition will be depression of a level likely to interfere with the patient's capacity to work in therapy. Prior or simultaneous treatment with antidepressants is indicated because severe depression is associated with poor outcomes in psychotherapy. If patients refuse medication, a trial of therapy may be offered, but not continued if no change is evident in 3–4 weeks.

2. If the patient is suitable for psychological treatment, is CAT the appropriate approach? In general, CAT is a safe initial therapy for a wide range of neurotic and personality disorders. While CAT requires active patient participation, patients on first presentation need not be expected to be 'psychologically-minded'. There are, however, exceptions:

- Patients with a clear preference for a different approach should be helped to find what they want elsewhere.
- Patients with major behavioural and symptomatic problems may be unsuitable or may need prior treatment and management by other means, for example detoxification for substance abuse, behavioural treatment for severe obsessional or phobic symptoms. Many patients with relatively minor symptoms, however, can be treated with CAT; in some cases therapy can incorporate direct treatment of the symptoms (for example, cognitive methods for bulimia, exposure programmes for avoidance) while in other cases the symptom, having been linked with the procedural system in reformulation, will be largely ignored and attention will be focused on the interpersonal and self-management procedures with which it is associated.
- The range of severity of the patients offered treatment will reflect the setting and the experience of the therapist. Actively suicidal patients are best treated in hospital services which can offer contact and, if necessary admission, at any time, without the direct involvement of the therapist. All such patients should have a clear understanding of what is available and how to make contact, and some rehearsal of how to deal with powerfully destructive feelings is appropriate. This also protects the therapist from the controlling use of suicidal threats. The same considerations apply even more strongly to patients with a potential for violence. Such patients should only be taken on after discussion with colleagues and in settings where other staff are readily accessible.
- Some therapists find some kinds of patient particularly difficult to work with. Unless this can be resolved in supervision, referral to another therapist is appropriate.

Therapy contract

During assessment and at the time of offering therapy, the nature of the offer being made and the expectations on the patient should have been discussed. In many settings it may be a good idea to have a written contract setting out these issues. The agreement should include the length of sessions, the number of sessions offered, the (limited or absent) right to contact between sessions, the expectations of homework and arrangements about holidays, missed sessions etc.

Conduct of sessions

It is preferable to see patients at the same time and place each week, but this is not always possible in health service settings. The adequacy of the soundproofing, and standard of decoration and furnishing of the room, should be at least decent, but this is not always possible in the current NHS. The patient should be seated at an angle which permits, but does not insist upon, eye contact, and a low table on which written and diagrammatic materials can be jointly perused should be provided. Note-taking during sessions is best avoided but, during the history-taking phase, may be necessary. Process records of the sessions should be kept, along with copies of the rather considerable amount of paperwork involved in CAT.

Audiotaping of sessions is a valuable basis for self-supervision and allows accurate process records to be kept; it should be part of the experience of all trainees. Excerpts can be taken to supervision. Patients should be permitted or encouraged to make tapes for their own use. The storage and ultimate disposal of the audiotapes should be treated with the same care as for written records; as an additional precaution patient's names should not appear on the tapes.

Sessions 1–3: gathering data and preliminary reformulation

The aim, in these early sessions, is to gain as extensive an understanding of the patient's experience as possible and to give the patient some experience of the kind of offer the therapist is making in order to recruit him or her to the work. The difficulties stem from the need to gather a full range of historical and diagnostic data, which encourages active questioning, while at the same time leaving choice of topic and theme as far as possible to the patient (because, as Balint says, if you ask questions all you get is answers). In addition, the problem procedures of some patients are likely to limit their capacity or willingness to reveal much about themselves.

At the first session it is best to say briefly what one has already gathered from the referral letter and invite the patient to expand on that. What they say and how they say it, supplemented by prompts to speak of particular phases or themes in their life or to talk about particular people, is usually enough to convey a fairly comprehensive view of the nature of the problem. It is always a good idea to rehearse the main themes at the end of the session to confirm that one has understood the story correctly; if possible it is also helpful to identify some underlying assumptions or recurrent procedural patterns. At the end of this session the Psychotherapy File (see Appendix 2.1) will be introduced, self-monitoring of recurrent moods or symptoms suggested and other work which may contribute to reformulation (e.g. life charts setting out the years of important events, previous illnesses or treatments, or family trees) may also be asked for. Where no previous psychological/psychiatric assessment has taken place, the gaps in the history and symptom profile gathered at this session should be noted and a small part of the next session should be devoted to covering the ground. Symptom questionnaires which may have been issued before the patient was seen should be inspected and evidence of symptoms not discussed in the session should be explored.

Over the ensuing two sessions the history will be amplified and. increasingly, the pattern of the therapeutic relationship will begin to emerge. This will usually, and preferably, include a developing working relationship, but will also convey aspects of problem procedures in most cases. Over-compliance and placation engendered by the hope for help may be useful in the short run, but need to be named and later resistance anticipated. Failure to complete agreed tasks or evasiveness or silence in the room must, obviously, be addressed, but in the form of a procedural description, which can usually be linked with the presenting difficulties, rather than of a disciplinary admonition. Less overt aspects of the interaction may indicate problem-related feelings and attitudes and may evoke corresponding countertransference feelings in the therapist, contributing to the understanding to be recorded in the reformulation.

To a large extent conflict between the 'cognitive' and 'analytic' components of CAT is minimal as all that takes place is aimed at the accurate understanding of the patient and the initiation of the therapeutic work. Only if, by 'analytic', is implied an unyielding transference-centred interpretative mode is the cognitive component intrusive. However, as far as possible, the introduction and discussion of cognitive tasks should be timed in such a way that it does not over-structure the session and block exploration. Conversely, in the more open-ended and exploratory aspects of the meetings, the need to link the material not just to immediate associations but to the wider, overarching understandings of the emerging reformulation must not be forgotten. (The wish on the part of therapists for more exploration and more history is usually a wish not to have to think about the reformulation yet.) Where the reformulation is difficult owing to the patient's failure to provide much to go on, early reformulation, describing this in terms of a problem procedure (which can usually be linked to life problems) is indicated. Such early, high-level, general reformulation engenders, in most cases, a more active participation, with amplification of the material, a fact which is central to the practice of CAT. There is no place for the prolonged siege conducted with low-level interpretations. Even the very distanced, untrusting patient, or the patient in whom the definition of the self seems to rest on not doing what is required, can often be reached by a high-level description of what is going on in the room. One should always remember that the consulting patient, however apparently obstructive, is there in order to change; reformulation offers an explanation of why it is difficult and does not convey criticism.

The reformulation session

This session will have been described in advance as being of a special nature and, for the therapist, even though most of the issues will have been discussed to some degree, it requires considerable preparation. Therapists need to gather together the information that they have collected and all the impressions they have received in the course of the sessions so far. It may help to read through the Psychotherapy File with the patient in mind, as well as checking through the items identified by the patients and already discussed. The draft of the reformulation, in writing, should be read out in the session, and the patient's comments and responses to this should be carefully noted. Reactions are often intense and serve to confirm the understandings and the sense of a felt working alliance, but placatory responses must be distinguished from acceptance, and rejection of parts as inaccurate and needing correction must be distinguished from responses which are expressions of a dismissive or envious procedure. The finalised written version, prepared after this meeting, will take note of these responses. Any parts deemed important but not accepted by the patient should either be omitted or included but noted as not agreed.

The reformulation process, devoted to the formation of the central tool of the therapy, is at the same time a lived example of collaborative, respecting and thoughtful relationship. Good CAT involves recruiting the patient to the task by: (a) clearly describing its joint nature, (b) encouraging full discussion of homework tasks, (c) timing interventions, leaving gaps etc. in order to elicit the patients' views, (d) making all suggestions in ways inviting comment and possible dissent, and (e) inviting patients to answer questions for themselves, before replying. The work orientation of CAT should not be misapplied; pauses and silences and tact provide the spaces into which the patient pours the material from which the understandings of the reformulation are built.

The written reformulation

The written reformulation letter is based upon interviewing, patients' self-monitoring, the interchange in the room, the patient's use of the Psychotherapy File etc. Many of the elements of the reformulation will have been discussed over the first three sessions. Re-presenting the story put together in a letter is, however, a powerful moment, serving to cement the therapeutic alliance in most cases. The letter should do all the following things:

1. Describe the patient's past experiences and name simply and directly the difficulties and pains of the life. This serves to validate experiences which have often been partially denied and can clarify what the patient was and

was not responsible for.
2. Describe the procedures used by the patient to cope. The word 'defence' is often felt to be critical and it is better to talk in terms of ways of coping or strategies.
3. Identify the currently operating Target Problems (TPs) and Target Problem Procedures (TPPs). These should be discussed in the letter, and should also be listed separately. An abbreviated list of TPs and TPPs will be transferred to the Rating Sheet.
4. Predict how the procedures may operate in the therapy relationship or describe how they may already have done so.

Target Problems and Target Problem Procedures

Target Problems (TPs) are descriptions of what is wrong. Listing the patient's own complaints, for example depression, fear of open spaces, difficult relationships, reminds us of what therapy aims to change; but we need also to list the problems which patients manifest but do not name, perhaps because they have come to see their distress as normal or their negative beliefs as true. Thus TPs may also describe problems such as 'never really enjoying anything' or 'being over-critical of myself'.

TPPs are an attempt to describe how the patient maintains the processes or creates the experiences which result in the TPs. A proper TPP description should indicate (a) what the person does, and (b) why revision has not taken place so far. Procedural description based on the Procedural Sequence Model would normally indicate the aim or intention (e.g. seeking intimacy, coping with daily life etc.) and descriptions should trace:

1. internal mental processes such as how things are seen and judged, the individual's intentions, predictions of capacity, choice of means
2. how the role or act is performed
3. external aspects such as other people's actions and responses, and the consequences of the acts.

Short-term summary versions of TPPs will be used on the Rating Sheet, but the fuller sequence should be clear from the letter or from the summary of TPs and TPPs at the end of the letter. Thus in the case of Traps, the circularity of the sequence—assumptions leading to actions, leading to consequences, leading to reinforcement of assumptions—should be spelt out. In the case of Dilemmas, it is important to note that dilemmas imply polarised choices to which the individual can see no alternative. Enactment of one pole serves apparently to confirm the narrow, polarised possibilities. In the case of external Snags the (often but not always false) assumptions of other people's responses should be named. In the case of internal Snags the use of phrases like 'as if your success would hurt your father' should be used. Although patients commonly use the Psychotherapy File accurately, it can be tempting to agree quickly with a provided description without checking out the patient's direct experience and without spelling out the whole sequence. Remember that a procedural description of thought and action carries with it implications for feeling (which feelings? expressed or repressed?) and for communication with, and control of, others.

Use of TPPs

Once TPPs are listed they are pivotal to the therapy. After reformulation, patients must have explicit homework assignments designed to teach them to recognise the occurrence of these Problem Procedures. Therapists must know their patient's TPPs; if you cannot tell your supervision group what your patient's TPPs are you are very unlikely to recognise their occurrence in the therapeutic relationship (transference). The aims of therapy will normally be the relief of Target Problems and the replacement or modification of Target Problem Procedures. Banal 'exists' or options, such as 'to live happily' are of no value. If such options are to be listed at all, this should be done only when the patient has shown a real grasp of the TPP and has begun to recognise its occurrence reliably.

The weekly rating of change (of the TPs and TPPs) on the Rating Sheet (see Appendix 2.2) is best done by the patient at the end of the session. It is often best to rate *recognition* in the early stages. Once this is achieved the rating may be applied to *revision*. It is important that therapists should consider each item and challenge ratings that do not accord with the patient's reported experience or way of being in the session. While some 'halo effect' is inevitable (i.e. while all ratings tend to move in parallel), closer examination will often show that change occurs at different rates and on different items, and its differentiation may be important. This joint rating serves to remind both therapist and patient of the procedures being tackled in therapy and hence has a focusing or scaffolding function in the course of therapy. It also serves as an example of realistic appraisal which patients then learn to carry out for themselves.

It is important to ensure that patients really understand the TPPs and that they do identify examples correctly. Their conviction and their application of the TPPs will not be completed all at once. As these TPPs are reliably identified through homework and in the sessions, the Exits or Aims or Alternative Procedures can be elaborated.

Sequential Diagrammatic Reformulation—SDR

People often find diagrams, or a combination of verbal descriptions and diagrams, more powerful than words alone. The more complex and poorly integrated the personality, the more it is the case that diagrams can convey sequences in a way that words cannot. Diagrams are therefore optional for many patients, but essential for some. The complexity of a diagram will reflect the use to be made of it; in general, the simplest necessary form can be used with the patient, but full diagrams help therapists anticipate covert transference.

Traps, Dilemmas and Snags in diagrams

Diagrams demonstrate sequences with lines, arrows and words. The basic patterns of Traps, Dilemmas and Snags can all be conveyed diagrammatically as in Figure 2.1.

Linking different TPPs

The value of diagrams is even greater where there are a number of procedures of importance, the relations between which need to be established, as in the example in Figure 2.2.

The Procedural Sequence Object Relations Model diagram

This is the most complete representation of how problem procedures are generated, connected and maintained. The core of the diagram should list the individual's *repertoire of reciprocal roles*. These generate (a) reciprocal role procedures, (b) self-management procedures (SMPs), including (c) symptomatic or avoidant procedures which have replaced unmanageable or forbidden roles.

In constructing the core, we draw upon the patient's history, way of being with us, and on our own countertransference (what the patient seems to make us feel or tries to make us do). The core represents the rules and expectations about relationships derived from those originally developed by the immature child and may include quite distorted or exaggerated patterns of both negative and positive roles. Simpler diagrams may be based upon the identification of a single internal role such as the unduly critical parent or the bad guilty child, or may identify the 'core pain'. However, by describing the complementary roles of the reciprocal role repertoire we get a richer, more explanatory account,

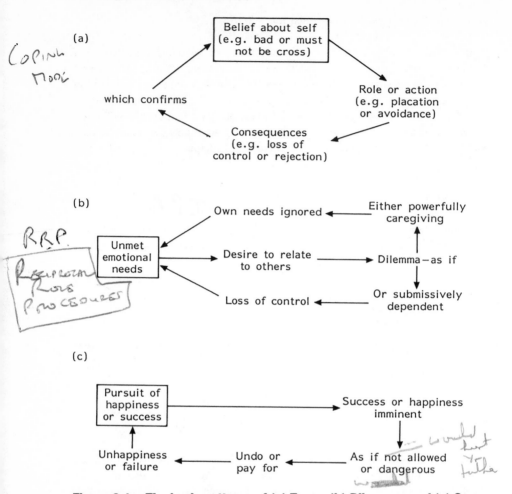

Figure 2.1: **The basic patterns of (a) Traps, (b) Dilemmas and (c) Snags**

and are less likely to identify the suffering roles but not the damaging ones. *The basic unit from which procedures are generated is a reciprocal role.*

Constructing sequential diagrams

The construction of the Sequential Diagram is based (a) on the history, (b) on identifying and describing manifest procedures (self-management, reciprocal role, defensive and symptomatic) and (c) on elaborating a core state model. Different people approach this task in different ways, but it is usually best in

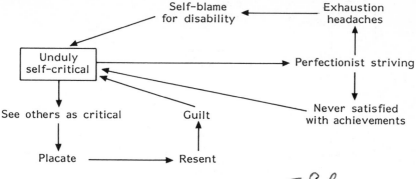

Figure 2.2:   Example of linked procedures $-T P P_o$
                         $TARGET\ PROBLEM\ PROCEDURES$

working with patients to complete the prose reformulation and the preliminary list of TPs and TPPs and/or diagrams of individual procedures before trying to build a complete diagram. In selecting the procedural loops to include in the diagram, try to produce the most economical version possible (some SDRs look like maps of Birmingham's road system). These will usually include:

1. the dominant 'coping mode' (e.g. placation, perfectionism, avoiding closeness)
2. the main SMPs (e.g. self-neglect, avoidance of emotions, symptomatic procedures)
3. the dominant RRPs (e.g. 'powerful care taker to submissive need' or 'contemptuous to contemptible').

Examples are given in Figure 2.3 of coping mode, interpersonal and symptomatic procedures plotted in this way.

Splitting: multiple self-states

Subjectively we are all aware of having different facets or sub-personalities but these are not unduly dissonant and we can usually mobilise the version of the self appropriate to the situation. In neurotic patients, such as have been discussed above, the main problem is one of an exaggeration or elimination of aspects of the range of procedures; e.g. no access to anger or only conditional self-acceptance. In more disturbed people showing a borderline personality structure there are usually two related problems: first the operation of more extreme procedures, and secondly the emergence of strongly contrasted alternative versions of the self. A common structure found in such people is summarised in the 'broken egg' diagram (Figure 2.4).

(a)

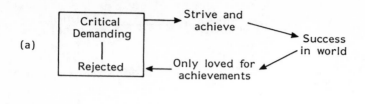

(b)

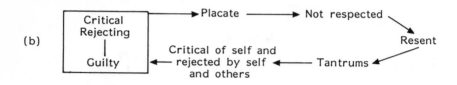

(c)

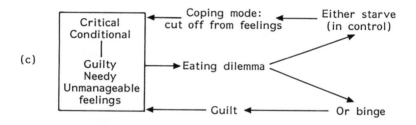

(d)

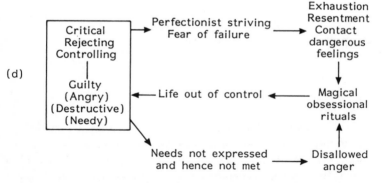

Figure 2.3:   Examples of procedures: (a) coping mode, (b) interpersonal, (c) and (d) symptomatic

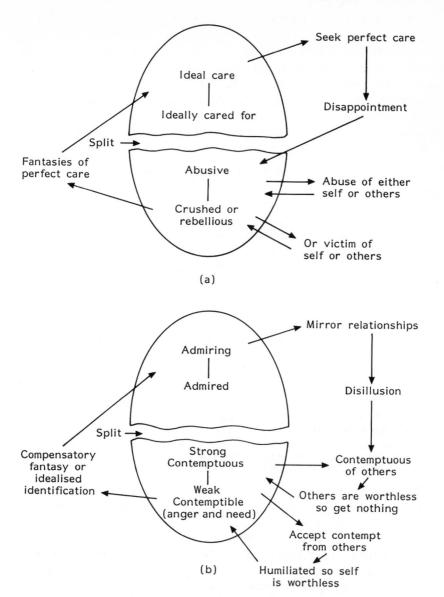

Figure 2.4:   Examples of (a) borderline personality, and (b) narcissistic personality

Splits of this sort are manifest in very polarised experiences and behaviours and in a subjective sense of discontinuity which may be witnessed or imposed upon the therapist if a state shift occurs in the therapeutic relationship. If, in treating such a patient, the therapist works only on the procedures relating to one or other core state, the therapy will be ineffective, for the basic need is for integration. This can only be achieved through the experience of all the aspects of the self being held in awareness (this is the use of the diagram for the patient) and through all being accepted and understood in a relationship (this is the use of the diagram for the therapist).

A state switch is an abrupt change between different states of being, each characterised by a different emotional tone, different symptoms and different patterns of self-management and of relating to others. It is important to seek to characterise these different states as accurately as possible and to ask the patient carefully to monitor shifts between the different states. (You may find that certain states are not very cooperative in this venture!) Patients may be helped to identify their different states by being given the following (derived from a form devised by Hilary Beard):

Recognising different states of being

1. First try to list the distinct, different states, and give each a name (for example 'Sulky Linda' or 'Bossy').

2. Take a separate page for each such name and, for each, describe: (a) How I feel towards others in this state; (b) How I feel inside myself; (c) How I think others feel about me; (d) How I judge or value myself when in this state; (e) What bodily feelings accompany this state? (f) What do I tend to do when in this state? (g) What do I try to avoid when in this state? (h) How do I comfort myself in this state? (i) How do I get out of this state?

It should be noted that what patients recognise as *states will be based on the subjective experience of a particular role. In the therapist's description of self-states* these will appear as one pole of a reciprocal role procedure. A full state switch involves a change in both poles, as in a shift from 'admiring–admired' to 'contemptuous–humiliated'; such switches usually have a profound impact on countertransference feelings. Other abrupt switches can occur within a given self-state, however, as a result of a role reversal, as in from 'abused' to 'abusing', or representing a change between alternative responses to a stably perceived reciprocal role, for example from 'compliant' to 'defiant' in relation to another seen as 'domineering'. The identification of separate self-states in terms of their reciprocal role repertoire is essential.

Once such states are defined, the transitions between them deserve particular attention, that is to say the sequential diagram must indicate state sequences as well as procedural sequences. Some of the procedures generated from one state can be seen to lead to a state shift, as in the broken-egg diagram. In many borderline patients a number of separate self-states can be identified. Commonly a main state reflects early experience, for example: 'Abusive contempt–humilated or rebellious'. Other patterns encountered are: 'ideal care–ideally cared for'; 'Emotionally blank zombie–unavailable or rejecting'; 'Unfeeling overactivity–threatening or critical'. But it is essential to work with the patient to describe the individual range. Remember that patients can enact either pole, and hence can attempt to elicit either reciprocal role (action, feeling) in you. An example of a Self State Sequential Diagram is given in Figure 2.5.

Projective identification

For some purposes, the core reciprocal role repertoire may be more usefully used as a guide to relationship patterns seen in terms of projective identification;

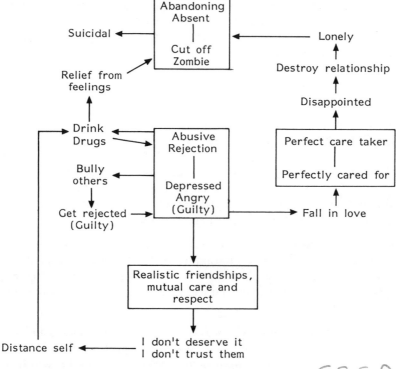

Figure 2.5:   Diagram showing four core states

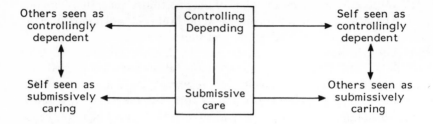

Figure 2.6:   Diagram of core repertoire indicating two patterns of projective identification

i.e. by demonstrating the way in which the various roles may be allocated to important others. The projected roles of a core state described as inner parent–inner child reciprocal roles are shown in Figure 2.6. This may be a helpful way of anticipating countertransference.

Any interaction between two people involves the 'meshing' of two matching RRPs. If the match is imperfect there will be some pressure on the other to reciprocate more exactly: we feel secure when we get back familiar responses. The more insecure we are, the stronger the pressure we exert on others to reciprocate. Figure 2.7 (designed by Mark Dunn) shows how, in relating, two role procedures mesh together.

Sessions 5–16: therapeutic change—general principles

Change is achieved by new understanding, new experience and new behaviour, with change in any one of these being reflected in changes in the others. CAT puts the main emphasis on *new understanding*, offering, in the reformulation, a new description of the patient's experiences and actions.

The *new experience* offered in CAT is, first and foremost, the cooperative, respecting and non-collusive relationship with the therapist. Therapists may also encourage patients to explore situations or aspects of their own natures which have been avoided, and will more generally suggest a testing out of old restrictions and predictions.

New behaviours are, in most cases, generated by the new understandings, but it may be helpful to discuss or rehearse in role play the alternatives to problem procedures, and revising avoidant behaviours may be helped by working out a formal programme of graded exposure.

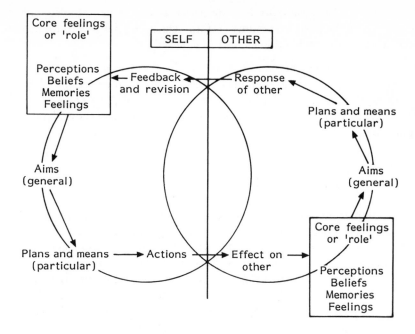

Figure 2.7:   Reciprocal role diagram

The uses of reformulation

The three 'Rs' of CAT are reformulation, recognition and revision, and much of sessions 5–16 will be concerned with the second of these. Recognition will be achieved through specific, focused homework tasks, such as keeping diaries recording particular procedures (e.g. a placation diary) or by keeping a diary of personally significant events or experiences which is subsequently linked by the patient to the TPPs or SDR. Some patients can achieve change simply through this kind of work, but many, notably those with the more disturbed and fragmented personality disorders, will need the therapist to recognise the problem procedures as they occur in the room, when they can be named and where collusion with them can be avoided or quickly corrected. Collusion can lead to missed sessions and premature termination.

The reformulation is the 'scaffolding' within which the patient's new construction is built. The therapist leaves as much of the work as possible to the patient, while maintaining the shape and offering support through the reformulation and the relationship. Here, as earlier, there is no conflict between the 'cognitive' and 'analytic' aspects of the task, for both are involved in the therapist's provision of an interpersonal experience, guided and described by explicit understandings, from which, by internalisation as competence grows, intrapsychic change is achieved.

The pace at which patients can learn to use the reformulation varies (but is faster than most dynamic therapists believe). The 'zone of proximal development', in respect of self-awareness, is often extensive, so the acquisition of new concepts with which to think about the self can mobilise a considerable untapped potential.

The course of therapy

No two therapies are alike and every session is different, but some overall patterns may be noted. Patients, whether initially untrusting, placatory or cooperative, are usually contained by the reformulation and sustained for the ensuing sessions, during which they will carry out homework tasks, apply their new understandings and be active and open in the sessions. Most will make real progress in their ability to identify problem procedures and will be able to begin to consider or try alternatives. However, usually around session 10–12, the approach of termination, inevitable shortcomings on the part of the therapist and the realisation that only so much has been achieved lead to a shift in mood and attitude and to the mobilisation of negative procedures. This may be presented in straightforward criticism, but will more often take the form of more subtle changes in atmosphere and of indirect or non-verbal messages. Their emergence will have been anticipated in the reformulation but this will not prevent the occurrence of covert countertransference collusion (e.g. maintaining a falsely positive idealised relationship, or by not acknowledging but conveying counter-hostility). The worst outcome is a missed session or a premature termination, the best is the subtle but insistent use of the reformulation to describe, in non-judgemental terms, what has happened. In the latter case a return to a basically positive but more realistic relationship will follow, and the return of negative feelings at termination can usually be accommodated in the same way. It is always important to note and permit or anticipate negative feelings at termination.

Some specific tasks and issues

Reviewing and rating progress—the Rating Sheet

The revised rating sheet now in use allows progress in *recognition* of TPPs to be rated in the early stages, with rating of *revision* following once this is secure.

When therapy is conducted in relation to the SDR, ratings can be made of the frequency/intensity with which problem procedural loops have been followed and of the occurrences of negative state shifts where multiple self-states are described.

There are two good reasons for carrying out ratings at every session. The first is that, carried out by the patient in discussion with the therapist, it is an exercise in accurate self-observation. The second is that it offers a chance to look back on both the content and the form of the session and to link these with the reformulation (a scaffolding function), incidentally giving the therapist a second chance to make sense of transference and countertransference feelings. Rating and the setting of homework should be carried out at the end of the session, the spontaneous flow of which (unless the patient is very distressed) should therefore be stopped an adequate time before the end.

Homework

The point and exact form of homework should be discussed with patients and the results, or the patient's non-completion, should always be considered at the next session. The main focus of homework in the first four sessions will have been on mood shifts, symptoms, behaviours; after reformulation the main focus will be on the recognition of problem procedures in everyday life.

Making procedural links in the session

A large proportion of what patients bring to the session in the form of memories, stories or dreams will turn out to be illustrations of their main procedures, and sooner or later most of their problem procedures will be manifest in the therapy relationship, either in behaviours such as lateness, disarming chat, direct anger or criticism, discounting what has been done and failures to do agreed homework, or in covert shifts in mood, conveyed indirectly and non-verbally. These may affect a whole session or set of sessions or they may emerge as a 'state shift' in the course of the session. The recognition of these transference manifestations may not be instantly possible and sometimes the pattern is only apparent in retrospect at the end of the session or after the session (or in supervision). Whenever recognised, all such links need to be discussed.

Making such links is a subtle task. I would like to acknowledge the work of Dawn Bennett in developing the following 'ideal' account of the stages:

1. The therapist acknowledges the expressed feelings of the patient or describes his/her sense of the feelings.
2. The nature of what is felt is explored and clarified in an open way.
3. The therapist invites the patient to link the feelings with the reformulation, or proposes how they might be linked. This may be amplified by linking the episode to earlier examples in the therapy, to relationships with others or with the childhood memories, *but the link with the reformulation will be the main focus.*
4. In the earlier stages, the patient's acceptance that a link exists needs to be amplified. Doubts and objections must be explored (*negotiation*), a resolved agreement reached (*consensus*) and the relation of the identified procedure to the whole reformulation, or to the SDR core procedural repertoire, should be established (*extension*).
5. Once recognition is achieved, alternatives to the identified procedure, already exemplified by the collaborative work, can be further explored through discussion, role play and so on, and this may lead to the identification of 'exits' from the current pattern.

Stagnation

Sometimes therapies which seem to go well lose their momentum; understandings are not translated into felt experiences or into new actions. At such a moment a review of the course of the therapy should be carried out, looking for possible collusive countertransference avoidance of difficult feelings and considering how far the history, for example of incomplete mournings or of unmanageable trauma, may indicate the need for a direct search for missing affects. The therapist may offer a safety within which the lost feelings can be explored or a relationship which can serve as a metaphor for the unresolved past (notably, termination serves this purpose in unmourned loss). In other cases possible ways of making feelings bearable can be discussed. Exploratory writing to the unmourned dead or confronting the abuser in imagination or through writing and other imagery can be helpful. Some ritual marking of the completion of the process may be suggested. These patients can evoke powerful countertransference feelings, as the therapist feels the feelings the patient cannot bear, and this may enable the load to be shared. In general, patients will only go as far as they can bear to go, and may be encouraged to explore, but, especially where major trauma or abuse have occurred, the therapist must be sensitive to the patient's ability to face their feelings and should never force the pace. Even in the absence of major loss or trauma some patients have great difficulty in translating their new understanding into new behaviour, either in the world of daily life or in the room with the therapist. Therapists will need to call upon a range of techniques to achieve movement, including 'shaking the transference tree', the explicit naming of countertransference, the use of role play or empty chair techniques or other non-verbal techniques. Some patients in this category may achieve useful understanding but little change from CAT; reviewing them at follow-up may show further change, but for others referral to alternative treatment to complete the work is appropriate; for example art therapy, psychodrama or group therapy may be indicated.

Difficult transference

Transference feelings can be difficult to deal with when they are very intense, when major dependency needs are expressed in a sexualised way, when feelings seem to be of a delusory intensity without evident awareness of their inappropriateness, and/or when they are aimed too unerringly at the therapist's countertransference vulnerabilities. To be able to contain such transference feelings in relative calmness and to show their relationship to central problem procedures is very therapeutic, but not easy. Any therapist faced with a very intense transference or aware of his or her unusual vulnerability to or preoccupation with a patient or noticing departures from the normal rules and limits of therapeutic practice should seek supervision urgently.

Termination and the goodbye letter

Therapy is often a profound and moving experience for both therapist and patient and termination is never easy. Nonetheless, in a time-framed therapy like CAT, there are very few indications for changing the contract. The fact of termination should be kept in awareness throughout the therapy by naming the number of each session, but its reality can still be experienced by patients as a desertion or betrayal. Such feelings may be expressed, but more often they are hidden or only hinted at. Failure to allow and deal with them lessens the chance of therapy being mourned in a way allowing the internalisation of a real but incomplete experience.

The goodbye letter from the therapist is a means of offering a realistic estimation of the changes achieved and of the work remaining; it should be accurate, linked with specific evidence, and should be discussed with the patient. The patient's goodbye letter is similarly an experience of self-evaluation. The therapist's letter should also name or predict the element of disappointment, sadness or anger, while at the same time 'permitting' the patient to take away a realistic memory of the therapist and a clear account of the understandings reached; in brief therapy the patient must continue to be a therapist to him or herself, and an ongoing internal conversation with the therapist should be encouraged. The period between termination and follow-up is an important one, in which it becomes clear how far the understandings have been taken on board, and decisions about the need for further follow-up, more CAT or other treatments are best left until this time, which is usually after three months. In cases evoking particular anxiety, a shorter interval or spaced sessions may be helpful without depriving the patient of the experience of termination.

The follow-up session

Anticipation of the follow-up can assist some patients to deal with termination and learn how much they have taken away from therapy. Quite a large proportion, however, do not attend, as much in cases that seemed to have gone well as in those with problems. This may reflect inadequate attention being paid to negative feelings at termination. For the therapist, it is an important opportunity to review the work of the therapy, free from the 'hello–goodbye' effects present at termination.

The semi-structured post-therapy interview used at Guy's CAT clinic is a good model for obtaining a reasonably accurate impression. Each of the presenting problems described in the reformulation and referral letter is discussed in turn, with detailed examples of any changes being elicited. In the course of this some patients will refer to their reformulation, but in all cases the details of the TPPs or SDR should be enquired after, both to see how far they are accurately remembered and/or are still being consulted, and also to seek evidence, in detail, as to whether they have been revised. Any new problem or important life event should also be discussed. On the basis of this interview the therapist should rate change and also ask the patient to give an overall rating for changes (a) in the problems and (b) for procedural change, on five-point scales (much better, better, unchanged, worse, much worse). General comments on the therapy may also be invited, and the patient should be asked if they feel they need further treatment.

Patients with residual difficulties who are still working with the therapy tools may be reviewed at a second follow-up, or may be helped with two or three 'top-up' sessions. Patients who have made good use of CAT in terms of understanding but whose access to feeling or ability to relate differently on the basis of their new understandings is little changed may be referred for group therapy (CAT allows little 'working through' time and some patients are socially too isolated to be able to apply the lessons of therapy in ongoing relationships) or to some other mode. If long-term individual therapy is available, some patients will be suitable for this. Patients who have made no real progress or who are worse should be reassessed, preferably by the team or individual who recommended them for therapy initially.

Psychometric testing

Apart from its research use, psychological testing before and after therapy has much to recommend it. The limitations of such tests are, of course, well known, but they remain of value (a) in indicating, crudely, the severity and type of difficulty of the patient group treated, and (b) in giving measures of change. The current battery of tests in use at Guy's CAT clinic consists of (i) the Beck Depression Inventory—BDI (Beck et al., 1961), (ii) the Symptom Check List—SCL 90/4 (Derogatis, Lipman and Covi, 1973), and (iii) the Inventory of Interpersonal Problems—IIP (Horowitz et al., 1988). The SCL 90/4 samples a range of symptoms, and discussing the highly scored items with the patient may amplify the history. The IIP's individual items are often worth discussing at the reformulation stage and the overall score gives an indication of the level of interpersonal difficulty and distress. Failure of elevated scores on these questionnaires to fall in the course of therapy strongly suggests an unsuccessful therapy, but it is also the case that scores can fall without all the issues being resolved. In institutional settings the audit of therapy services would normally need to include some psychometric tests.

Of other paper-and-pencil tests. Repertory grid testing, used extensively in CAT in relation to research (see Chapter 10), may also have clinical applications, and with the widespread availability of computers is quite within the reach of the interested therapist.

References

Beck, A.T., Ward, C.H., Mendelson, M., Mock, J. and Erbaugh, J. (1961). An inventory for measuring depression, *Archives of General Psychiatry*, **4**, 561–571.
Derogatis, L.R., Lipman, R.S. and Covi, M.D. (1973). SCL90: an outpatient rating scale, *Pharmacology Bulletin*, **9**, 13–20.
Horowitz, L., Rosenberg, S., Baer, G., Ureno, G. and Villasenor, V.S. (1988). Inventory of interpersonal problems: psychometric properties and clinical applications, *Journal of Consulting and Clinical Psychology*, **56**, 885–892.

Appendix 2.1 The Psychotherapy File—An aid to understanding ourselves better

We have all had just one life and what has happened to us, and the sense we made of this colours the way we seen ourselves and others. How we see things is for us, how things are, and how we go about our lives seems 'obvious and right'. Sometimes, however, our familiar ways of understanding and acting can be the source of our problems. In order to solve out difficulties we may need to learn to recognise how what we do makes things worse. We can then work out new ways of thinking and acting.

These pages are intended to suggest ways of thinking about what you do; Recognising your particular patterns is the first step in learning to gain more control and happiness in your life.

Keeping a diary of your moods and behaviour

Symptoms, bad moods, unwanted thoughts or behaviours that come and go can be better understood and controlled if you learn to notice when they happen and what starts them off.

If you have a particular symptom or problem of this sort, start keeping a diary. The diary should be focused on a particular mood, symptom or behaviour, and should be kept every day if possible. Try to record this sequence:

1. How you were feeling about yourself and others and the world *before* the problem came on.
2. Any external event, or any thought or image in your mind, that was going on when the trouble started, or what seemed to start it off.
3. Once the trouble started, what were the thoughts, images or feelings you experienced.

By noticing and writing down in this way what you do and think at these times, you will learn to recognise—and eventually have more control over—how you act and think at the time. It is often the case that bad feelings like resentment, depression or physical symptoms are the result of ways of thinking and acting that are unhelpful. Diary-keeping in this way gives you the chance to learn better ways of dealing with things.

It is helpful to keep a daily record for 1–2 weeks, then to discuss what you have recorded with your therapist or counsellor.

Patterns that do not work, but are hard to break

There are certain ways of thinking and acting that do not achieve what we want, but which are hard to change. Read through the lists on the following pages and mark how far you think they apply to you.

Applies strongly + +   Applies +   Does not apply 0

TRAPS

Traps are things we cannot escape from. Certain kinds of thinking and acting result in a 'vicious circle' when, however hard we try, things seem to get worse instead of better. Trying to deal with feeling bad about ourselves, we think and act in ways that tend to confirm our badness.

Examples of Traps

1. Fear of hurting others Trap

Feeling fearful of hurting others* we keep our feelings inside, or put our own needs aside. This tends to allow other people to ignore or abuse us in various ways, which then leads to our feeling, or being, childishly angry. When we see ourselves behaving like this, it confirms our belief that we shouldn't be aggressive and reinforces our avoidance of standing up for our rights.

People often get trapped in this way because they mix up aggression and assertion. Mostly, being assertive—asking for our rights— is perfectly acceptable. People who do not respect our rights as human beings must either be stood up to or avoided.

2. Depressed thinking Trap

Feeling depressed, we are sure we will manage a task or social situation badly. Being depressed, we are probably not as effective as we can be, and the depression leads us to exaggerate how badly we handled things. This makes us feel more depressed about ourselves.

3. Trying to please Trap

Feeling uncertain about ourselves and anxious not to upset others, we try to please people by doing what they seem to want. As a result (1) we end up being taken advantage of by others which makes us angry, depressed or guilty, from which our uncertainty about ourselves is confirmed; or (2) sometimes we feel out of control because of the need to please, and start hiding away, putting things off, letting people down, which makes other people angry with us and increases our uncertainty.

4. Avoidance Trap

We feel ineffective and anxious about certain situations, such as crowded streets, open spaces, social gatherings. We try to go back into these situations, but feel even more anxiety. Avoiding them makes us feel better, so we stop trying. However, by constantly avoiding situations our lives are limited and we come to feel increasingly ineffective and anxious.

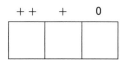

5. Social isolation Trap

Feeling under-confident about ourselves and anxious not to upset others, we worry that others will find us boring or stupid, so we don't look at people or respond to friendliness. People then see us as unfriendly, so we become more isolated from which we are convinced we are boring and stupid—and become more under-confident.

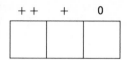

6. Low self-esteem Trap

Feeling worthless, we feel that we cannot get what we want because (a) we will be punished, (b) others will reject or abandon us, or (c) as if anything good we get is bound to go away or turn sour. Sometimes it feels as if we must punish ourselves for being weak. From this we feel that everything is hopeless, so we give up trying to do anthing—which confirms and increases our sense of worthlessness.

DILEMMAS (False choices and narrow options)

We often act as we do, even when we are not completely happy with it, because the only other ways we can imagine, seem as bad or even worse. Sometimes we assume connections that are not necessarily the case—as in 'if I do *x* then *y* will follow'. These *false choices* can be described as either/or or if/then *dilemmas*. We often don't realise that we see things like this, but we act as if these were the only possible choices.

Do you act as if any of the following false choices rule your life? Recognising them is the first step to changing them.

Choices about myself
I act AS IF:

1. Either I keep feelings bottled up or I risk being rejected, hurting others, or making a mess.

2. Either I feel I spoil myself and am greedy or I deny myself things and punish myself and feel miserable.

3. If I try to be perfect, I feel depressed and angry: If I don't try to be perfect, I feel guilty, angry and dissatisfied.

4. If I must then I won't; it is as if when faced with a task I must either gloomily submit or passively resist (other people's wishes, or even my own feel too demanding, so I put things off, avoid them).

5. If I must not then I will; it is as if the only proof of my existence is my resistance (other people's rules, or even my own feel too restricting, so I break rules and do things which are harmful to me).

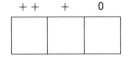

6. If other people aren't expecting me to do things, look after them etc., then I feel anxious, lonely and out of control.

7. If I get what I want I feel childish and guilty; If I don't get what I want, I feel frustrated, angry and depressed.

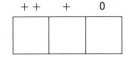

8. Either I keep things (feelings, plans) in perfect order, or I fear a terrible mess.

Choices about how we relate to others
I behave with others AS IF:

	+ +	+	0

1. Either I'm involved with someone and likely to get hurt, or I don't get involved and stay in charge, but remain lonely.

	+ +	+	0

2. Either I stick up for myself and nobody likes me, or I give in and get put on by others and feel cross and hurt.

	+ +	+	0

3. I'm either a brute or a martyr (secretly blaming the other).

	+ +	+	0

4. (a) With others either I'm safely wrapped up in bliss or in combat.
   (b) If in combat, then I'm either a bully or a victim.

	+ +	+	0

5. Either I look down on other people, or I feel they look down on me.

	+ +	+	0

6. (a) Either I'm sustained by the admiration of others whom I admire, or I feel exposed.
   (b) If exposed, then I feel either contemptuous of others or I feel contemptible.

	+ +	+	0

7. Either I'm involved with others and feel engulfed, taken over or smothered, or I stay safe and uninvolved but feel lonely and isolated.

	+ +	+	0

8. When I'm involved with someone whom I care about, then either I have to give in or they have to give in.

	+ +	+	0

9. When I'm involved with someone whom I depend on, then either I have to give in or they have to give in.

	+ +	+	0

10. As a women, either I have to do what others want or I stand up for my rights and get rejected.

	+ +	+	0

11. As a man, either I can't have any feelings or I am an emotional mess.

SNAGS

Snags are what is happening when we say 'I want to have a better life, or I want to change my behaviour but . . .'. Sometimes this comes from how we or our families thought about us when we were young; such as 'She was always the good child', or 'In our family we never . . .'. Sometimes the snags come from the important people in our lives not wanting to change, or not able to cope with what our changing means to them. Often the resistance is more indirect, as when a parent, husband or wife becomes ill or depressed when we begin to get better.

In other cases, we seem to 'arrange' to avoid pleasure or success, or if they come, we have to pay in some way, by depression, or by spoiling things. Often this is because, as children, we came to feel guilty if things went well for us, or felt that we were envied for good lick or success. Sometimes we have come to feel responsible, unreasonably, for things that went wrong in the family, although we may not be aware that this is so. It is helpful to learn to recognise how this sort of pattern is stopping you getting on with your life, for only then can you learn to accept your right to a better life and begin to claim it.

You may get quite depressed when you begin to realise how often you stop your life being happier and more fulfilled. It is important to remember that it's not being stupid or bad, but rather that:

1. We do these things because this is the way be learned to manage best when we were younger.
2. We don't have to keep on doing the now we are learning to recognise them.
3. By changing our behaviour, we can learn not only to control our own behaviour, but also how to change the way other people behave to us.
4. Although it may seem that others resist the changes we want for ourselves (for example, our parents, or our partners), we often under-estimate them. If we are firm about our right to change, those who case for us will usually accept the change.

Do you recognise that you feel limited in your life:

1. For fear of the response of others? (for example, success *as if* it deprives others, *as if* others may envy me, or *as if* there are not enough good things to go around.)

+ +	+	0

2. By something inside yourself? (For example, I must sabotage good things *as if* I don't deserve them.)

+ +	+	0

DIFFICULT AND UNSTABLE STATES OF MIND

Some people find it difficult to keep control over their behaviour and experience because things feel very difficult and different at times. Indicate which, if to blank them off and feel emotionally distant from others.

1. How I feel about myself and others can be unstable; I can switch from one state of mind to a completely different one.

+ +	+	0

2. Some states may be accompanied by intense, extreme and uncontrollable emotions.

+ +	+	0

3. Other states may be accompanied by emotional blankness, feeling unreal, or feelng muddled.

+ +	+	0

4. Some states are accompanied by feeling intensely guilty or angry with myself, wanting to hurt myself.

+ +	+	0

5. Other states are accompanied by feeling that others can't be trusted, are going to let me down, or hurt me.

+ +	+	0

6. Yet other states are accompanied by being unreasonably angry or hurtful to others.

+ +	+	0

7. Sometimes the only way to cope with some confusing feelings is to blank them off and feel emotionally distant from others.

+ +	+	0

Appendix 2.2　The Rating Sheet

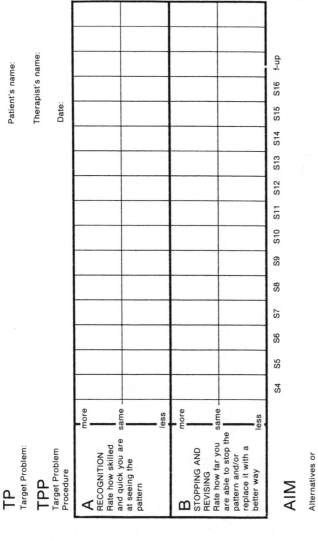

Patient's name:

Therapist's name:

Date:

TP
Target Problem:

TPP
Target Problem
Procedure

A
RECOGNITION
Rate how skilled
and quick you are
at seeing the
pattern

more ─
same
─ less

B
STOPPING AND
REVISING
Rate how far you
are able to stop the
pattern and/or
replace it with a
better way

more ─
same
─ less

AIM

Alternatives or
exits:

S4　S5　S6　S7　S8　S9　S10　S11　S12　S13　S14　S15　S16　f-up

3 Very brief psychotherapeutic interventions with deliberate self-harmers

Pauline Cowmeadow

There is a need for an effective treatment of patients who deliberately do themselves harm, whether through poisoning or injury, because of the frequent repetition of such acts and the increased risk of suicide. In the course of a controlled intervention study (Cowmeadow et al., in preparation) in which patients admitted to hospital after deliberate self-harm were allocated randomly to either eight sessions or a single session of psychotherapy (Cowmeadow, 1994), I gained experience of very brief interventions with this difficult group of patients. My interests were two-fold: firstly to explore the advantages of a psychotherapeutic approach, and secondly to assess the benefits of a single psychotherapeutic session, offered as soon as possible after the initial assessment. This chapter describes a model and some case studies, based on my work with deliberate self-harmers, in a single psychotherapeutic session. This model combines general psychodynamic elements with specific elements from the CAT approach.

Deliberate self-harm

Repetition of deliberate self-harm is common. A number of studies have shown that between 12% and 25% of patients treated for deliberate self-harm repeat within one year (Hawton and Catalan, 1982). Furthermore, there is an increased risk of suicide; in the year following an episode of self-harm the risk is 100 times higher than in the general population (Kreitman, 1989) and the overall lifetime risk is 27 times that of the general population (Hawton and

Cognitive Analytic Therapy: Developments in Theory and Practice, Edited by A. Ryle
© 1995 John Wiley & Sons Ltd

Fagg, 1988). It has been noted that between a third and a half of all suicides are preceded by an episode of deliberate self-harm, often a comparatively short time before the fatal event and often treated by a professional (Kreitman, 1989). This represents a powerful argument for providing an effective intervention at the time of the self-harm episode, to prevent both repetition and suicide by severing the deliberate self-harm–suicide link.

Difficulties of providing effective treatment

The difficulties include the range of problems—emotional, personal and interpersonal—of these patients; the high proportion of patients with personality disorders; and the lack of any clear agreement about the best form of treatment, which is reflected in the wide variation in clinical practice (Hawton and Fagg, 1988). This patient group is characterised by very poor compliance with treatment; typically only 30% attend follow-up appointments after initial assessment (Moller, 1988). However, it has been noted that compliance may be improved by early intervention and continuity of care—that is, the same person doing both assessment and treatment (Moller, 1988). Another difficulty is that these patients often provoke rejecting and hostile attitudes in those who attempt to help them (Ramon, Bancroft and Skrimpshire, 1975). In addition, these patients are often very distressed and thus may cause high levels of anxiety in staff which may be difficult to contain.

Important treatment characteristics

The observations above suggest that an intervention most likely to be helpful should have the following features:

1. Treatment should take place early, as soon as possible after the episode of self-harm.
2. Treatment should be provided by the same person who did the assessment.
3. Treatment should be psychotherapeutic in approach, thus providing a framework within which the patient's distress may be taken seriously and his or her anxiety contained. Also, a psychotherapeutic approach addresses countertransference difficulties, in that reactions aroused in the therapist may be understood as enactments of the patient's interpersonal difficulties.
4. Treatment should include a problem-solving component which aims to help patients find alternative solutions to their difficulties so they do not need to resort to self-harm.

Before describing how I have combined these four elements in a single psychotherapeutic session, offered to patients shortly after assessment for a deliberate self-harm act, I shall review briefly the literature on single-session therapy.

Single-session psychotherapy

There have been many studies of brief psychotherapy, but reports of change occurring in five or fewer sessions are more rare (Barkham, 1989). Information about the potential usefulness of single-session psychotherapy comes from three areas: studies of 'dropouts' from therapy; follow-up studies of patients who received psychotherapy assessments but no treatment; and reports of planned brief interventions of between one and three sessions.

Several studies, mainly from the USA, have looked at the reasons given by patients for discontinuing therapy after a single session. These studies showed that, contrary to the therapists' assumptions, many patients failed to return because they felt they were satisfied with the help they had received (Talmon, 1990; Silverman and Beech, 1979). The author of one of these studies concludes that: 'Single-session encounters between mental health professionals and their clients are remarkably common. Not only is their frequency underestimated, but more importantly their therapeutic impact appears to be under-estimated as well' (Bloom, 1981, p. 180).

The second area of relevance is follow-up studies of patients assessed for psychotherapy who did not receive treatment. David Malan and others at the Tavistock Clinic (1975) followed up 45 patients two and eight years after the initial assessment. Twenty-three patients (51%) were judged to have improved symptomatically, and 11 (20%) showed evidence of psychodynamic change, as judged from therapists' reports of the first interview and from patients' comments about the interviews at follow-up. The psychodynamic changes were similar to those that might be expected from long-term psychotherapy. The authors concluded that 'Powerful therapeutic effects may follow from a single interview' (p. 121).

The two therapeutic factors that were identified as being important in dynamic change were 'insight' and the patients being brought face to face with the necessity to take responsibility for their own lives. The authors commented that these patients, when seen at follow-up, showed a new ability to resolve a situation, first by self analysis and then by taking appropriate constructive action on the insight achieved. This resulted in a new way of handling emotional difficulties. Other changes included patients being able to work through feelings with other people involved and the breaking of vicious circles between patients and their environment. These changes appeared to have been facilitated by the single diagnostic interview, and the authors concluded:

'Clearly psychiatrists who undertake consultations should not automatically assign patients to long term psychotherapy or even to brief psychotherapy, but should be aware of the possibility that the single dynamic interview may be all that is needed' (p. 126).

The third area of information about single-session therapy comes from accounts of brief interventions of between one and three sessions. Freud described two cases of patients who were treated in a single session of psychoanalysis: Katharina (Breuer and Freud, 1893) and Gustav Mahler (Freud, 1960). More recently, Bloom (1981) has described a model for 'single-session focused therapy', the aim of which is to 'break through an impasse in the client's psychological life' (p. 182). Davanloo (1980) has given accounts of planned two-session dynamic psychotherapy, and Talmon (1990) has described an approach to single-session therapy in terms of 'maximising the effect of the first (and only) therapeutic encounter'. He emphasises flexibility of technique and an active approach. Barkham has described a model of 'Two Plus One Therapy', in which patients are seen for two sessions one week apart, followed by a third session three months later.

Common themes from studies in all three areas are, firstly, that the therapeutic impact of single psychotherapeutic sessions may be under-estimated; secondly, that the therapeutic power of single sessions may be maximised by active interventions by the therapist; and lastly that these interventions should aim at increasing the patient's insight into his or her difficulties so as to discover new ways of handling emotional difficulties.

Single-session therapy and deliberate self-harm

Various studies of psychodynamic psychotherapy with deliberate self-harm patients have described the difficulties and general issues that may arise in working with these patients (Tabachnick, 1961; Birtchnell, 1983; Campbell and Hale, 1991; McGinley and Rimmer, 1992). There are, however, no reports of single psychotherapeutic sessions with this group of patients. One of my research interests was to explore the potential therapeutic value of the single psychotherapeutic session, which I thought might be especially relevant in the treatment of deliberate self-harmers because they frequently do not return for treatment after initial assessment.

Practical details

All patients received a full clinical assessment as soon as possible after their admission, before the psychotherapy session. Patients needing antidepressants or inpatient treatment were excluded from the project. During the assessment, particular emphasis was placed on a detailed reconstruction of the events, including the patient's states of mind and emotions, leading up to the self-harm act. Typical patterns in relationships and in reactions to important figures in the patient's life were identified. In this way, information was gained about problem behaviours or feelings which would be the focus for the single psychotherapy session. After assessment, the patient was given a copy of the Psychotherapy File (see Appendix 2.1 in Chapter 2), and asked to read it before the psychotherapeutic session, which usually took place about one or two hours later.

The patients were told that the aim of the session was to look in more detail at some of the problems that had emerged in the assessment interview, with a view to clarifying the cause of these difficulties and identifying alternatives to self-harming behaviour. Patients were also told that they would be asked to attend follow-up appointments in three months and one year but they could request a further session at any time.

A model for single-session psychotherapy with deliberate self-harmers

My starting point for doing psychotherapy with patients who have harmed themselves deliberately is Neil Kessel's (1965) description of the predicament of patients who have taken overdoses:

> Distress drives people to self poisoning acts: distress and despair, unhappiness and desperation. . . . Nobody takes poison a little or a lot, to live or to die, unless at that moment he is distressed beyond what he can bear and so desperate that he cannot see a more rational solution. He does not think that no solution exists, but he cannot himself find it. The suicide says, in effect 'There is no way out', but people who poison themselves are saying 'I cannot see a way out'. They find themselves trapped. They are desperate; and their distress drives them to an action that is both stupid and, at the same time, a blow for liberation, to an action that is both senseless and purposeful (p. 1336).

There is wide variation in what may be achieved in a single psychotherapeutic session, depending on the intensity and nature of the patient's distress and how well motivated he or she is to understand the internal causes of the problems, rather than attributing everything to external events. Despite this variation, it is possible to describe a number of therapeutic factors and aims that are involved in a single psychotherapeutic session:

1. Restate the problem in terms of specific emotions and anxieties, such as rage, despair, guilt, fear of rejection.
2. Encourage the expression of emotions and provide containment.

3. Identify problem feelings and behaviours, such as angry outbursts.
4. Describe procedures that reinforce problem feelings and behaviours, especially those linked with actual or perceived rejection from others.
5. Link problem procedures with past experiences.
6. Discuss alternative procedures.
7. Provide a brief reformulation, which may be in prose or diagrammatic.

The self-harm act is often presented by the patient as a reaction to external events but always represents powerful internal states or conflicts which must be addressed therapeutically if repetition and future suicide are to be prevented. When the emotions underlying the distress have been acknowledged, these may be linked to maladaptive procedures which will be seen to be derived from early experience. Alternative strategies will be discussed, and a brief reformulation may be drawn up with the patient.

In summary, the single psychotherapeutic session responds to the predicament of the self-harmer, as described by Kessel, by combining a therapeutic understanding of the patient's distress with a problem-solving approach. I will now illustrate the use of this model with some case examples.

CASE 1

Mr J was Italian, aged 22. He had recently come out of prison and was trying to find work and somewhere to live. He had lost a job as a waiter and was having arguments with the friend in whose council flat he was staying. He felt guilty about imposing on his friend's hospitality but felt exploited by her because she expected him to do baby-sitting and housework. His guilt was compounded when his friend received a bill from the council for £1000 for the rent. Feeling increasingly depressed and anxious, he asked his GP for help but felt fobbed off with a prescription for diazepam with which he overdosed three days later.

Mr J expressed feelings of anger and despair, initially towards the council who were refusing to help him find a flat. He described his feelings before he took the overdose as: 'I felt fed up, couldn't handle any more, and wanted to block everything out. I felt everyone was looking down on me, despising me. I felt I wasn't going to get anywhere on my own and that no-one would help me. I felt desperate and hopeless.' He strongly identified with the description of the Placation Trap in the Psychotherapy File, recognising that behaving in this way often caused him to feel taken advantage of and furious.

The focus of the psychotherapeutic session was his sense of worthlessness and his placatory behaviour within relationships. He attempted to improve his self-esteem by trying to please others and this often led to his feeling exploited, resentful and guilty. This cycle was described to him in the form of a diagram (Figure 3.1). This linked his childhood experience of having been threatened and beaten by a very critical stepfather to internalised self-critical and blaming attitudes which reinforced his feelings of worthlessness.

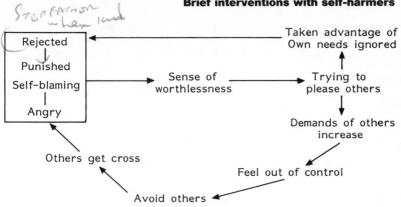

Figure 3.1: Diagrammatic reformulation for 'J'

Mr J found this a helpful description of his difficulties. He became less angry and described how in some situations he had been able to set limits on the demands of others and that this had resulted in an increased sense of his own worth. Mr J was given a copy of the diagram, but was lost to follow-up because he moved out of the area.

CASE 2

Mr B was a 24-year-old unemployed man who took an overdose after a violent argument with his girlfriend during which he smashed up their flat. The argument was precipitated by her threatening to leave, because of his mounting aggressive behaviour. He described himself as feeling increasingly depressed, tense and 'on a short fuse' for three months since he had lost his job. This occurred after he was accused of threatening behaviour towards his workmates.

He was the only child of his parents but was brought up with step-siblings who were the children of each parent's previous marriages. He was envied by his step-siblings, who regarded him as spoilt and fortunate in having two parents living together. He described himself as 'idolised' by his mother, who had high expectations of him. This put him under considerable pressure to succeed. He said he did not want to be 'special' but just to be 'normal'. He dropped out of school and ran away from home. His father was a physically intimidating man who had the potential to be violent. Although he was never violent towards Mr B, he often felt frightened of and intimidated by him. He described how frightening it was when his father beat up a young man who had insulted his wife.

In the psychotherapeutic session, Mr B was very tense and angry, demanding: 'What's the point of all this?' I asked him what he thought his main problem was. He replied: 'my violent tendencies'. I then explained that the purpose of the session was to try to understand this problem in more depth and if possible to find some solutions. He then calmed down considerably and talked about how his aggressive feelings were affecting his life in all areas; not only at work and with his girlfriend whom he felt made unreasonable demands on him, but also sometimes with strangers by whom he easily felt criticised. He was very self-conscious about his appearance and thought that people made comments on this. Sometimes he would resort to aggressive behaviour towards himself, banging his head on the wall in frustration. Underlying much of these aggressive feelings and behaviour appeared to be the fear of being judged as a failure, which seemed to have its origins in childhood.

From the psychotherapy file he identified placation and bottling up his feelings as most relevant to his difficulties. He talked about a terror of losing control and a fear of what he might do if his aggressive feelings got the better of him. His difficulties were formulated diagrammatically as shown in Figure 3.2.

The patient was then asked if he could think of any alternative strategies for dealing with his anger so that it did not escalate into violence. With little prompting, he made seven suggestions. These included: drinking less; taking more physical exercise and seeking mental stimulation; avoiding situations in which he anticipated being exploited; remembering the positive aspects of his relationship with his girlfriend; when he felt himself getting wound up, talking to a helpful friend or getting out of the situation to give himself time to think.

When Mr B was seen for follow-up four months later, he reported considerable improvement. He had had only one further violent outburst, had been getting on better with his girlfriend and had started on a training course. He felt less depressed, more relaxed and had remembered all seven alternative strategies and was putting most of them into practice.

Thus the single psychotherapeutic session appeared to have helped Mr B mobilise his own resources for dealing with increasingly difficult aggressive feelings that were having a destructive effect on all areas of his life.

CASE 3

Miss C was an 18-year-old college student living with her mother and younger sister. She took an overdose after an argument with her mother in which she felt treated unfairly. The background to this was that, due to her mother's intending remarriage, there had been increasing arguments between her sister and her mother. Miss C was very worried that her mother's marriage would result in the breakup of the family. Despite her own anxiety at losing a close relationship with her mother and having to move to a different house, in which she feared her stepfather would 'make all the rules', she suppressed these feelings in trying to help her younger sister come to terms with the situation. 'I've been feeling so upset but couldn't talk about it. . . . No-one seemed to understand how I was feeling, but all the time I was trying to understand how they were feeling, trying to sort it all out. . . . I just got too much.' She expressed anger because she felt that everyone expected her to be 'solid and coping and not in need of support'. Even her boyfriend seemed unaware of her feelings.

Her parents had divorced when she was eight; her father had left home which upset her greatly because she was very attached to him. She remembers feeling insecure, fearing that he was dead and that the house might be broken into by a man who would attack her, her mother and her sister. Despite these anxieties she

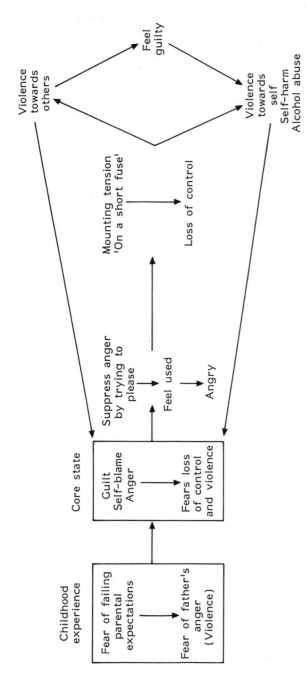

Figure 3.2: Diagrammatic reformulation for 'B'

remembered thinking that she had to be 'strong', that it was up to her to take her father's place and protect her mother and sister. It seemed her sense of security was based on the continuity of her mother, sister and herself being a threesome, and that the threat of having to include her mother's fiancé was very disturbing, and perhaps also caused her to feel displaced in her mother's affections.

Problem procedures identified in the session with Miss C included: looking after others at the expense of herself; feeling that she must be 'strong', thus ignoring her own needs and feelings, then becoming angry because others failed to offer her support when she felt she needed it. Miss C had good insight and recognised how this pattern of coping had developed since her father's disappearance, and also how this contributed to her overdose because she despaired of anyone being interested in how she felt. At three months follow-up, although the difficult situation with her mother's remarriage and housemove remained, she was bottling up her feelings less and talking more to her boyfriend, her mother and also friends at college. She remained anxious about the effects of her mother's relationship with her fiance on her own relationship with her mother, but seemed more tolerant of him and better able to cope with her feelings of rejection by her mother.

These themes were discussed again when Miss C was seen one year after her overdose. By this time, her mother had married and the family had moved outside London. Miss C expressed her sadness about the changes in her life, but also acknowledged that the time had come for her to lead a more independent life.

Miss C was seen, in all, for three sessions over a year and these seemed to be very helpful in assisting her to negotiate a difficult phase of her life.

Conclusions

My experience suggests that single psychotherapeutic sessions with deliberate self-harmers may have several important benefits:

1. Because the psychotherapeutic intervention is combined with assessment and often takes place on the same day or very shortly after assessment, problems of compliance are avoided in that the patient does not need to return for treatment.
2. Providing treatment as soon as possible after the episode of self-harm makes it more likely that the painful feelings which are often relevant to core anxieties are still accessible.
3. Becuase the assessment and treatment are done by the same person, relevant information gleaned at assessment may be reframed in a psychotherapeutic way during the therapeutic session.
4. A psychodynamic psychotherapeutic approach ensures that close attention is paid to the patient's distress and psychotherapeutic skills are used to contain the patient's anxieties and unmanageable feelings. The psychotherapeutic approach also emphasises the therapeutic relationship which is particularly important for patients who may arouse difficult countertransference reactions and who often feel very alienated, and anticipate rejection and criticism.

5. The problem-solving component helps to alleviate distress and despair by suggesting the possibility of alternative solutions.

There are, however, two important limitations of single-session therapy. From a practical point of view, an assessment of a self-harm patient followed by single-session therapy is time-consuming, usually taking a minimum of three hours. However, it could be argued that a thorough assessment followed by a therapeutic session which aims to prevent repetition of self-harm is a more effective use of professional time than giving appointments for future treatment which most patients do not attend. I believe that a therapeutic intervention closely combined with assessment should be provided for every patient who is admitted for deliberate self-harm, and that this may represent a potentially effective approach to the problem of repetition and suicide.

A second limitation of this approach is that some patients need more than one session; they are often those with serious personality difficulties or those with longstanding depression. However, a single psychotherapeutic session combined with assessment forms a good basis for further psychotherapy. Provided this is done by the same therapist, taking a psychotherapeutic approach from the start creates a therapeutic alliance which makes it more likely that the patient will return for further therapy. This was borne out by my experience with the group of self-harmers in my research project who were allocated to an eight-session therapy. All of these received a first psychotherapy session, similar to those described above, on the same day or a few days after assessment. These patients subsequently showed a much higher compliance than expected, in that 50% of them attended all eight sessions, completing their therapy, and four-fifths of them attended at least once after the initial intervention (Cowmeadow et al., in preparation).

This finding appears to confirm the effectiveness of the single psycho-therapeutic session described above. In summary, the crucial elements of this approach are: continuity of care; early intervention; a psychotherapeutic approach that aims to make emotional contact with the patient and help him or her feel that the difficulties are being taken seriously; and a problem-solving element, that offers hope because taking a different perspective on apparently insuperable difficulties carries the possibility of finding new solutions. In conclusion, there is a strong argument for providing this type of psycho-therapeutic intervention to all patients who present with an episode of deliberate self-harm, no matter how trivial this may initially appear to be.

References

Barkham, M. (1989). Exploratory therapy in 2–1 sessions. I: Rationale for a brief psychotherapy model, *British Journal of Psychotherapy*, **6** (1), 82–88.

Birtchnell, J. (1983). Psychotherapeutic considerations in the management of the suicidal patient, *American Journal of Psychotherapy*, **37**, 24–36.

Bloom, B.L. (1981). Focused single-session therapy: initial development and evaluation. In: Budman, S.H. (Ed), *Forms of Brief Therapy*, pp. 167–216, New York, Guilford Press.

Breuer, J. and Freud, S. (1893). Studies in hysteria. Republished 1944 in J. Strachey (ed), *The Complete Psychological Works of Sigmund Freud*, Vol. 2. London, Hogarth Press.

Campbell, D. and Hale, R. (1991). Suicidal acts. In: Holmes, J. (Ed), *Textbook of Psychotherapy in Psychiatric Practice*. Edinburgh, Churchill Livingstone.

Cowmeadow, P. (1994). Deliberate self-harm and cognitive–analytic therapy, *International Journal of Brief Therapy*, **9**, 135–150.

Cowmeadow, P., Ryle, A., Watson, J. and Savournin, R. (in preparation). An intervention study using brief psychotherapy with deliberate self-harmers.

Davanloo, H. (Ed) (1980). *Short-term Dynamic Psychotherapy*. New York, Jason Aronson.

Freud, A. (ed.) (1960). *Letters of Sigmund Freud*. New York, Basic Books.

Hawton, K. and Catalan, J. (1982). *Attempted Suicide*. Oxford, Oxford University Press.

Hawton, K. and Fagg, J. (1988). Suicide and other causes of death following attempted suicide, *British Journal of Psychiatry*, **152**, 359–366.

Kessel, N. (1965). Self poisoning, *British Medical Journal*, 1265–1270 and 1336–1340.

Kreitman, N. (Ed) (1989). *Para-suicide*. Chichester, John Wiley.

Malan, D.H., Heath, E.S., Bacal, H.A. and Balfour, F.H.G. (1975). Psychodynamic changes in untreated neurotic patients. II: Apparently genuine improvements. *Archives of General Psychiatry*, **32**, 110–126.

McGinley, E. and Rimmer, J. (1992). The trauma of attempted suicide, *Psychoanalytic Psychotherapy*, **7** (1), 58–68.

Moller, H.J. (1988). Compliance. In: Platt, S.P. and Kreitman, N. (Eds), *Current Research on Suicide and Para-suicide: Selected Proceedings of the Second European Symposium on Suicidal Behaviour*. Edinburgh, Edinburgh University Press, pp. 164–172.

Ramon, S., Bancroft, J.H.J. and Skrimpshire, A.M. (1975). Attitudes towards self-poisoning among physicians and nurses in a general hospital, *British Journal of Psychiatry*, **127**, 257–264.

Silverman, W.H. and Beech, R.P. (1979). Are drop-outs, drop-outs? *Journal of Community Psychology*, **7**, 236–242.

Tabachnick, N. (1961). Countertransference crisis in suicidal attempts, *Archives of General Psychiatry*, **4**, 64–71.

Talmon, M. (1990). *Single Session Therapy*. Oxford, Jossey-Bass.

4 Treating eating disorders using CAT: two case examples

Francesca Denman

This chapter recounts the experiences of a group of therapists at a major psychiatric hospital who have been treating patients presenting with severe eating disorders, using Cognitive Analytic Therapy (CAT). Two patients who had different presentations and underlying target problem procedures (TPPs) are discussed. The cases illustrate the range of difficulties encountered by CAT therapists in managing the different presentations.

Background

Eating disorders are now a relatively common problem in psychotherapeutic practice, but no approach to treatment has gained clear pre-eminence. These patients can be among the most challenging to treat and their symptoms can be of life-threatening proportions. CAT was thought a possible approach to try because, while both psychodynamic and cognitive–behavioural approaches appear to have something to offer, they also both present distinctive difficulties. CAT, insofar as it integrates both these approaches, might be able to offset the weaknesses of one approach against the strengths of the other.

Cognitive–behavioural treatments seemed to be good at achieving symptomatic improvements in some patients but frequently appeared to leave emotional issues untouched. Furthermore, things could go wrong in these treatments because the therapist could be seen by patients as a coercive parent and was, in consequence, liable to reproduce some common aspects of their

Cognitive Analytic Therapy: Developments in Theory and Practice, Edited by A. Ryle
© 1995 John Wiley & Sons Ltd

family background. On the other hand, psychodynamic treatments addressed emotional and motivational issues well but frequently symptoms did not improve and therapists could appear uninterested in the acutal physical deterioration of their patients.

CAT combines insights from psychodynamic therapy (particularly object relations theory) with techniques and insights from cognitive therapy. It achieves this combination by using a distinct theory of human behaviour, thought and feeling called the Procedural Sequence Model (PSM) (see Ryle, 1990 and Leiman, 1992). Normal goal-directed behaviour and pathology are discussed in terms of procedural sequences, and therapeutic efforts are directed to altering maladaptive procedures in a beneficial direction. CAT neglects neither behaviour nor emotions nor thought; rather, all three are incorporated within the procedural concept.

The context in which the two cases described below were treated was of a specialist treatment centre which takes tertiary referrals from around the country. In consequence patients tended to be at the more severely unwell end of the spectrum of eating disorders, and many had to travel a considerable distance for their therapy sessions. The unit has both outpatient and inpatient services and this is well known to most patients. As a result some patients may be thought by their therapists to be angling for admission, while others whose weight loss or electrolyte levels become medically threatening may be considered to need admission rather than continuing outpatient treatment.

The therapists on the unit were all experienced in managing eating-disordered patients. As therapists they mainly had experience of using cognitive and behavioural interventions. They were all in the process of learning how to use CAT, but none was a complete beginner and none had fewer than three previous CAT cases. CAT was regularly supervised by a relatively experienced CAT supervisor (C.D.) at weekly intervals in a small supervision group of three or four members.

Because of their sensitive nature, these cases have been extensively disguised. Both patients were female.

CASE 1: Severe anorexia

N's anorexia had started gradually two years before referral, following an illness which involved vomiting and weight loss and a visit to an aunt with anorexia who had told N how terrible she looked. N had also suffered a series of losses in the years leading up to her illness. Her brother and current lover had been killed in a car crash some years previously. Then N had an abortion which she had concealed from everyone except her GP. More recently her best friend had died and she had herself been involved in a serious car crash. N's anorexia was now very severe.

She had been treated locally by psychiatric services and then by the local eating disorders unit, to no avail, and was now referred to the unit. N was severely under-weight. She starved herself rigorously, and although she did not binge or induce vomiting she was often spontaneously sick after eating.

N's relationship with her parents was complex. Her parents' marriage was strained and at times it seemed that they were on the point of separating. N's mother would frequently give up work to look after N, watching her eating and ensuring she could not vomit after meals. N complained bitterly about being chaperoned in this way, but covertly she colluded in her mother's over-concern by losing weight sharply whenever her mother was not present. At a family meeting before therapy, N's mother alternated between an adult but over-concerned mode of relating to her daughter and a complicit, giggly, childish one—leaning over and whispering to N that things would be all right. Her father, while more realistic about the seriousness of the situation, limited his involvement to practical help and declined emotional involvement. It is also possible that he drank rather too much.

At work N was under-achieving. She felt put upon by her boss but was unable to confront him. Often she would agree to perform tasks she knew she would be unable to complete in time because she could not bear to say No. Her subsequent failures to deliver were then held against her. N kept her eating disorder a secret at work and this often precluded her from attending or enjoying office functions of various sorts. N's social life was also restricted in other ways. She had had a variety of short-lived relationships with men which left her feeling 'picked up and put down'.

The therapy

N found it difficult to address psychological issues. If she did address them, she showed a remarkable capacity to dissociate. For example, one week she discussed the death of her brother and became upset and terrified by the force of her feelings, but this seeming breakthrough was entirely negated the following week when she said she did not remember the content of the previous session. N restricted her involvement in therapy. She was invariably late for sessions and often doodled during them. If she was challenged about her lack of progress and involvement in the therapy she would blandly promise to get better by next week!

N's therapist felt a number of things towards her patient. She sometimes felt confused, as though she had not got a grip on the case; or she could feel practical and technical, advising N but also subtly minimising the extremity of N's misery and distress. At other times the therapist felt as though her patient was 'quite a little madam' and wanted to shake her, feeling contemptuous and thinking of her as a weak, silly and spoiled girl.

In therapy the therapist's understanding of N's story was embodied in a diagram (Figure 4.1) which was discussed with N.

N was able to see that the diagram might apply to her and she did then begin

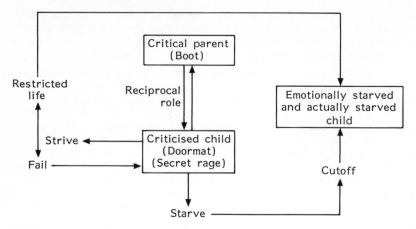

Figure 4.1: The SDR of 'N'

to make some modest gains in weight. However her progress was limited. At the end of therapy, the therapist suggested in her goodbye letter that N might be feeling 'picked up and put down' in a therapy which had not got to the heart of things, just as she sometimes felt in relationships with men. Importantly, N was, at that point, able to say that she had hoped that her case would be serious enough to warrant admission to the inpatient unit and that she had felt that outpatient treatment had belittled the severity of her condition and, in some way, branded her as making a fuss. N and her therapist then became aware of the dynamic force of N's split off, longing for perfect care and her need to avoid the repeated disappointment of that need, even at the cost of forfeiting success.

Follow-up

N subsequently had a period of treatment on the inpatient unit and gained weight rather well at that point. While her CAT therapy was not successful in helping her to gain weight, it did begin a process of psychological awareness which allowed her to use inpatient admission in a way which would probably not have been possible before therapy.

Comment

N is typical of one group of patients who present to the eating disorders unit and who have the anorexic picture of low weight and low body mass index.

They may also have some bingeing or vomiting behaviours but these are not severe. Psychologically the most prominent features are restriction of psychic life because of an evident terror of, or need to avoid, emotions; perfectionistic striving; and a reciprocal role procedure of 'perfectly self-denying care giver (doormat) to perfectionistic luxuriating and demanding recipient (boot)'.

The extreme restriction of psychic life is accompanied by a major lack of psychological mindedness and this presents a considerable obstacle to a psychologically based therapy. The typical feel which these patients give to their therapist is one of 'heavy going'; every gain seems achieved only after trudging for some time through an arid desert. The way that CAT approaches these cases is to try to identify the procedures by which emotionality is avoided, restricted and denied. CAT aims to describe these procedures in relation to the childhood atmosphere in which they were fashioned. It tries to show how the procedures were originally an adaptive attempt to cope with an emotionally difficult or overwhelming situation, but now have become restrictive, and inapplicable. The therapist tries to make plain the 'as if' nature of assumptions that emotions cannot be dealt with in a supportive atmosphere, which may in itself help to contradict those assumptions.

It is important to gain an understanding of the procedures which result in requests for more therapy of various sorts. If further therapy is sought only because of the failure of the current approach, then progress is unlikely. This is because complaints by the patient that they are starving need to be met (gently) with a demonstration of the fact that they have been starving themselves, rather than with the provision of more food which they can refuse. While effective self-starving continues it does not really matter how much more food or therapy is offered. However, sometimes further therapy is sought as a result of a new insight. This was the case with N and in such cases there may be progress. This is especially likely if the new insight includes greater awareness of the fact of, and reason for, emotional and physical self-starving.

CASE 2: Bulimia nervosa with an unintegrated personality

J was living in the house of one of her previous therapists, and concurrently with her CAT she was receiving acupuncture, herbal remedies and long-term psychodynamic psychotherapy. She was still under the care of a psychiatrist who had referred her to the eating disorders unit because she was complaining to him that the treatment offered to her by his unit was not making her better. J's long-term psychotherapist was represented by her as being keen for her to receive help for her eating disorder so that he could get on with other aspects of her therapy. The ex-therapist with whom J was cohabiting had taken her into his house in order to help J with her eating disorder. However, J said that her ex-therapist did not know that she was still bingeing and vomiting about three times a day. As a result she kept secret her CAT sessions at the eating disorders unit. Unfortunately this meant that periodically J had to cancel her CAT sessions in order to take her ex-therapist, who was himself chronically unwell, to hospital for treatment of one sort or another.

The therapy

Understandably J's CAT therapist was extremely unclear what sort of help she could offer. She felt overwhelmed by the amazing variety of care givers in J's world, and was by no means entirely sure if it would be wise to add to them. J's therapist felt, in her own countertransference towards J, an uncharacteristic urge to slap J and bring her to her senses. This urge was provoked by the contrast between (a) J's repeated avowal that CAT therapy was the best thing she had ever had and surely doing her huge amounts of good, and (b) her lack of tangible progress, her failure to do any of the assigned out-of-session tasks, and her habit of cancelling sessions. In addition to J's therapist's countertransference, the supervision group and supervisor had a further countertransference towards J which would best be described as impotent curiosity in relation to J's platonic but rather irregular relationship with her previous therapist.

J did not initially talk much about her family background, and so reformulation at session 4 was completed without details of her past life. The therapist was, however, amply provided with direct experience of J which allowed the construction of an SDR (see Figure 4.2).

J was, as one might expect, immediately hugely impressed by the diagram, instantly announcing it the most helpful thing she had ever seen. Sadly, though, J contrived to leave the SDR behind in the therapist's office! However J did, after a while, begin to make some changes. She spoke for the first time about her family background, which not surprisingly (because abuse is so common in these patients) contained a story of physical abuse tinged with sadomasochistic sexuality by her middle-class father, and of an uncaring and detached mother who had her own health troubles—which she visited on her daughter.

The SDR, based mainly on countertransference, can be seen to be fairly concordant with J's history. The therapist's countertransference paralleled to some extent the role of the father in relation to the patient, while the patient's adoring transference towards the therapist reflects the wish for an ideal carer. In the supervision group we felt we were in the role of useless watching mother in relation to the role of the previous therapist, who himself partly embodied the roles of abusing father and of sick mother. Other ineffective mothers were scattered around the helping network. J's chief symptomatic procedures issuing from and maintaining this set of states included angry sabotage

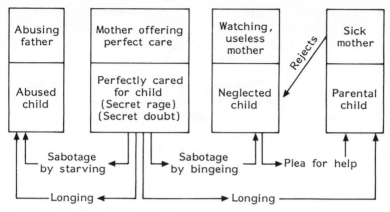

Figure 4.2:   The SDR of 'J'

(although the rage was well concealed) of the seemingly good parent, and rapid uncritical acceptance of the food offered by that parent without true assimilation because of the repressed doubt engendered by the unconscious awareness that the good parent was grotesquely over-idealised.

After the second session in which the diagram was used, J did begin to make some changes. The therapist was able to show how accepting the diagram uncritically and then sabotaging it by leaving it behind were actions which the diagram itself could predict. After that session J went home and told her ex-therapist about her continuing bingeing and vomiting. Usefully she received a sensible response which, while not being rejecting, was also not over-involved. J allowed her long-term therapist and her CAT therapist to communicate with one another, so reducing the fragmentation of mother figures which was such an effective part of J's sabotaging behaviour. J also began to take the diagram around with her and was able to think about the way she was living her life using the diagram. Her bingeing and vomiting did decrease (but not stop).

Comment

J's case is fairly typical of a group of patients who have bulimic symptoms and also suffer from marked personality disorganisation, although she is not a particularly severe example. Other cases seen by the unit include patients with severe self-harming behaviour, patients who have made apparently false allegations of sexual abuse against a sequence of therapists, and patients who have features of Münchausen's syndrome. In all such cases the approach taken by the CAT therapist is to emphasise the severe lack of integration in the personality as the primary feature which needs attention before specific procedures are tackled. In J's case the drawing of a diagram of self-states with a few procedures sketched in helped both the therapist and the patient towards this aim.

Bulimics with concurrent severe illness such as asthma or diabetes deserve mention because they present therapists with difficulties which are especially acute. These patients are able to add dysfunctional illness behaviours to the usual repertoire of behaviours present in eating disorders. Additionally they often succeed in pulling their physicians into the same kinds of loops of coercion and collusion as ordinary eating-disordered patients get into with their families and carers. Often these patients are already bitter about the damage which their physical illness has worked on them. Part of the motivation which drives both their continuing eating disorder and their abuse of medication is an enraged urge to spoil. Because of this, therapy has to take up the work of mourning for the damage already done. Also, the time limit means that limitation must be faced by the therapist (as much as the patient) very early in therapy. Limitation is a useful break on the dynamics of therapeutic omnipotence and despair that can easily infect these cases.

Discussion

Both these cases presented typical problems to their therapists in assessing levels of insight and motivation, and in working out how to increase them. Because therapy is an exercise in which a motivation to change (at least at some level) is a prerequisite, the most important task facing CAT therapists in dealing with these patients is to find some area of motivation and to mobilise it. Therapists also need to identify the reasons why insight is lacking in order to help increase it.

With anorexic patients the level of motivation for treatment is often very low. Young anorexics may have been pushed into therapy by family pressure, and so their motivation for treatment may be bound up in a very literal way with family dynamics which are implicated in the causation of their illness. This may be the reason why family therapy could be the most helpful intervention (Dare et al., 1990). Anorexics lack insight into the practical aspects of their condition, such as realistic weights to attain and body image, but they also lack insight of a more conventional sort in the form of psychological mindedness.

In the successful cases of this kind that were seen at the eating disorders unit, the common feature was the establishment of some kind of joint relationship with the therapist combined with some moves in relation to the external situation—for example talking in a new way to mother or father. Patients who did well seemed to seize on that aspect of the reformulation which meant most to them and to make it their own in some way. This feature is gratifyingly in accord with the theoretical stress within CAT on the use and value of joint tools (Leiman, 1992) as ways of creating and shaping new psychological meanings, which can then act both as the sources of motivation and as centres of insight.

However, in relation to some of the most severe anorexic patients—and particularly those who combine severe anorexic symptoms with bulimic pathology—CAT, at least as practised at the eating disorders unit, does not, so far, appear to be very successful. These patients appear unable to tolerate the timetable of therapy. They come to some appointments, then cancel several, then promise to turn up, and finally drift away. The writing of either simple reminder letters, or interpretive letters or supportive and encouraging ones, does not help them to return. One feature of at least some of these patients treated unsuccessfully at the eating disorders unit was a combination of distance from the unit and extremely severe life circumstances. One patient had a dying mother, and another patient laboured under the double disadvantage of extreme poverty and employment difficulties.

In such cases an active brief therapy like CAT may be too demanding on the patient, who feels over-stretched; but possibly any therapy conducted at such a distance would have the same unsatisfactory outcome. It is tempting to draw an analogy with the idea of a baby who is too hungry to think and, in consequence, needs a mother to think for it. This analogy in some form lies behind the urge to admit the patient for feeding or to offer more intensive psychotherapy. Such efforts can be successful; but often the problem is that these patients have procedural sequences in place which perpetuate the chronic starvation, which then in turn destroys the capacity to make the mental space needed for the revision of the procedural sequences maintaining the starvation. In keeping with this idea, it is striking that in these severe patients the pressure for admission which characterised some of the anorexics was not there; rather, they just drifted away.

In contrast to the procedural causes which characterise lack of insight in the anorexic group, the lack of insight in multi-impulsive bulimics arises from their lack of personality integration. This gives rise to a range of personality states that are occupied sequentially, each of which lacks to some degree the moderation, complexity and flexibility of a fully integrated self. Consequently in such patients insight and motivation may vary depending on the current state, and because of incomplete access to new learning between states therapists may 'successfully' treat a state only to find their work abolished by a state shift that is precipitated, for example, by the end of therapy. This was the case with J whose first reaction to and acceptance of the SDR was shallow, and abolished by a state shift as she left the session. Personality integration must precede other interventions. For this reason the treatment of multi-impulsive bulimics with CAT does not differ very much from the treatment of other kinds of patients with unintegrated personalities.

The stress must be on obtaining a reasonably accurate and empathic description of the sequential states occupied by the patient and the reasons for shifts between them. Key pieces of evidence used in delineating these states include the therapist's countertransference experiences, descriptions of encounters with others, and the patient's history. Once the states have been described the patient is encouraged to try to learn how to identify them using a variety of techniques. Clearly such an activity is in itself insight-promoting, and furthermore it is, in the words of one patient, 'off the diagram'. The use of this joint tool and activity contributes (it is to be hoped) to the building up of a new state or situation with a more general overview.

Two central features of CAT are that (a) it is undertaken as a consciously joint exercise by patient and therapist, and (b) it stresses the concept of procedures as units of goal-directed action. The aim of this chapter has been to demonstrate how both these features of CAT work out in the practice of treating patients with eating disorders. A central theme has been to show how CAT's stress on joint activities and on procedural thinking is helpful in work with patients whose motivation and insight are most often ambivalent or lacking.

References

Dare, C., Eisler, I., Russell, G.F.M. and Szmukler, P. (1990). Family therapy for anorexia nervosa: implications from the results of a controlled trial of family therapy, *Journal of Marital and Family Therapy*, **16**, 39–57.

Leiman, M. (1992). The concept of the sign in the work of Vygotsky, Winnicott and Bakhtin: further integration of object relations theory and activity theory, *British Journal of Medical Psychology*, **65** (3), 209–222.

Ryle, A. (1990). *Cognitive Analytic Therapy: Active Participation in Change. A New Integration in Brief Psychotherapy*. Chichester, John Wiley.

5 CAT in groups

Norma Maple and Ian Simpson

As both practising CAT therapists and group analysts, our experience of working with patients within the NHS and in private practice has shown us that brief individual CAT is a very good preparation for longer-term group therapy. Patients who have followed this path tend to stay longer in their groups and have good insight into the psychological mechanisms which lie behind their difficulties. They are more self aware, less likely to act out and can use the richer, interactional dynamic of the group to put into practice learning from the earlier dyadic relationship with their CAT therapist. After an individual CAT and an appropriate gap, a patient can take the opportunity in a group to explore the meanings of their procedures in a dynamic environment where they receive instant feedback. In a long-term group they are also given the opportunity to experiment with new ways of being and thus consolidate new behaviours into more successful interpersonal procedures outside the therapy setting.

This led us to wonder, along with other CAT colleagues, whether there was not a place for even further integration of the models: whether CAT understandings, tools and practice developed successfully in brief individual therapy could be combined with the theory and practice of group analysis into one integrated model. We were aware of some of the common features of both models:

1. a basic psychotherapeutic stance with the objective of providing a safe setting within which troubled individuals are able to explore their difficulties with the help of (an) empathic other(s)

Cognitive Analytic Therapy: Developments in Theory and Practice, Edited by A. Ryle
© 1995 John Wiley & Sons Ltd

2. engagement of the patient into an active collaboration aimed at verbalising and giving meaning to a range of symptoms
3. the belief that through understanding the effect we have on others and our contribution to dissatisfying interactions, we can draw on our creative energies to challenge dysfunctional behaviour and develop more constructive ways of relating.

Both theory bases also have common features. Group analysis comes from traditional psychoanalysis but focuses on the social origins of interaction and develops ideas from object relations theory and self psychology, amongst others, to inform its theory of group practice. CAT's own roots are also in the ideas of object relations theory amongst other theories of psychological and social development. CAT understands the origins of neurosis through the Procedural Sequence Model as belonging to reciprocal role procedures. These derive from actual experience in the child's historical and social context, mediated by the tools, language and ideas in use within the family and culture. These seemed not too disparate in essence, although the use of and focus on such understandings in the treatment models differ in detail.

We were also aware of what might seem conflictual in the two modes. CAT is an active model using an educational stance to provide the patient with access to new or repressed feelings, understandings and behaviour. Written material has a high profile in this work and suggestions as to tasks aimed at self-monitoring and changing behaviour are offered overtly by the therapist. CAT is individual and brief. Dependency and regression is kept to a minimum and the rational, coping, cognitive functions of the patient are actively enlisted and engaged alongside emotional expression in the search for change. By contrast, a group analysis can take some years of once- or twice-weekly sessions. In group analysis, dependency is encouraged; the patient expresses thoughts and feelings in the group and comes to new understandings at her or his pace, and the length of the therapy is related to the individual need. Group analysts offer a listening stance and conduct rather than lead their groups, confident as to the power of the group to heal, nurture and provide an environment where long-lasting change can take place.

Below, we discuss some thoughts, experiences and conclusions drawn from our attempts at integrating these two models, both theoretically and in practice.

Group analysis

Group analytic psychotherapy is practised in a range of settings both in the NHS and in private practice in this country and throughout Europe, with the standard model being one conductor to eight patients in a slow, open group, meeting once or twice weekly. Patients stay in the group for varying lengths of time ranging from months to many years, and in due course discuss with the group when it will be the appropriate time to leave.

In brief, group analytic theory rests on the premise that the essence of human beings is social rather than individual, unconsciously as well as consciously. The individual organism is the basic biological unit but the basic psychological unit is seen as the group (Hopper, 1980; Napolitani, 1980). Whilst the individual can seem separate and isolated from the group and the community, this separation, whilst palpable, is an artificial one. The terms are complementary as in the Gestalt notion of figure and ground, with the space between the isolate and the group the fertile ground for therapy. Neurotic symptoms are disguises for what cannot be expressed in communication, and in the group—the setting where difficulties originate—communication can be developed from autism through to interaction. In the group, everything that happens involves the group as a whole as well as the individual. The individual is understood as a nodal point for the group and is often the spokesperson for the group as well as for her/himself.

Group analysis provides a setting for analysis in the group, by the group including the group conductor. The psychoanalyst S.H. Foulkes, the originator of group analysis, saw the group analytic experience as an opportunity for 'ego training in action' (Foulkes, 1964) where it is the conductor's role to provide and protect the setting and its boundaries. Within this safe space the group provides opportunities for energy hitherto invested in symptoms to be translated into shared communication. All communication is relevant, whether verbal or non-verbal, and this communication can be on several levels: for example, present relationships; individual transference towards each other and the conductor; shared and projected feelings and fantasies often from early developmental stages; as well as a primitive level of archetypal universal images. The conductor leaves as much as possible to the group and refrains from directing or pulling material into consciousness; rather, the conductor waits for the point where it is possible just to tip preconscious material into the public arena.

An important aspect of the group analytic experience is that of socialisation, where collectively patients constitute the psychological norm from which their individual symptoms deviate (Foulkes, 1948); thus 'normal' reactions are reinforced and neurotic reactions corrected. The other side of this is that difference, felt and actual, is also experienced, be it of race, gender, class, sexual orientation or handicap. In this respect, individual views of normality are challenged and modified.

Foulkes likened the group situation to a 'hall of mirrors' (Foulkes, 1984) and linked the group experience to that of the early caretaking experience where mirror reactions help in the developing differentiation of the self from the not-self. In the group, the individual comes to see more and more of himself through identifying parts of himself in others and by reflections back from other members and the group conductor. The experience of receiving care from other members and learning to give care in return, of finding oneself playing a familiar role in the group/family, of having this identified by other members, and eventually attempting a wider range of role behaviours and of receiving greater understanding from others in return, are but some of the factors in the diversity of the group experience that contribute to a highly versatile and eminently creative forum for therapy.

Attention to the group process as described above, initially by the conductor and increasingly by group members, allows group members to learn to hear and be heard and to care and be cared for, to observe others and then themselves in interaction, and through this ultimately to develop a capacity for more fulfilling relationships within and outside the group. Therapy within a group can also provide a sense of other people being reliable and concerned, which may be highly appropriate for individuals whose early parenting was fragile or unreliable. Unlike in individual therapy where the therapist can seem an omnipotent mediator of power, in the group the caretaking qualities are shared as if in a family and negative transference onto the person of the conductor can be more contained and manageable. Other group members can help someone experiencing a negative transference, which might otherwise lead to great difficulty or even to dropout in individual therapy, by pointing out the reality of the behaviour and the therapeutic stance. There is a sense, too, of Winnicott's 'going on being' quality to group therapy (Meinrath, 1992) where the individual in turn can also seem less omnipotent. For instance if a session is missed, in contrast to that of individual therapy, the group can be thought of as taking place and continuing its existence despite one member's absence, thus increasing the sense of stability and commitment.

With all these factors contributing to group therapy as a therapy of choice, it seems unnecessary but relevant to point to the factor of economy. In group analysis, eight people can be seen by one worker in the time that would otherwise be devoted to an individual patient.

How compatible are CAT theory and group analysis?

The theory base of CAT, the Procedural Sequence Model (PSM), identifies the development of the individual's dominant interactional procedures as reciprocal role procedures and uses these understandings to guide the course of therapy. Procedures are sequences of mental processes, action, environmental events and outcomes which take place in pursuit of a given aim. Procedures are interrelated hierarchically, from sub-procedures such as those aimed at basic self-care (e.g. tying shoelaces) through to higher-level procedures aimed at, for example, career progress. Object relations theory and Vygotsky's developmental psychology (Wertsch, 1985) inform the CAT view of human aim-directed activity being learned and shaped in the early relationships with parents and other figures who represent both care and control. Learning takes place within these interpersonal interactions and leads, through the process of internalisation, to intrapersonal functioning where the internal dialogue re-enacts the earlier interrelational experience in self-care and self-control.

Problems arising from distortions and conflicts in these early interactions lead to difficulties and limitations in later life through unsatisfactory relationships and conditional views of the self. Of particular concern to CAT therapists are the role procedures related to the maintenance of psychological self-care and of social interaction; in other words reciprocal role procedures concerning care and control in self-to-self and self-to-other relationships. Here, personal and acquired beliefs and values, together with perception and appraisal of thoughts, memory, meaning and feeling, followed by action which produces responses and consequences, are all involved. In CAT, these procedures are accurately identified in collaboration with the patient and are described and presented to the patient in various ways in the reformulation; subsequent therapy is aimed at challenging dysfunctional procedures and finding more satisfying alternatives. Thus making links between the interpersonal and intrapersonal, both in the patient's history and therapy, are the focus of work in CAT and fit most appropriately with the group task. By helping patients, fellow group members and the therapists make sense of reciprocal role behaviour, CAT tools and descriptions can be a useful adjunct to the group structure in offering a greater sense of containment and for helping people to engage with the group.

This is particularly relevant for individuals whose early containing experiences were fragile and fragmented and whose reciprocal roles developed accordingly. In 'A theory of thinking' (1967), the psychoanalyst Bion suggested that, in the complexities of life in a group, the adult tended to regress to earlier stages of development as she or he struggles to make contact. If the process is to be manageable and meaningful, the SDR—a tool of reflection, identifying and describing meaning and affect in interaction—has much to offer. Whilst the 'child' part of the patient in the child-derived pole of the reciprocal role procedure can be sharing anxieties and feelings in the group, the 'adult' part becomes more able to observe self and others, with the ability to think, although under attack, supported through the use of the diagram.

Mirroring too has particular connotations for CAT. Whilst identifying and observing the mirroring roles in other members is a powerful part of any group experience, CAT sees the transforming effect of therapy as requiring both the experience and the commentary/conceptual tools as described above. Similarly, CAT can equally contribute to ego training in action with its invitation to the patient to see her or his reciprocal role procedures as patterns of behaviour which have been developed to cope with difficult situations. The group provides a stage where corrective adjustments may be made.

Foulkes, like Bion, saw that the group experience raises 'deep conflict and characteristically brings up the early family situation, Oedipal situation and ... (members) are really afraid to become independent, a kind of fear of freedom' (Foulkes, 1975). Such issues raised by the group and in the group, affected by the nurturing experience found there, are influenced not only by the group members' own experience of their early family situations, but also by social and cultural aspects and expectations appertaining to these. For example, living in a society which believes that families provide the best environment within which to bring up children, leads us to groups where such values are initially accepted unquestioningly and where those with unsatisfactory family experiences struggle with their envy and longing for an idealised stereotype.

As family situations are changing in a social environment where women and men are now questioning the roles expected of them, we need to recognise that the institution of the family has inbuilt dynamics which have been accepted as the norm, often unquestioningly so. Just as these dynamics have affected our social policies and individual desires, so they have also affected the development of psychoanalytic theories which have influenced our therapeutic practice.

Stereotypically, mothering roles in our post-industrial society have been passive, nurturing and caretaking, with fathering being seen as active, independent and repressive of emotions. Father brings the outside world into the hitherto private sphere of the nursing dyad. Whilst his actual involvement with his children's day-to-day care has remained a limited and certainly optional role over the centuries, our society has supported an acceptance of the father's dominance in his provision for the family. We have given him, in the guise of the doctor and psychoanalyst, the authority to prescribe for good mothering, for example, from his only experience of that situation, that of a child in relation to a more powerful mother. In recent years, of course, women and men are attempting to challenge and modify these stereotypes to something more appropriate to a gender-sensitive environment. Women are beginning to speak out from their experienced position as mothers whilst men struggle to find a way to express their fatherhood appropriately.

So what, if anything, does this mean for group therapy? In psychoanalysis, Freud developed the idea of the analyst as a reflective screen, keeping as much of her or his personality as possible outside of the analytic situation. Foulkes recognised the need for a greater involvement in the group than the purely analytic stance in his definition of leadership in group analysis (Foulkes, 1964). He moved from the essentially narcissistic concentration of the Freudian model and the analytic neutrality of the analyst to a point where the individual in relation to the group is the focus of the experience.

In group analysis, the group conductor is responsible for the dynamic administration of the group and for holding the boundaries of the setting. During the sessions, she or he maintains a stance of careful listening and is ready to protect the group from situations that might threaten the safe space. Whatever the actual gender of the group leader, a stance of mainly careful listening during the sessions could be seen as passive, rather than active father or mothering. It is in this respect that the activity of the CAT therapist could, in our view, bring an additional quality to the group conductor's role, in a way analogous to the struggle of the male in our society to find an active fathering role that is neither intrusive nor abusive but allows for creativity in the true meaning of potency.

So it seems that within a brief model, there is room for both a nurturing, care giving and depriving mother/group therapist as well as a potent and educative father/group therapist, one who by facing both the internal and external worlds, provides containment yet brings the advantages and disadvantages of the external reality to the child/patient's experience. The danger of over-dependence on therapists is also guarded against in CAT by the model of sharing and collaboration, of handing over to the patient the therapist's understanding of their problems in written reformulations, in descriptive diagrams and goodbye letters etc. This can remain so whether support for change comes from an individual or from a group, and indeed the group could be viewed as the forum of choice.

A final advantage that CAT can bring to group therapy is that of researchability. Group analysis as a model has all the difficulties of evaluation of psychoanalysis and finds itself open to criticism of the subjectivity of its assessments of effectiveness. This position leaves open questions such as which patients are best served by group analysis and which are not. In the reality of scarcely resourced settings, as well as in the interest of group workers wishing to research their efforts, CAT can bring to group therapy one of its other strengths, that of a capability for evaluation.

Can we integrate CAT theory and group analysis?

Consider the following questions:

1. How adequately could a brief CAT group experience explore individual difficulties?

2. Who is suitable for a brief CAT group?
3. What effect would the relatively brief time-span have upon the group process?
4. How would the tools of traditional CAT practice be used in a group context?
5. How would the activity of the CAT therapist combined with the demands of a brief therapy group affect the therapists and the therapeutic stance?

Before attempting to answer these questions, we shall discuss some of our experiences of brief cognitive analytic group therapy.

St Thomas's Hospital Group 1 (STH1)

Two brief CAT groups have been run at St Thomas's Hospital. Both drew patients from referrals to the psychotherapy unit. The first group was facilitated by a senior registrar and a clinical psychologist. Neither of the facilitators was a trained group conductor, although one was participating in some group work training. This group was supervised within the unit by one of us (I.S.), a trained group analyst. Eight members started and seven finished. One woman left after only a few sessions, and one was admitted as an inpatient after a psychotic episode near the end of the therapy but did return to the group.

Research data was collected from the members and the group also utilised the traditional 'tools' of CAT. Each member was given an individual written reformulation subsequent to some individual sessions with one of the facilitators. Similarly an SDR was drawn up for each member. Members met both conductors prior to the start of the group but worked with only one on the SDR and reformulation. The group's life-span followed the pattern of individual CAT and was for 16 weeks. Four of these were with the facilitators working on the SDR and reformulation, the remaining 12 were in the group. Members were invited to read their reformulations out to each other or they could ask someone else to do this. SDRs were put together on one A4 sheet and these were made available during the sessions and collected by the conductors at the end of the sessions. Group members were also asked to complete a repertory grid (Watson, 1970) before the start of the group section, midway through and at the end of therapy, and everyone was asked to write a goodbye letter. Two papers describing this experience are reviewed in Chapter 10.

Day Hospital Group (DHG)

Dr Dilys Davies, a clinical psychologist and CAT therapist of George Eliot Hospital, Nuneaton, facilitated a day-unit group. This group comprised four men and two women, longstanding attendees of the unit for whom the staff felt that basic unit attendance had little more to offer. The group had weekly sessions for a period of four months. The members were given individual reformulation letters and SDRs and then developed, in the group, a group model of the common reciprocal roles by identifying the common parent-derived and child-derived roles being acted out in the group. These were as follows:

- *Parent*
  powerful
  abusing
  punishing
  conditional love
  precarious security

- *Child*
  powerless, helpless   abandoned
  abused, victim   insecure
  worthless   unimaginable terror
  rage (retaliation)   fear
  guilt (magic)   isolation, loneliness
  precarious dependence

This became a powerful group exercise bringing together members who on the surface would seem to have little in common, to a point where they functioned as a very cohesive group, sufficiently so as to challenge the ending and to continue to meet once monthly as an ongoing self-help group.

Counsellor Training Group (CTG)

In another setting, a CAT group has been used to help in training counsellors. In Wokingham, Berkshire, Jane Melton, a CAT therapist and counsellor trainer, has utilised this forum to facilitate group members' understanding of their own reciprocal role procedures prior to their working with clients' problems. The group comprised three men and three women, who were either counselling trainees or were considering undertaking training, and ran for ten sessions. This group used before and after measurements which identified a clear numerical increase on the scoring of awareness of reciprocal role behaviour by the end of the group. This work points towards the effective use of CAT groups for couples work (Melton, 1994).

Guy's Hospital Group (GH)

One of us (N.M.) conducted a 24-session CAT group at Guy's Hospital where the seven group members were mainly patients who had already had an individual CAT but at follow-up had asked for, and been assessed as needing, more therapy. This group format had four individual sessions to clarify an SDR, based on, but not always the same as, the reformulation used in the previous therapy, prior to 24 group sessions with a single group conductor.

Particular features in this group were an initial extreme difficulty in sharing, which was finally successfully addressed by a group reformulation letter prepared by the conductor describing the group process and the dominant reciprocal roles in operation:

GH group reformulation

We came together in November with each person wanting something from the group. C hoped for help with her panic attacks, agoraphobia and fear of being with others in public. A and Y to deal with the anxiety and fear that makes them feel unable to cope at work or socially. N and G had experienced abuse in early life that left them fearful of trusting others, whilst M and P had been disappointed by those who should have cared for them unconditionally and felt isolated, alone and guilty.

The group raised hopes of finding help for these problems but also anxieties about aggression and attack. In the first session people spoke of group therapy they had seen on TV where people confronted each other about their behaviour and also of the doctors who had variously let group members down. So even at the beginning, it seemed difficult to think that we could achieve a group where people could be cared for, nurtured and supported as they tried to find new ways of sharing themselves with each other and expressing their vulnerabilities.

The group seemed quickly to become a place where people feared to expose themselves and their feelings. The diagrams that we had worked on individually, were kept by the individuals and handed back to me at the ends of the group rather than shared with each other. N spoke of depression and her fear of letting others see behind her 'mask' and did not return to the group. Subsequently, P and G showed us their vulnerable sides and then did not return. It also seemed that I, perhaps like some of your mothers, might be too fragile or too self-absorbed to be able to help or to protect people from abuse.

Currently those members remaining with the group are confronting the dilemma of keeping the group a seemingly safe and 'comfortable' space where people are pleasant to each other. This is in contrast to an outside world that seems so full of frustration, disappointment and the threat of violent attack. But it is as if 'safe and comfortable' is also a way of masking real feelings and real communication and satisfaction in being together meaningfully.

There is a sense that belief in the group as a valuable experience for help towards changing lives remains with me alone rather than the members. It is as if the group is still being experienced as the unsatisfactory families you once had and longed to escape from rather than an opportunity to find more support and nurture in a new environment, where people can be heard, cared for and appreciated for who they are, and not for the masks they have learned to wear.

In summary, it is as if in the group to date it has felt necessary to be

- **either** masked, isolated but safe, keeping true thoughts and feelings inside for fear of ridicule, aggression, rejection or disappointment.
- **or** vulnerable, exposed, and likely to be looked down on, rejecting others before they can reject or abuse me.

The opportunity exists in the group to create a setting where vulnerabilities, difficulties and true selves can be valued for what they are, can be shared appropriately and the group strength employed to give people more options in their future relationships outside. But this requires taking risks and opening up to change within a group committed to helping themselves and each other. I invite the group to make such a commitment to themselves, to opt in to our experience together and find in the group a place where new understandings can be gained and your future lives considerably enhanced.

N.M.

This had the effect of bringing the group together and group interaction finally took place, culminating in a genuine sharing and caring for each other and the development of a group ethos. Subsequently, people dared to describe and share some powerful anxieties; one man told the group that he had thought he was HIV-positive and the group gave him sufficient confidence to go for an AIDS test, whilst one woman spoke of her real fears of being a bad mother to the son of whom the group knew she was over-protective. Independent research which included before and after interviews with the group members confirmed the group reformulation as being the mobilising therapeutic factor towards group cohesion and change. Group cohesion, of course, is one of the main therapeutic factors identified by Yalom (1985) as contributory to successful outcome in group therapy.

St Thomas's Hospital Group 2 (STH2)

This group was facilitated by one of us (I.S.) a group analyst, and the senior registrar who had led the first St Thomas's group. Six members started and all finished, although one member's attendance was erratic and another missed several sessions and had to be seen individually prior to her return. The model used was as described for the first St Thomas's group and some of the group experience is discussed below.

Early sessions in any group are likely to mobilise considerable anxiety. This group swung between anger at being dependent on powerful figures 'who could shove you around irrespective of your wishes or needs', to the opposite position of complete independence. They speculated about whether or not they needed the facilitators there. They had their reformulations and their SDRs; maybe they could do without us? They seemed to be desperately seeking a way out of the painful anxiety generated by the group situation. Accordingly they swung between extremes of total dependence, and the loss of self-identity which goes with that, to a fantasy of complete separation from safe, containing structures. Being able to express their ambivalent feelings towards each other and the facilitators helped them come to terms with the group. This was assisted by the facilitators understanding and containing the angry feelings.

Gradually the anxiety lessened, although in a brief group with ending always in sight, this is never very far away from the surface. As the initial anxiety lessened, members were more able to individuate and relate to the others reciprocally. As they began to work, their individual patterns began to emerge:

J, a young woman in her late twenties, who presented with relationship difficulties and a fear of group situations, was very resentful in the early sessions. She was angry with the facilitators (largely indirectly) and often asked why a group had been chosen for her instead of individual therapy. Her early group behaviour closely followed the patterns outlined in her SDR (see Figure 5.1).

P, a young man in his mid-twenties, often narcissistically preoccupied, also began to conform to the patterns in his SDR. He too had presented with relationship difficulties and he eagerly joined with the others in expressing his ambivalence about being in a group. However, he always kept a wary eye on the facilitators and he was quick to repent if he thought he might incur their wrath.

E, a young woman in her mid-twenties, who presented with problems of lack of confidence and low self-esteem, was invariably quiet and withdrawn for much of each session. As her SDR highlights, she gave little of herself spontaneously and invariably had to be coaxed into contribution by the facilitators.

K, in his mid-thirties, who complained of tiredness and lethargy at work and at home, found no difficulty in identifying and sharing with other members. He seemed to be the one who was most at home in the group and the others began to look to him as a unifying and stabilising influence. Following the pattern in his SDR, he worked hard trying to make the group work and he would often take up someone else's case when he felt they needed support.

B, in her mid-thirties, who presented with difficulties at work and in her personal relationships, managed to stay aloof and apart from the other members. She had a dismissive and contemptuous manner which helped to keep her at a distance. She seemed very defended and quite reluctant to risk exposing herself to closer contact. This behaviour conformed closely to that outlined in her SDR.

C, in his late twenties, who was concerned about recent violent and self-destructive losses of control, appeared distant and introverted during the early sessions. However, he often came to the defence of the facilitators when they were under attack. This mirrors his fear, reflected in his SDR, of close or intimate contact with others and it also highlights his propensity to get into self-destructive situations.

The behaviour patterns of the members was fed back to them through the use of the SDRs and through group and individual interpretations. This was soon being done by the group members as well as by the facilitators. As the group progressed through its middle stage into the last few weeks, some changes became apparent. The following example of the modification of a reciprocal role procedure took place during these later stages of the group.

P, who was convinced the other members would not like him if he followed the patterns of his SDR, was pleasantly surprised when they not only tolerated his acting out and occasional episodes of outrageous behaviour, but also emphasised how much better he was when he was not trying to be something he was not. He found this difficult to comprehend and was very resistant. Similar types of exchanges took place between the group members and C, E, J, K and, to a lesser extent, B. All these interactions resulted in established patterns being challenged and changed behaviour being reinforced and supported. This was achieved through either the group as a whole or one particular individual standing for a parental figure. This dynamic was in addition to the transference relationships with the facilitators.

Group process Scapegoating is a process common to all groups. It occurs when one individual or easily identifiable group of individuals takes or is given unwanted or unmanageable feelings which belong with other group members or with society. In a small group this is usually associated with a displacement of feelings about the facilitators away from these figures and on to some unfortunate individual. There may be a fear that the facilitators will not be able to cope with powerful feelings and that they might collapse or be destroyed. Alternatively, they might retaliate and attack group members or destroy the group. It is therefore felt safer to place these difficult feelings elsewhere.

A scapegoat may be a willing or unwilling victim of this process. However, what invariably happens is that they carry the unwanted feelings and may act these out by behaving in certain ways within the group boundaries or by being driven away for the greater good of the group as a whole. This is primarily a preconscious process in which the scapegoat sacrifices himself or herself, or is sacrificed, so that the other members may survive. In this group, although P often seemed the most likely candidate for the scapegoat role and he did find himself flirting with it in several minor ways, E was the one chosen for sacrifice.

E did not return after the third session. During the fourth session it was revealed (by P, interestingly enough) that the whole group had gone to the pub after the last session. This of course, was a direct rebellion against 'sensible' parental advice, as all group members knew that outside social contact was disapproved of for reasons of group cohesion and safety. It is quite common

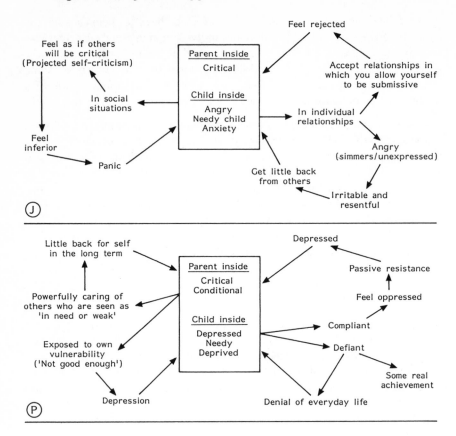

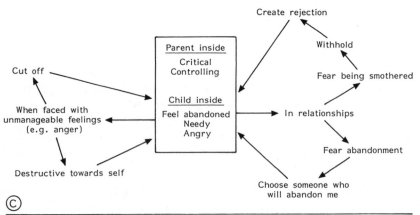

Figure 5.1:   SDRs of the group members of STH2

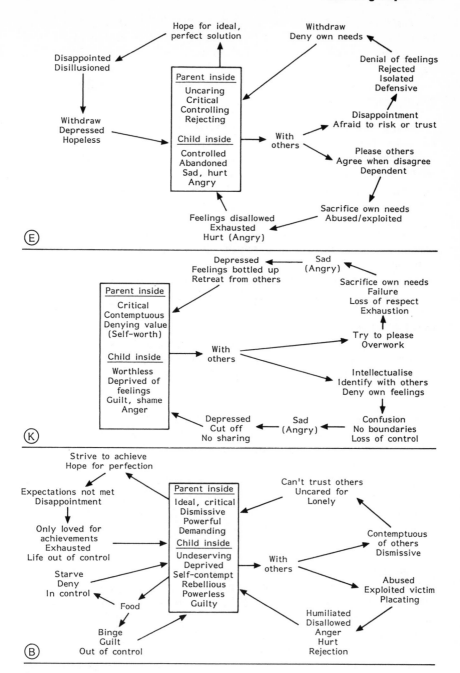

Hope for ideal,
perfect solution

Withdraw
Deny own needs

Disappointed
Disillusioned

Denial of feelings
Rejected
Isolated
Defensive

Parent inside

Uncaring
Critical
Controlling
Rejecting

Disappointment
Afraid to risk or trust

Withdraw
Depressed
Hopeless

Child inside

Controlled
Abandoned
Sad, hurt
Angry

With
others

Please others
Agree when disagree
Dependent

Sacrifice own needs
Abused/exploited

Feelings disallowed
Exhausted
Hurt (Angry)

(E)

Depressed
Feelings bottled up
Retreat from others

Sad
(Angry)

Sacrifice own needs
Failure
Loss of respect
Exhaustion

Parent inside

Critical
Contemptuous
Denying value
(Self-worth)

Try to please
Overwork

Child inside

Worthless
Deprived of
feelings
Guilt, shame
Anger

With
others

Intellectualise
Identify with others
Deny own feelings

Depressed
Cut off
No sharing

Sad
(Angry)

Confusion
No boundaries
Loss of control

(K)

Strive to achieve
Hope for perfection

Can't trust others
Uncared for
Lonely

Expectations not met
Disappointment

Parent inside

Ideal, critical
Dismissive
Powerful
Demanding

Only loved for
achievements
Exhausted
Life out of control

Contemptuous
of others
Dismissive

Child inside

Undeserving
Deprived
Self-contempt
Rebellious
Powerless
Guilty

Starve
Deny
In control

Abused
Exploited victim
Placating

With
others

Food

Humiliated
Disallowed
Anger
Hurt
Rejection

Binge
Guilt
Out of control

(B)

for members to test group boundaries by meeting before or after a session and many have a fantasy that the group would be better if members could meet outside; but it is unusual for the whole group to go somewhere together. This suggests that a very powerful reciprocal role procedure in relation to the facilitators was in operation here and that this was intensified by the brief group experience.

During the sojourn in the pub, the group was discussed and E stated that she felt out of place, uncomfortable and uncertain as to whether or not she had anything useful to contribute. Perhaps, she wondered, it would be better if she left? It then seems that she was encouraged to do just that. One member (J) accompanied her on the bus home and it appears that E decided not to return after their conversation.

E was offered an individual appointment with one of the facilitators. She attended and was persuaded to return. She rejoined in the sixth session and remained until the end. She returned to face her fears of unworthiness and rejection and therefore handed back to the other members the vulnerabilities they had tried to place with her. If she had left, the others could have rationalised the whole episode by feeling sorry for her or felt superior because they had what it took to survive while she had not. As it was they all had to face what had happened together and the scapegoating issue was brought openly into the group dynamic. Everyone had to deal with their own feelings of vulnerability and explore their fears of becoming the one who was 'lost' or unwanted. E's return prevented the escape from these uncomfortable issues.

This episode happened in the middle period of the therapy when there appeared to be a desire for group cohesion and the wish to get down to work. Alongside this pressure to conform to some sort of commonly acceptable standard, there seemed to be a search for the right qualities required to be a 'good' group member. Other examples of scapegoating have occurred at the beginning and the endings of brief groups when anxiety is high. Attempts at scapegoating are likely to occur in any group during certain developmental stages, but they emerge in brief groups in a way which suggests an added intensity and a heightened sense of urgency.

It is common for anger to be directed at facilitators at various points in group therapy, but it is normally an individual or perhaps a couple who will take up the scapegoat roles. For the full group to act in concert points to a desperate attempt to over-identify with the group as a whole at the expense of individual autonomy and judgement. There is always a delicate balance between individuality and group membership and the work for the members is to find this balance, to maintain a separate identity whilst staying in relation to the group.

J managed to stick it out. Despite her constant unspoken criticism and resentment, she was able to be more in touch with the anger and pain which lay behind her intransigence. She found an exit by expressing her anger rather than letting it simmer, and in her follow-up interview she admitted that she had found the group helpful. She said that shortly after the end she had been strong enough to take a major decision about her current relationship. She credited the group experience for this.

P was eventually able to break free from his ambivalence. He also seemed to make some limited gains by identifying the maladaptive patterns into which he fell when he confronted painful feelings. However, he was not able to stop his old ways. He missed several sessions including the last and found it hard not to play the clown or act as if he were superior to everyone else. At follow-up he asked to be referred for longer-term therapy where, sadly, here too he stayed trapped in his patterns and left unsatisfactorily after a year.

E came back and faced her problems. The scapegoat was not sacrificed but she still found it impossible to relate freely and openly to the others and kept herself hidden and inaccessible. The fact that she returned was significant and an exit of sorts, but any gain was limited and her negative self-image pulled her inexorably back. She would have benefited from longer therapy but missed the opportunity as she left the district shortly after the end of the group.

K managed to risk anger. Around the middle of the group's life, he complained angrily about not getting enough from the facilitators. He was rewarded by a tacit acceptance of this request which coincided with the facilitators' feelings that it was appropriate for them to be more active at this stage of the group's development. At follow-up, he said the group had helped him. He was more relaxed at work and his relationships were going better. In fact, he had decided to get married soon. He had found a clear exit from his primary dilemma and felt that this had enabled him to have more confidence in his own judgements and to risk saying what he was feeling.

B probably gained the least from the experience. She revealed herself on only one occasion. Undoubtedly she got something from sharing with the others and recognising that she was not the only one with problems. Nevertheless her desire to stay in control was very powerful. She decided to join a long-term group and, at the time of writing, is still in that group. Progress has been slow as she continues to find it difficult to relinquish control. At follow-up, she agreed she had gained some insight into her negative patterns and that she understood more about her lack of boundaries. The brief group does, however, seem to have been a useful introduction to therapy for her and this is significant in itself.

C achieved quite a lot. About halfway into the group he re-established contact with his mother and began to explore a very painful episode of his childhood, his father's mysterious death/suicide. He was surprised and gratified by his mother's positive response. This was his first tenuous step towards acknowledging that he had unresolved feelings. Towards the end of the group he was also able to share the problems he had in his current relationship. Speaking about this and having this accepted by the group was very important to him. He felt validated and understood in a new way. In his follow-up, he was positive about the group experience and recognised that he had begun work he may need to continue in the future.

Group epilogue Two members (B and P) went on to long-term group therapy. For them the experience was useful in opening up areas which they felt needed further work, and it provided a model of therapy in which they felt relatively comfortable. One member (C) contacted the unit 18 months later to ask for further therapy and was referred on. E left London to live elsewhere and we have not heard further from K and J subsequent to follow-up.

Discussion and evaluation

Brief group psychotherapy can be seen as a pragmatic response to NHS waiting lists. More people can be given the opportunity to participate in psychotherapy, and certainly the provision of long-term individual and to a lesser extent long-term group therapy is constrained by limited resources. Therefore an exploration of what can be achieved in a brief CAT therapy group must be a worthwhile enterprise.

Although it may be the case that something is better than nothing, this cannot be used as a justification for 'placebo' therapies or for those that are second-rate. Brief individual CAT has shown that it is a safe first intervention, and there is no evidence to show that it is any less effective than once-weekly psychodynamic therapy. In reality, very few CAT patients go on for longer-term therapy. CAT can enable individuals to see the benefits of talking about their problems within a professional structure, and its focused and cognitive elements can quickly give a sense of gaining some control over their lives. With prospective patients drawn particularly from disadvantaged groups, CAT is wide enough to lend itself to an educative function which can enhance contact and encourage engagement in the therapeutic process.

Brief CAT groups appear to have been a positive experience for most of the participants in the groups described above. Without question, the patterns outlined in the SDRs emerged in the group dynamic and were acknowledged and recognised by all the group members. What is unresolved is whether or not the time-span of the group gave them sufficient space to work through these therapeutically.

Duration

Ultimately this question rests on the aims and objectives set for the exercise. If these were limited to acknowledgement and recognition then the groups were reasonably successful. If these were to make perceptible changes in behaviour then it is not so easy to make a satisfactory evaluation. As in individual CAT, some people seemed able to take on the cognitive reframing of their problem areas, use understandings from the SDRs etc., and to employ what they had learned very quickly. This resulted in quite major shifts for some whilst others found it more difficult. In the STH2 group, K and C for example both made significant gains and J achieved what she wanted. On the other hand, E, having been rescued from the sacrificial altar upon which she had placed herself, had difficulty in seeing this as a positive step, rather viewing continuing in the group as being returned to the torture chamber. B and P remain unable to relinquish their old procedures.

We would see this outcome as not unusual for any therapy setting where there will always be some who can use the experience more readily than others. As with individual CAT, we would expect change to continue (and sometimes only to commence) subsequent to the group's ending but outcomes from this and the other CAT groups in operation currently are being collected with a view to informing further the development of the model.

On balance it seems that 12 weeks of group time is too short. Whilst some members of the St Thomas's groups were able to make positive changes, others did not move at the same pace. This, of course, is a phenomenon which is common to all groups in their various stages of development, and individuals change in relation to the particular needs and psychological patterns they bring with them. The temptation is to think that more change could have been achieved and consolidated if there had been a longer time to work things through. The findings of Butcher and Koss (1978) support this view with their suggestion that 25 weeks is an appropriate duration for a brief group, whilst Budman and Gurman (1988) suggest 65 sessions of one-and-a-half hours for a time-limited group for those with chronic and severe difficulties in intimate relationships.

In CAT groups, as in individual CAT, we are aware that the issue of time and the denial of time must be confronted throughout the therapy. Despite this there will still be individuals who can only function fully in the last few sessions. For others, the approaching time boundary will be responded to with anger and/or regression. Therefore, although we are not convinced that a longer time will necessarily produce twice as much consolidation, we do feel that 24 sessions for a standard CAT group may be a more appropriate time limit than 12. This is the model currently in use at Guy's Hospital and the experience seems to suggest that it is a good time span for a brief group. However, there still needs to be some flexibility as there may be instances where the ending needs to be staggered according to the needs of the members.

The example of the DH group supports this view. Here group members, patients from a day unit for the chronically mentally ill, seemed to choose an ending which was appropriate to their needs at the time. The group, initially very disparate people coming from very different ends of the social and educational spectrum, decided, as ending came, that they wanted to continue meeting. They chose monthly sessions in which they could revisit the setting where they had struggled to make sense of the histories of abuse that they had in common.

Some of our anxiety as therapists is tempered by the inherent flexibility of the CAT model in terms of extending endings or adapting the therapist's techniques as we have discussed. Careful composition of the group is equally important and the difficulties of assessment and selection must be acknowledged.

Selection and group composition

For successful referrals, brief CAT groups need to show that they can be a 'good enough' or even more than 'good enough' intervention for a range of identifiable patients and/or particular problem areas. To do this we must establish an appropriate yet flexible structure and a subtle and comprehensive assessment to discriminate who are the most suitable recipients.

Not surprisingly, it seems that brief groups are most appropriate for those people who are functioning reasonably well in the world outside, and have a relatively stable social network. This is particularly true for individuals who have come from backgrounds where emotional expression was suppressed. A brief therapy can greatly ease their sense of separateness and difference. They can be reassured that they are not going mad or are bad because they feel angry or are depressed. Sharing thoughts and feelings can be liberating and these individuals can find themselves acknowledged and validated as 'normally neurotic'. Patients with presenting symptoms ranging from panic attacks, post-traumatic stress disorder, depression, phobias and eating disorders have all responded well in our groups.

It is when we come to consider the more 'borderline' patients that concerns arise. As described in Chapter 1, there is sufficient evidence to show that individual CAT can have a powerful therapeutic effect on borderline personality disorder in a high proportion of cases. This may not be the case in brief groups and we need to research this area more fully before anything definitive can be said. The high levels of anxiety together with the added elements of competitiveness and rivalry which a brief group experience throws up, may feel dangerous and threatening for such individuals whose experience of parental figures and family life will have included little of the containment necessary for integration. Yet these patients will often demonstrate a strong commitment to the group, finding in this setting a 'holding containment' not available elsewhere in their chaotic lives.

There is growing evidence in the groups we have experienced that some of these patients do survive very well in a brief group. Outcomes from STH1, the membership of which included three members with borderline personality disorder and one with narcissistic personality disorder diagnoses, showed that the group was able to hold all but one member and only two required further therapy subsequent to the completion of this group. We are also aware that, for instance, the borderline personality disorder diagnosis does not represent a homogeneous category of patient; within this group patients may have markedly differing characteristics and will respond best to differing therapeutic interventions.

A large number of our NHS patients will, however, be classified within the range of this diagnosis and we are looking at ways of responding to them. In group analysis, we would suggest up to two 'borderline' patients in a group of mainly neurotic patients could be a good mix and to the benefit of all. However, in brief CAT groups, because of the heightened intensity of the interactions, it may be better to attempt to avoid a situation where only one or two patients in a group would have such pronounced difficulties. One option might be to develop specifically 'homogeneous' groups of all 'borderline' patients. These groups might well be of longer duration, be co-led of choice and allow for some adjunctive individual therapy to support group membership.

There is also the possibility of a pre-group structured workshop. This would provide an opportunity for prospective members to gain an experience of what it would be like in a group before making a commitment to join and for the facilitators to assess the individual's ability to relate in such a setting. It is hoped, as described by Yalom (1985), that this would also help with some of the difficulty of early dropouts, something that can be more easily handled in a long-term open group than in one that is closed and brief.

An alternative is to consider attempting to provide a common working focus for the group such as that developed by Dr Davies in Nuneaton. Here the common focus in the group was that all were coming to the end of their time in the day unit and a supportive structure developed around this theme, minimising some of the more rivalrous and competitive aspects. Much more work needs to be done in this area but preliminary findings do seem to indicate that a broad range of patient difficulties can be worked on in a CAT group.

Group cohesion and CAT tools

Unless there is a quickly developing sense of cohesiveness and trust in a short-term group, it is unlikely that the group will be viewed by members as providing a valuable experience. In CAT groups, as in individual CAT, the reformulations and SDRs give a clear focus which helps to initiate a sense of cohesion. Members also have a common group language from the beginning through the use of diagrams in their individual sessions and then gradually through sharing them in the group. On balance, the SDRs are a valuable tool in a CAT group although there are times when attempts are made (both by members and even facilitators!) to use them to block, hinder or avoid difficult issues. If the facilitator(s) are aware of SDRs being used defensively, draw attention to this and interpret its meaning in the context of the group, then the impact can be reduced. Members gradually become more fluent at translating the patterns on the SDR into interactions in the group. They become more proficient at observing themselves and other members. For STH2 as the group progressed, the A4 sheet containing all the SDRs (Figure 5.1) became a shared and common group focus. It became a fluid map showing where individuals were at any point on the group's journey.

Different groups use SDRs differently. In the St Thomas's groups, SDRs were shared at the first session. In the GH group, members were invited to share but were only confident enough to do so towards the middle of the group life. This group made an ending 'ritual' of giving each other copies of the SDRs of the group to take home—symbolically as if 'transitional objects'.

When we consider use of the written reformulation letters, a question revolves around when this is done and for what purpose. Reading them in the first session, as in the St Thomas's groups, proved cumbersome and ineffectual with the anxiety of the first session making it difficult for members to take in other people's material. Also the actual process of reading them aloud felt rather dry and detached, leaving little opportunity for interaction. This was in contrast to the graphic simplicity of the SDRs. However, very effective use was made of reformulations in two other group formats as we have mentioned. In these instances written reformulations were used in much the same way as containing or holding interpretations, which encompass the whole group or address all individual members separately, might be made during a long-term analytic group. These provide a timely focus and understanding of underlying issues which contain anxiety and lead to a recognition of the shared enterprise members had undertaken, while emphasising that individual autonomy could exist alongside group cohesiveness. In this way group analytic techniques can fit well into the methodology of brief group work.

Issues for group conductors/facilitators

Although the facilitators should be relatively active in a brief CAT group, they need also to strive against creating too much dependency upon themselves. This is a challenge best overcome by being clear and direct, keeping the members focused by using the SDRs and concentrating on current events in members' lives. Although the facilitators may weave in an examination of some historical material, for the most part this should be directed to identifying similar patterns of relating in the here-and-now, whether enacted inside or outside of the group.

Strict boundaries are also important and, although they can sometimes foster a mystique or leader-centred focus, they are necessary to contain anxiety and to create an atmosphere of confidentiality and trust. This can be difficult for inexperienced facilitators, but there is for all CAT group facilitators, as for individual CAT therapists, a tension between the openness of our collaborative stance and our overriding responsibility to provide a safe space where overwhelming feelings can be explored safely.

Transference issues and characteristic modes of dealing with authority figures will certainly arise within the group context. The dilemma for the facilitators in CAT groups, as in individual CAT, is how to address these and allow the here-and-now reciprocal role invitations sufficient exploration to be understood without engaging into an enactment. They should be addressed and interpreted as in any group with the transference identified as belonging with the facilitator(s) if this is appropriate.

Research aspects can become a vehicle for compliance/non-compliance transference issues if the facilitators are involved in the practical aspects of collection of material. For this reason, it is easier for the administration and collection of research data to be done by someone unconnected with the group. This also allows for material such as group repertory grids to be compiled with constructs relating to the group facilitators included. If members are aware that group facilitators are collecting such material, it may well influence their ability to respond to the grid spontaneously.

In individual CAT, endings can be a painful and potentially anxious time for the therapist. In the group some of this anxiety can be mediated and held by the group experience. The members and the group as a whole are able to share, hold and contain some of the loss and separation difficulties which emerge. Ending thus becomes something of a shared property, taken on by everyone and not left either with the facilitators or with those individuals prone to carry the painful aspects for others. Interestingly, in the St Thomas's groups there was a strong desire for group members to meet after the group ending, indicating that the ending was not fully dealt with within the group boundaries. Dr Davies' group have avoided an ending by arranging for monthly meetings, and the Guy's group has arranged for a group follow-up rather than individual. This all suggests that there are difficulties in the intensity of the CAT brief group experience that makes dealing with endings particularly intricate. It might also relate to the life experiences of many of the patients referred for these groups, in which there figured a predominance of fragile care or of abuse, neglect or abandonment. Therapists also can have their own personal difficulties with endings.

This all emphasises the importance of having experienced facilitators responsible for brief CAT groups. The anxiety and tensions generated require careful handling and facilitators need to be trained to recognise the varied and complex group processes which take place. It may be that the best way to facilitate these groups is to use co-conductors. This does have resource implications but the ability to establish trust and safety early on in the life of the group would probably be enhanced if two facilitators were present. This is not to suggest that one person could not run a CAT group perfectly well, but rather to note an area for further research.

If brief CAT groups are to be facilitated by therapists with very little or no training, then a training programme built into the experience would be essential. This should include academic input to increase their knowledge and understanding of group processes and the way in which individuals function in a group context. A contemporaneous experience for the trainee group facilitators in a group might also be considered, as well as the possibility of trainees acting as co-conductors with more qualified therapists.

Conclusions

Our emerging research evidence (Duignan and Mitzman, 1994) and current experience described above appear to suggest that this integration has much to offer. It certainly seems that a brief CAT group intensifies feelings and processes which would take longer to unravel in a longer-term group. In a CAT group there is no time to sit back or rest on our laurels, but neither is it always possible in a slow/open group to deal with everything, to take our time and pick our spot either. Overall our impression is that the experience of a CAT group is more probably akin to travelling to America by luxury aircraft as opposed to taking a leisurely cruise on an ocean liner. Whilst the outcome may be something approximately similar, the process will have both advantages and disadvantages and certainly a different purpose and meaning.

To continue the metaphor, piloting a CAT group requires close attention, a strict adherence to boundaries and careful monitoring of interactions. Obviously not all issues touched on will be able to be developed in a brief CAT group, but the limited time-frame clearly helps facilitate an atmosphere in which participants are eager to work quickly. There is an urgency and tension in a CAT group which gives its own flavour, with the intensity bringing out underlying group processes very quickly and members can feel exposed and unnerved. On the other hand, there is much to work with and members are forced to take up difficult and challenging interactions almost immediately. This can be exciting, stimulating and creative, and if the facilitator(s) can provide the safety and containment sufficient to enable a sense of cohesiveness, the enterprise has considerable potential. Whilst we are not proposing it as a *replacement* for longer-term individual or group therapy, we hope we have said enough here to suggest that, for certain patients and for certain problems, brief cognitive analytic group therapy, viewed as an intervention in its own right, may have much to offer.

References

Beard, H., Marlow, M. and Ryle, A. (1990). The management and treatment of personality disordered patients: the use of sequential diagrammatic reformulation, *British Journal of Psychiatry*, **156**, 541–545.

Bion, W. (1967). A theory of thinking, In: *Second Thoughts: Selected Papers on Psychoanalysis*. London, Heinemann (reprinted by Maresfield Library, 1990).

Budman, S.H. and Gurman, A.S. (1988). *Theory and Practice of Brief Therapy*. London, Hutchinson.

Butcher, J.N. and Koss, M.P. (1987). Research on brief and crisis oriented therapies. In: Garfield, S. and Bergin, A.E. (Eds), *Handbook of Psychotherapy and Behavior Change*, 2nd edn, pp. 725–768. New York, John Wiley.

Duignan, I. and Mitzman, S.F. (1994). Measuring individual change in patients receiving time-limited cognitive analytic group therapy, *International Journal of Short Term Psychotherapy*, **9** (2/3), 151–160.

Foulkes, S.H. (1948). *Introduction to Group Analytic Psychotherapy*. London, Heinemann (reprinted by Maresfield Library, 1983).

Foulkes, S.H. (1964). *Therapeutic Group Analysis*. London, Allen & Unwin.

Foulkes, S.H. (1975). *Group Analytic Psychotherapy: Methods and Principles*. London, Gordon & Breach (reprinted by Maresfield Library, 1986).

Hopper, E. (1980). Discussion on paper by Marie Jahoda, 'Individual and group', presented at the Seventh International Congress on Group Psychotherapy, Copenhagen, August 1980.

Mann, J. and Goldman, R. (1982). *A Casebook in Time-Limited Psychotherapy*. New York, McGraw-Hill.

Meinrath, M. (1992). Safety in numbers: tackling primitive anxiety in the group.

Unpublished paper, Institute of Group Analysis, London.

Melton, J. (1994). Unpublished MSc dissertation, United Medical and Dental Schools, Guy's and St Thomas's Hospitals, London.

Napolitani, D. (1980). Beyond the individual: the relationship between subject and group in a group-analytic perspective. Paper presented at the Seventh International Congress of Group Psychotherapy, Copenhagen, August 1980.

Watson, J.P. (1970). A repertory grid method of studying groups, *British Journal of Psychiatry*, **117**, 309–318.

Wertsch, J.V. (1985). *Vygotsky and the Social Formation of Mind*. Cambridge, Mass., Harvard University Press.

Yalom, I.D. (1985). *The Theory and Practice of Group Psychotherapy*, 3rd edn. New York, Basic Books.

6　Early development

Mikael Leiman

My interest in a closer examination of early development has been inspired by my experience of the frequent presence of the patient's non-verbal procedures in the consulting room. Both neurotic and more severely disturbed patients enact such patterns that seem to be more or less articulated. Sometimes they have the structure of a reciprocal role procedure which invite me to play the complementary role. In some cases the pattern is much less clear, creating either a strong feeling in me or sometimes only a somatic sensation.

In object relations theory these phenomena have been described in terms of countertransference and projective identification. While clinically useful, both concepts seem to be limited by their attempt to account for intersubjective processes without articulating how they are mediated; i.e. what happens 'in between'. Countertransference refers to processes that take place in the therapist. Projective identification presupposes the concepts of projector and recipient and describes their interchange that seems to dissolve the separateness of the two subjects. Yet it does not clearly spell out the process that mediates such a merger. If we accept the common opinion of the primitive nature of projective identification, then by studying very early development we might elucidate its peculiarities (Leiman, 1994a).

Another line of interest in very early development has been stimulated by my long-lasting enthusiasm for Vygotsky's theory of sign-mediated activity (Leiman, 1994b). His remarks concerning the problems in defining the object of psychological research are, even nearly seventy years after their publication, still very relevant.

Cognitive Analytic Therapy: Developments in Theory and Practice, Edited by A. Ryle
© 1995 John Wiley & Sons Ltd

Vygotsky claimed that psychology had run into a methodological crisis mainly for two reasons. First, it had been unable to define its object of study so that the complexity of our mental activities, and especially their deeply developmental nature, could be properly addressed. Secondly, psychology's persisting tendency to adopt explanatory principles from alien disciplines, such as elctrodynamics, biology or neurophysiology, produced very restricted models of psychological phenomena that led to an increasing fragmentation in psychology (Zinchenko, 1985).

Vygotsky asserted that no study of the human mind can bypass the issue of meaning and proposed *sign meaning* as the fundamental unit for the analysis of psychological processes. All human beings are born in a historically formed world. The experience of previous generations is stored in the tools by which we transform nature to meet our needs and in sign systems that carry both our practical and our social experiences in a symbolic form.

The ability to use socially created signs in communication and in the regulation of our mental processes is the fundamental feature of the human mind. When we tie a knot in a handkerchief we create a sign for the thing we want to remember. When we speak we make use of the immense store of verbal signs with a rich history of joint social usage.

An important feature of signs is their ability to contain meaning. However, by examining the outer appearance of the sign we cannot see its content directly. Sign meanings are created by the activities into which the sign is brought as a mediator. These activities become internalised in the sign. The knot in the handkerchief remains a knot for an observer who does not know that it was made to remind the person that he should make a phone call next morning.

Vygotsky was convinced that by approaching mental phenomena as sign-mediated activities we shall retain the specific quality of the human mind. We can be faithful to the specific approach of our discipline and shall not obscure psychological analysis by using alien explanatory principles.

If we take Vygotsky's plea seriously, we should approach mental phenomena by ways that retain their social and interpersonal origins. We should never lose sight of meaning that permeates every form of mental activity. We should also regard man's relation to the world as a mediated relationship. We do not have a direct access to the 'reality out there'. We encounter the world with our tools and signs that, inevitably, channel our relationships to it.

In this chapter I apply the notion of sign mediation to some aspects of early development. I begin by presenting a few critical remarks on the currently popular use of attachment theory as the explanatory principle in the studying of very early development. I then discuss two phenomena, namely cross-modal perception and attunement, as they are presented by Daniel Stern (1985) in his seminal work *The Interpersonal World of the Infant*. I first introduce his interpretation regarding the nature of the phenomenon and then provide a restatement in the light of the theory of sign-mediated activity.

Attachment theory as an alien explanatory principle

Attachment theory, originally summarised by Bowlby (1969, 1988), has stimulated much empirical work on early development and is becoming increasingly popular in our attempts to understand the infant's way of being in the world.

I have some methodological misgivings concerning the use of attachment theory as an explanatory framework for the dynamics of early development. I do not object to attachment as a phenomenon. I do believe that the biosphere, humankind included, is based on the principle of unitedness and interdependence. We are in need of one another in a much deeper sense than as objects of our drives or as relievers of our basic needs. In this sense attachment is indeed ingrained to the fabric of our corporeal life. As a psychologist, my doubts are directed against the importing of both concepts and explanatory models from biology in order to account for attachment.

Bowlby was very explicit on this issue. He wrote:

> The key concept is that of a behavioural system. This is conceived on the analogy of a physiological system organised homoeostatically to ensure that a certain physiological measure, such as body temperature or blood pressure, is held between appropriate limits. In proposing the concept of a behavioural system to account for the way a child or older person maintains his relation to his attachment figure between certain limits of distance or accessibility, no more is done than to use these well-understood principles to account for a different form of homoeostasis. (1988, p. 29)

The principle of homoeostasis and the concept of behavioural system restrict our view of activity so that it begins to appear as a self-regulating movement within permissible upper and lower limits. It also ignores the role of signs as the fundamental mediators in any activity.

As a scientific concept, behaviour had its heyday as the main descriptive unit of psychological analysis about five decades ago. Its inadequacy to account for the complexity of human activity gradually led to its abandonment. Now it seems to have been resurrected, with some cybernetic overtones, essentially with the same content with which James Watson embodied it at the beginning of this century.

An illustration of the effects of employing biological explanatory principles in the psychological analysis of early development is Bowlby's (1969) account of the developmental timetable for attachment. He concluded that attachment becomes fully developed around the first year and that the 'behavioural systems continue to be very readily activated' until about the third birthday of the child.

Winnicott's (1974) theory of transitional phenomena suggests that attachment can be recognised much earlier and that it is mediated by symbolic means. For a baby of five or six months, transitional objects begin to act as powerful signs of the mother's presence. Human beings create and maintain modes of attachment primarily by using signs, and transitional objects are one of its first clear manifestations. While acknowledging the phenomenon, Bowlby regarded the symbolic role of these objects as a superfluous construction. He suggested:

> A much more parsimonious way of looking at the role of these inanimate objects is to regard them simply as objects towards which certain components of attachment behaviour come to be directed or redirected because the 'natural' object is unavailable. (1969, p. 312)

Because the concept of behavioural system does not include mediational processes that employ the use of socially created signs, such processes appear, for the behaviourist, as epiphenomenal. Symbolic mediation is rejected as an unnecessary complication.

An impoverished account of the structure of activity tends to support another line of reductionist thinking in attachment theory. It is the frequent referring to the innate, biological roots of attachment. Such a line of thinking is very apparent in the current popular research into the biological basis of attachment patterns (de Zulueta, 1993; Spangler and Grossman, 1993).

Ainsworth presented a typology of three main attachment patterns (Ainsworth and Witting, 1969) that was based on her observations of infants from middle-class American homes after two brief separations from the mother. She called this the 'Strange Situation' assessment. This typology is based on clusters of behavioural responses that the infants tended to emit after reunion with the mother.

In the early studies, approximately two-thirds of the infants presented cues that were categorised as 'secure attachment'. Two main types of 'insecure attachment' were also derived. One-fifth of the infants displayed patterns that were termed 'avoidant'. These infants appeared indifferent to mother's departure and reappearance. Gaze aversion and other similar cues were used to classify infants into this group. About 12% of the sample were classified as 'anxiously attached'. When reunited the infants tended to show a lot of angry ambivalence, both wanting to be close and, at the same time, resisting the mother's efforts to soothe (de Zulueta, 1993).

Main and Solomon (1990) added a category of insecure attachment pattern that they termed 'disorganised'. This seems to be a surplus class for seemingly confused babies that did not show clear signs to be classified under the other headings.

The attempt to understand the biological basis of these behaviourally established categories has led to a number of studies that try to correlate various physiological, neurological, or endocrinological measurements with the main types of attachment patterns. Statistically significant correlations have indeed been established and, as de Zulueta (1993) notes in her excellent summary of current attachment research, 'attachment . . . is now known to have a biological substrate which is affected by experience at a biochemical and physiological level' (p. 44).

The problem with such correlative efforts lies in the typological approach to activity. The soundness of the current classification of attachment patterns can be, and has recently been, questioned. In their meta-analysis of 32 studies from eight different countries that used Ainsworth's main categories, van Ijzendoorn and Kroonenberg (1988) found the occurrence of the patterns varied greatly. Intracultural variance was 1.5 times as large as the variance across different countries. The originally established distribution of the three types can scarcely be applied to any other sample than to mother–infant couples from middle-class American homes. This raises at least two issues. Firstly, there must an enormous variation of attachment patterns across different social groups and local communities, if the categories are reliably established. Secondly, the process of classification, using greatly varying behavioural cues to generate highly abstract type descriptions, may be beset with flaws.

As if sensing the imminent fragmentation of the categorising system, Spangler and Grossman (1993) voiced their concern about the variability of attachment patterns and suggested that their existence can best be supported by establishing biological indicators that will discriminate the categories. To their satisfaction, there are endocrinological variables that seem to distinguish the securely attached type from the insecure attachment patterns in the Strange Situation experiment.

It is too early to make any final judgement about the biological validity of behavioural classifications in the attachment research. However, this approach is methodologically virtually identical with the individual differences tradition in the psychology of intelligence and personality types. Both represented an attempt to understand human activity in terms of trait classifications. Both showed a developmental path of ever-increasing descriptive categories. Both finally collapsed in the 1960s under the pressure of the necessity of adding finer and finer discriminations and due to the fact that virtually any physiological, psychological, or even social variable showed some correlation with the behavioural trait descriptions.

For example, the simple two-factor model of intelligence, presented by Spearman at the beginning of this century (1904), ended up as a factorial model with 120 ability categories (Guilford, 1967). Every presentation of a new classification was followed by a heated debate on the relative importance of hereditary endowment versus environmental influence. Our physiological and biochemical measurement instruments are, of course, much more sophisticated today than four decades ago. However, the methodological logic of attachment research is based on the assumption that simple behavioural descriptions can be related meaningfully to biological variables. I would be quite surprised if this methodological weakness did not in the long run produce an outcome similar to what happened to differential psychology as a scientific tradition.

Development as the emergence of new mediational structures

No study on early development can bypass Daniel Stern's fundamental account offered in his book *The Interpersonal World of the Infant*. His aim was to bridge the gap between experimental research and clinical understanding that has characterised the field for decades, by exploring what the findings of experimental infant research might imply for our clinical psychoanalytic theories of early experience.

Stern encapsulated nicely the underlying issue in the varying psychoanalytic timetables for the emergence of autonomy by showing that different theorists have simply focused on different aspects of the child's activity, when choosing their criterion. Thus although Freud and Erikson saw the first true sign of autonomy in the independent control of bowel functioning at around two years of age:

> Spitz . . . placed the decisive encounter in the ability to say 'no' at fifteen months or so. Mahler . . . considered the decisive event for autonomy and independence to be infant's capacity to walk, to wander away from mother on their own initiative, beginning at about twelve months. (Stern, 1985, pp. 20–21).

Stern argued that the infant's gaze behaviour, becoming a sophisticated mode of interaction during the period from three to six months, could equally well be regarded as an early sign of autonomy.

Stern's insight shows how important it is to understand the mediated nature of our psychological processes. He uses this understanding to describe the principal mode of mediation in the phases of the development of the early self.

I shall now readdress two phenomena—amodal perception and attunement as described by Stern—basing my review on the notion of sign-mediated activity. I have chosen these two because they represent fundamental forms of mediation within a specific developmental phase. *Amodal* (or cross-modal) *perception* is an integrating mental 'mediational device' that can be seen to operate during the very first weeks of life. *Attunement* is the gradually emerging mode of interpersonal communication during the latter half of the first year.

I want to discuss these phenomena because both seem to contain puzzling aspects that allow for a range of interpretations. I shall try to examine how the developmental theory of sign mediation might account for these intriguing phenomena. At the same time the concept of *sign* may be illustrated.

Amodal perception

Newborn infants seem to have an amazing ability to recognise external objects by making inferences across different sensory modalities. Stern introduces the phenomenon by presenting Meltzoff and Borton's experiment on 3-week-old babies (1979). The infants were blindfolded and given, alternatively, one of two differently shaped pacifiers to suck. After the baby had some experience of sucking, the pacifier was removed and placed side-by-side with the other one. The blindfold was removed. The infants performed a quick visual comparison and then looked more at the nipple they had just sucked (Stern, 1985, pp. 47–48).

Echoing Meltzoff and Borton, Stern concluded that infants are predesigned to master such cross-modal inferences, as no learning seems to be needed. Amodal perception would then be an innate capacity. This capacity rests on the infant's ability to distil highly abstract perceptual qualities, such as shaped, intensities, temporal patterns, etc.

The issue of cross-modal perception has been a natural consequence of the traditional understanding of perception in experimental psychology. Perception was regarded as an internal 'function' that operated on the 'raw data' produced by the sense organs. In cognitive psychology this operation was interpreted as the act of fitting a schema on incoming information, commonly defined in terms of the sense modality that was being studied.

This conceptual distinction between sense data and perception has resulted in a long-running inner tension within the psychology of perception. On one hand there have been those who argue for the utmost purity of sense data in order to be able to say anything of the laws of perception. This line of research is still popular within psycho-physiological studies. On the other hand, beginning with the 'New Look' researchers like Bruner, there has been a strong wish to understand the more complex relationships between sensation and perception. Studies on cross-modal perception are a natural outgrowth of this line of thinking. However, they have still retained the classical methodological point of view, distinguishing between sense data and perception as an act of categorisation of this data.

Studies of adult perception have indeed shown that people make inferences by using cues that enter via different modalities. Thus perception has more clearly appeared to be a mental activity. When such studies were modified to trace the early origin of perceptual inferences, the researchers found out that even infants were able to perform such inferences. Studies of early cross-modal perception was a logical extension of such research into the very first days of the neonate.

The studies, cited by Stern, do show that 30-day-old babies can perform inferential mental acts that permit them to recognise the pacifier they had been sucking. They do not let us draw any conclusions about 'innate abilities of amodal perception'. Our habitual methodological approach to mental activity, regarding it as a 'function' or a 'capacity', instead of mediated activity, produce over and over again the seemingly puzzling findings that then seduce us into neurophysiological or biological speculation.

Amodal perception as sign-mediated action

When Walton and Bower (1993) conclude that infants have abilities 'to relate information picked up through different modalities', they are right. However, babies do not 'pick up information', they perceive things and events. They do not live in a subjective world of abstract shapes, or 'stimulus intensities', but in the concrete world with all its richness. Hearing, seeing, smelling and sensing this world does not break it up into distinct sets of information that should then become coordinated by some innate mental instance. That is our way of describing the matter, an outcome of our preferences to approach perception through information processing analogies.

Instead of arguing for preprogrammed abilities to relate abstract information, we should study the extremely subtle forms of sign mediation involved in perceptual activity. Seeing, touching and hearing are sensory activities that serve to establish mediational links with the environment, which for human beings is always socially created and meaningful. They aim at generating signs of the objects and happenings, signs that will serve as psychological tools for appropriate orientation in the complex world.

Bakhtin maintained that signs are not mere representations but 'true carriers' of the object they designate. Every sign contains a layer of meanings that it has received from the object it signifies (Voloshinov, 1928). Metaphorically speaking, the sign acts like a prism that compresses the total spectrum of the light emitted by the object into a single beam, yet containing the whole spectrum.

Following this line of thinking, we may assume that the sign of the presented object contains *more information*, to use the traditional cognitive expression, than what seems to be there as modality specific sense data. The nature of 'information', comprised in the sign, depends on the manner in which the sign was created. By sucking the nubby pacifier, the infants in Meltzoff and Borton's experiment established an active connection with the pacifier, with all its specific attributes being present in the mouth.

It would be quite one-sided to understand mediational relationships only as an impact of external phenomena on passively receiving subjects. It is not the sign that acts on the infant. It is the infant that brings the sign into being. There would not be anything that could be called a sign without the neonate's activity that establishes his or her relation to the object and creates the sign as a mediator. The presence of the caregiver must, however, also be taken into account. Signs arise in the interpsychological territory and they are, to use Voloshinov's (1928) definition of words, *two-sided acts*.

I want to illustrate these complex relationships by two vignettes. A few-days-old baby grabbed the edge of his blanket and pulled it over his face. His mother noticed the baby's movement and said to him 'Oh, you want to hide your face! Is there too much light in the room?' Here the mother invested the baby's embryonic movement with intentionality. For her, it was a complete action aimed at protecting the baby from too much light. The mother could also have said 'Oh, you naughty boy, you want to hide from your mother!' In that case the whole contextual meaning of the bay's movement would have changed. The baby's movement *became a meaningful sign to the mother*. He originated it as a motor act, but the mother made it meaningful by her interpretation. It became a new kind of mediator in the joint sequence that determined the mother's response. It became a sign for the mother and she saturated it with her responsive understanding. Repeated occurrences of the pattern would eventually 'teach' the meaning of the sign to the baby too.

This aspect of jointly created sign meanings is illustrated by the second vignette. This is a case described by Cramer (Brazelton and Cramer, 1991). Juan was a 2-month-old boy who had regurgitated feedings since birth. His mother was convinced that he would die and asked for a consultation at the clinic that offered joint parent–infant therapy.

> Soon after the clinician started talking with this mother, she reported that she was still very upset about the death of her brother, three months before the baby's birth. She was then encouraged to talk more about this event and described her last visit to him in the hospital; he was emaciated, smelt very bad, and kept regurgitating (he was at the terminal stage of intestinal cancer); this impression was so powerful that she fainted. The brother died soon thereafter. She had not felt up to going to his funeral. She didn't cry once. the process of mourning had not taken its normal course.
>
> What was remarkable was that *while she was describing* this painful scene, Juan suddenly regurgitated. The clinician then simply said: 'He regurgitates like your brother did.' (Brazelton and Cramer, 1991, p. 140)

Juan's natural regurgitations had been interpreted by his mother as the sign of imminent death. At the same time they seemed to be 'a sign of life' of her dead, but unmourned, brother. We may understand the particular power of regurgitations for the mother as being a true re-enactment of an extremely traumatic and tragic event in her life. By the age of two months, Juan too had well understood the particular significance of regurgitations and was seemingly able to use them appropriately as communicative signs.

I now want to return to Meltzoff and Borton's experiment. Viewed from the vantage point of sign mediation, it seems to contain a confusion. An external observer, cannot, in fact, determine in advance what the particular signs of the pacifier (that begin to mediate the infant's perceptual activity) will or should be. However, the observers did just that when they decided, in their experimental design, that the abstract quality of *tactual shape* should be the decisive sign of the object. They believed that even the infants would act by employing the same sign. In this regard they were exactly like the mothers in the above vignettes. They invested the baby's eye movements with meaning. Yet we do not know what the infant's *act of sucking* created as the specific sign of the pacifier. We are thus puzzled by our own, premature, interpretation when we claim that the infants were able to recognise the shape of the pacifier when it was re-presented.

Meltzoff and Borton seem to be aware of this when they write 'Obviously, these initial experiments do not isolate the exact nature of the information perceived as invariant across the different modalities'. Yet they fall back on their adult reasoning when they conclude 'However, they [the experiments] suggest that neonates are capable of using and storing surprisingly abstract information about objects in their world. This information must be abstract enough, at least, to allow recognition of objects across changes in size and modality of perception.'

I would like to suggest that it is not the abstract perceptual quality (i.e. the shape) as such that directed the infants' recognition. Their active relationships with the pacifier, creating adequate signs, began to mediate their perceptual activity in the setting where the pacifier was physically re-presented.

Amodal perception as an act of signifying

There is another fascinating aspect about amodal perception. It is the infant's ability to establish mediational links between two phenomena and treat the other phenomenon as a true sign of the first one. This is illustrated by the studies of cross-modal matching. By three weeks of age infants seem to be able to match levels of sound intensity with specific levels of light intensity. They are also capable of relating auditory temporal patterns with structurally similar, visually presented temporal patterns (Stern, 1985).

Here we may see the very first form of symbolic activity. There are no inherent or biologically determined connections between the two presented 'data sets'. The connection is established by the common context and the joint activity of the experimenter and the baby.

The experiments, quoted by Stern, fall short of elaborating the infant's activities because they approach the phenomenon as a perceptual ability. I would like to suggest that by understanding cross-modal matching as a rudimentary form of joint signifying activity, and not a 'capacity', we could open up exciting lines in the study of symbol formation. Attunement, to be discussed below, could then be seen as a developed, and much more complex, form of signifying activity, contributing directly to the emergence of speech—that is, verbally mediated acts of signification.

On the basis of the experiments of amodal perception, Stern concluded that infants distil the abstract properties of complex stimuli or qualities of perceptual material. 'These abstract representations that the infant experiences are not sights and sounds and touches and nameable objects, but rather shapes, intensities, and temporal patterns—the more 'global' qualities of experience' (ibid., p. 51). In the light of sign mediation this view represents an impoverished account of the rich mediational relationships that are embedded in our most rudimentary perceptual activities. The baby does not enter a world of empty abstractions but a very concrete environment where everything is potentially meaningful and can be adopted as a device through which the environmental relationships are shaped and further enriched.

Affect attunement

I shall now jump over several transforming periods in early development and address the phenomenon called 'affect attunement' (Stern, 1985). Attunement indicates an interpersonal process whereby the mother and the infant seem to share and communicate internal feeling states during ongoing activities.

> Affect attunement, then, is the performance of behaviours that express the quality of feeling of a shared affect state without imitating the exact behavioural expression of the inner state. (Stern, 1985, p. 142)

Stern gives a number of illustrations. I shall reproduce two of them in order to illuminate his understandings of the phenomenon and, later, to provide an alternative account based on sign mediation:

- A 9-month-old girl becomes very excited about a toy and reaches for it. As she grabs it, she lets out an exuberant 'aaaah!' and looks at her mother. Her mother looks back, scrunches up her shoulders, and performs a terrific shimmy with her upper body, like a go-go dancer. The shimmy lasts only about as long as her daughter's 'aaaah!' but is equally excited, joyful, and intense.
- An $8\frac{1}{2}$-month-old boy reaches for a toy just beyond reach. Silently he stretches toward it, leaning and extending arms and fingers out fully. Still short of the toy, he tenses his body to squeeze out the extra inch he needs to reach it. At that moment, his mother says, 'uuuuuh...uuuuuh!' with a crescendo of vocal effort, the expiration of air pushing against her tensed torso. The mother's accelerating vocal–respiratory effort matches the infant's accelerating physical effort.

Attunement seems to be base on cross-modal matching. The mother tracks the experiential flow of the infant's behaviour by reproducing its pattern in a *different* sense modality.

Stern emphasises the difference between attunement and such alternative conceptualisations as 'intersubjectivity', 'echoing', 'mirroring' or 'empathy'. For him, these are either too inclusive (intersubjectivity, mirroring) or mix up cognitive and affective elements in complex interpersonal communication (empathy). Stern connects attunement with amodal perception, maintaining that both depend on the human ability to abstract patterns, shapes, and intensities of concrete behaviours.

According to Stern, the main function of attunement is to share the infant's affective experience without any attempt to change his or her ongoing activity. Purposeful misattunements occur when the mother, deliberately, over- or under-matches the intensity, timing, or behavioural shape of the infant's action sequence. Stern calls this *tuning* and regards it as a mode of emphatic communication. The mother 'slips inside of' the infant's ongoing action and then affects its course by creating a mismatch in its flow.

An alternative conceptualisation

In order to generate an alternative view of what might be going on in the phenomenon of attunement, I shall use Stern's second illustration of the boy reaching for a toy and examine it in the light of the development of reaching as described by Vygotsky (1978).

Vygotsky claimed that, initially, there is nothing more than the baby's unsuccessful attempt to grasp something beyond its reach. When the mother comes to the child's aid by investing the movement with a meaning, the situation changes radically. Grasping becomes a gesture *for others* (Vygotsky, 1978). It becomes a communicative sign. In this example Vygotsky showed how vital is the intepreting role of the caregiver in transforming the action into such a sign. The caregiver invests the infant's movement with meaning and completes the action sequence by handing the desired object to the infant.

As soon as this basic, concretely mediated sequence has been established, the infant's movements begin to attain communicative functions. At first, the baby is still unaware of the communicative aspect of reaching. The action of the baby is directed toward the object rather than at the mother (cf. Clark 1978). Although there is structured co-activity, it does not yet represent *intentional communication.*

Vygotsky's example of pointing shows how the earliest communicative signs are formed within object-oriented actions. They are, initially, the baby's movements in the joint sequence, beginning to signify the order and continuity of the process. They are *anticipatory signs* produced by the baby. embedded in the sequence. They signal the ordered continuity of the joint action sequence. The importance of anticipatory signs in such sequences is confirmed by the fact that, very early on, infants exhibit surprise or discontent if an established action sequence is diverted from its expected course.

Anticipatory signs attain their function as communicative devices only through the reliable mediation performed by the caregiver. She understands the baby's motor acts in the sequence as meaningful signs and responds according to her interpretation of this meaning.

Intentional communication would never emerge unless the caregiver did not let her interpretation of the infant's utterance affect her next move in the joint action sequence. The utterance will then become a meaningful sign that determines what is to come next. If the expected flow of action is diverted, the infant usually increases the force of his utterances to make things happen as they should. The caregiver that is not too insensitive then re-adopts her role. I believe that such 'negotiations', occurring in the course of action, eventually help the infant to conceive of the communicative function of his utterances.

Having attained this dual mediating position (as anticipatory signs that may also be used as 'negotiable' signs to direct joint action) the infant's utterances become decontextualised, to use the Vygotskian term, from the concrete flow of the sequence. They may now be used to *signify* the anticipated action sequence by reproducing its significant moments without the object, so to say. When this happens the emergence of gestures may be witnessed. 'A gesture, in this case the reach, emerges as a gesture because it is not simply produced in order to get an object but in order to produce an effect on another in order to get an object' (Clark, 1978, p. 249).

We may now return to Stern's second illustration. Long before the phenomenon described in that vignette, the infant has already learnt that he can use his repertoire of motor and vocal utterances as meaningful signs and that his mother understands what is going on. He has developed a rich language that can be used intentionally, both in the still necessarily joint action sequences and in the service of completely new spheres of playful communication and independent activity.

In the example, the boy acts independently trying to grab the toy. He performs an object-oriented action and does not call the mother for help. To borrow Winnicott's remark, he acts in the absence of the present mother. However, this independent action unfolds in the interpsychological space in which it also has a potentially communicative role. His mother makes this explicit by reproducing the final part symbolically, by vocalising the pattern in his effort of grasping. This may be called the first instance of joint reflective activity. The mother creates a vocal metaphor of the action. What is extremely important here is the use of signs that allow a new target, the infant's personal action sequence, to be represented symbolically.

It would not be quite right to say that the mother echoes the infant's action. She does more than that. She intones it, in the sense of expressing the emotional pattern of the sequence. Intonation reflects or, more truly, spells out the sense of the action. This sense is established in the space that unites object-oriented action with communication. We may ask whose feelings, actually, create the specific quality of the boy's grasping, because the mother's intonation becomes an inseparable part of the act.

Stern's examples of attunement are good illustrations of the interpersonal origin of feelings. He defines attunement as the sharing of inner experiences, thus assuming that the pattern and the nuances in the feelings state would be intrapsychological. This is a vast topic, and I can here only lay bare the issue involved. In most current theories of emotion, feelings are associated with internal need states or other similar, physiological phenomena. This has perpetuated the unfortunate conceptual separation of emotions and cognitions. It has also obscured the view that feelings are yet another mode of mediational devices that carry the basic properties of the sign.

The mother's responsive understanding of her child's mode of grasping for the object is quite different in the two vignettes above. The baby girl seems to approach the toy with a self-confident exuberance. Her mother, certainly, emphasises the aspect of joyful success in the action. She dramatises the triumphant possession of the toy. The boy approaches the object more cautiously. His action is slower, and there seems to be the aspect of effort which his mother elaborates with her utterance.

We do not know anything about the history of these two mother–child couples. We do not know how much the mothers' symbolic enactments expressed their personal way of meeting the world. The two different modes of grasping might thus reflect the pattern by which the mothers tended to address issues of handling or possession. Using the Bakhtinian notion of the sign (Leiman, 1992), we would be tempted to speculate that the mother's attunement contains her lifelong experience of the modes of possessing things. Her non-verbal utterance is a symbolic micro-universe, presented to the baby during the sequence. The baby cannot know, of course, all the embedded aspects of this communicative sign. Nevertheless, they are there. By 'choosing' her expression the mother tells the baby about the nature of things, about the sense in getting them and in handling them.

To sum up, attunement as an interpersonal phenomenon becomes possible when joint action sequences have been replaced by the infant's independent actions and when communication has been separated from object-oriented activity. They now come together in a complex mode, permitting the use of communicative signs as a symbolic reflection of activity.

Everything proceeds without verbal signs and yet we may speak of a rich non-verbal vocabulary that is established in such attunements. The eventual appearance of words does not seem so mysterious when we recognise how complex phenomena, such as action sequences, can be mediated by meaningful signs that are established jointly in the context of early independent activity.

The main function of attunement, as the intonated representation of action by signs, is substantiated by the experiments in which the mother deliberately introduces a mismatch in her attunement. Stern showed that if the mother introduced a new set of reflecting signs (approaching the infant from behind, putting her hand on his bottom, and giving him a jiggle) this did not interrupt the infant's ongoing action sequence if it *intoned* the action accurately. If it did not, the infant stopped and looked at the mother. In such perturbations the infant interpreted the jiggle as a sign to pay attention to the mother, not as a symbolic reflection.

Stern's experiment also shows that, at the age of seven months or later, the jointly created and used signs have become quite idiosyncratic. They form a truly intimate language that cannot be arbitrarily replaced by something else. The perturbations had to be tailored individually for each mother–infant pair. Perhaps this is the clearest difference between non-verbal and verbal modes of sign mediation. Baby and mother create their joint communication by elaborating a highly individualised set of non-verbal signs. When words are being introduced they bring with them their socially determined meaning and patterns of usage. This is a great addition to the store of mediational devices. However, introducing words does not break the continuity in the infant's experience. He has already adopted the principle of using signs both in communication and in the regulation of action patterns.

Understanding early development in therapy

Cognitive Analytic Therapy is about changing problematic patterns of internal and external activity; i.e. procedures. What is then the role of understanding early development when conducting therapy? It is easier to argue for the relevance of developmental knowledge in therapies that emphasise reconstruction. In CAT, however, uncovering the disawowed parts of the patient's personal history is not the principal aim of treatment. In some cases successful therapy can be achieved with hardly any knowledge at all of the patient's childhood experiences. Is, then, the issue of early development only a cosmetic device that justifies the 'analytic' in the name of the approach?

I believe that developmental knowledge is directly relevant for CAT in two ways, at least. Firstly, knowing something about the processes of early development is vital for understanding how complex procedures are formed; that is, how interpersonal and internal activity patterns emerge and how they relate to each other. Such a thesis will help us create a developmental model of psychotherapy process that seems to follow the 'laws' for the formation of psychological phenomena in general.

CAT is based on the joint creation of symbolic tools that begin to mediate the patient's maladaptive action patterns. Exploring very early development reveals to us, in the simplest possible manner, how signs are born. Although we deal with adults and, frequently, work with quite complex symbolic tools, the processes by which such tools emerge in therapeutic discourse are remarkably similar. Signs are born at first on the interindividual territory. The quality and colouring of this territory is an inseparable part of the signs that begin to mediate joint understanding. This contextual dynamics of sign mediation holds true at all developmental stages but studying early development permits us to disclose its structure in the clearest possible manner.

Secondly, every human being displays a myriad of activity patterns in which 'primitive' mediation structures are embedded within more 'advanced' processes, and vice versa. Understanding early development alerts the therapist to the vast array of potential personal experiencing and action and helps her or him to detect the signs of rudimentary processes that may interfere with more complex forms of activity.

Even quite disparate schools of therapy now seem to subscribe to the thesis that severe mental disorders have an early origin. The views tend to differ with regard to the kinds of adverse early experiences that are emphasised. Severely disturbed persons usually suffer from dissociated states of being that contain primitive, often non-verbally mediated, action sequences. Without an adequate conception of early forms of sign mediation and the interpersonal context out of which they get formed, we would not be able to enter such sequences by our responsive understanding. Accurate 'attunement', to use Stern's concept, represents the specific mode of joint reflective activity of primitive action sequences in therapy. It is the therapist's task to find symbolic descriptions that will match the patient's experience and his or her idiosyncratic usage of signs.

Acknowledgement   Nordic Academy for Advanced Study has contributed to the preparation of this chapter.

References

Ainsworth, M.D. and Witting, B.A. (1969). Attachment and the exploratory behavior of one-year-olds in a strange situation. In: Foss, B.M. (Ed), *Determinants of Infant Behavior*, vol. 4, pp. 113–136. London, Methuen.

Bakhtin, M. (1984). *Problems of Dostoevsky's Poetics*. Edited and translated by Caryl Emerson. Manchester, Manchester University Press.

Bowlby, J. (1969). *Attachment. Vol. 1: Attachment and Loss*. Harmondsworth, Penguin (second edition 1989).

Bowlby, J. (1988). *A Secure Base: Clinical Applications of Attachment Theory*. London, Routledge.

Brazelton, T.B. and Cramer, B.G. (1991). *The Earliest Relationship: Parents, Infants and the Drama of Early Attachment*. London, Karnac Books.

Clark, R.A. (1978). The transition from action to gesture. In: Lock, A. (Ed), *Action, Gesture, and Symbol: The Emergence of Language*, pp. 231–257. London, Academic Press.

de Zulueta, F. (1993). *From Pain to Violence: The Traumatic Roots of Destructiveness*. London, Whurr Publishers.

Guilford, J.P. (1967). *The Nature of Human Intelligence*. New York, McGraw-Hill.

van Ijzendoorn, M.H. and Kroonenberg, P.M. (1988). Cross-cultural patterns of attachment: a meta-analysis of the Strange Situation, *Child Development*, **59**, 147–156.

Leiman, M. (1992). The concept of sign in the work of Vygotsky, Winnicott and Bakhtin: further integration of object relations theory and activity theory, *British Journal of Medical Psychology*, **65**, 209–221.

Leiman, M. (1994a). Projective identification as early joint action sequences: a Vygotskian addendum to the Procedural Sequence Object Relations Model, *British Journal of Medical Psychology*, **67**, 97–106.

Leiman, M. (1994b). Integrating the Vygotskian theory of sign-mediated activity and the British object relations theory. *University of Joensuu Publications in Social Sciences*, No 20.

Main, M. and Solomon, J. (1990). Procedures for identifying infants as disorganized/disoriented during the Ainsworth Strange Situation. In: Greenberg, M.T., Cicchetti, D. and Cummings, E.M. (Eds), *Attachment in the Preschool Years: Theory, Research and Intervention*. Chicago, University of Chicago Press.

Meltzoff, A.N. and Borton, W. (1979). Intermodal matching by human neonates, *Nature*, **282**, 403–404.

Spangler, G. and Grossman, K.E. (1993). Biobehavioral organization in securely and insecurely attached infants, *Child Development*, **64**, 1439–1450.

Spearman, C. (1904). General intelligence: objectively determined and measured, *American Journal of Psychology*, **115**, 201–292.

Stern, D.N. (1985). *The Interpersonal World of the Infant: A View from Psychoanalysis and Developmental Psychology*. New York, Basic Books.

Voloshinov, V.N. (1928). *Marxism and the Philosophy of Language*. Cambridge, Mass., Harvard University Press (1973).

Vygotsky, L.S. (1978). *Mind in Society: The Development of Higher Psychological Processes*. Edited by M. Cole, V. John-Steiner, S. Scribner, and E. Souberman. Cambridge, Mass., Harvard University Press.

Walton, G.E. and Bower, T.G.R. (1993). Amodal representation of speech in infants. *Infant Behavior and Development*, **16**, 233–243.

Winnicott, D.W. (1974). *Playing and Reality*. Harmondsworth, Penguin Books.

Zinchenko, V.P. (1985). Vygotsky's ideas about units for the analysis of mind. In: Wertsch, J.V. (Ed), *Culture, Communication, and Cognition: Vygotskian Perspectives*. Cambridge, Cambridge University Press.

7 CAT in relation to cognitive therapy

John Marzillier and Gillian Butler

Cognitive Analytic Therapy (CAT) is an avowedly integrative therapy. It has its theoretical roots in object relations theory, Kelly's personal construct theory, cognitive and behavioural science and developmental psychology. The therapeutic approach includes aspects of psychoanalysis (e.g. the interpretation of transference and countertransference), behaviour therapy (e.g. goal setting), cognitive therapy (e.g. challenging irrational beliefs), personal construct therapy (e.g. reappraisal of personal meaning), transactional analysis (e.g. parent–child–adult roles) as well as features that are unique to CAT such as the Sequential Diagrammatic Reformulation (SDR). The relative brevity of the therapy (between 12 and 24 sessions) is designed to make it affordable to public services and accessible to most clients. With this background CAT might be seen as the magpie of psychotherapies, snatching up the treasures of others and claiming them for its own. A more positive view would see CAT as one of a new breed of integrative psychotherapies which attempts to combine the best aspects of the traditional schools into a rich and potent mixture that has greater impact than the original recipes.

Aware of potential criticism of atheoretical eclecticism, Ryle (1990, 1994a) has sought to develop a theoretical model which he claims underpins the uniqueness of the approach. He originally called this the Procedural Sequence Model (PSM). *Procedures* are defined as 'linked sequences of mental and behavioural processes' guiding purposive action. *Sequences* describe the order in which procedures follow one another. These are normally hierarchical, with higher-order procedures (e.g. to enjoy life) being served by lower-order ones

Cognitive Analytic Therapy: Developments in Theory and Practice, Edited by A. Ryle
© 1995 John Wiley & Sons Ltd

(e.g. to take care of my health) and by specific sub-procedures (e.g. not to smoke cigarettes). The sequences include both feedforward and feedback loops, with seven stages being worked through from defining the act to reviewing and revising the procedures and aim.

Psychological problems are viewed as the persistent use of ineffective or harmful procedures. CAT specifies them as Traps, Snags and Dilemmas and the goal of therapy is to identify and modify these maladaptive patterns. Successful therapy should lead to patients learning more effective procedures and thereby feeling more able to identify and manage the problems that brought them to seek help in the first place. Ryle (1990) acknowledges that the PSM is a cognitive theory in the broadest sense. Within a broad cognitive framework, CAT has claimed allegiance to theorists such as Kelly, Vygotsky, Mead and Bruner and to the constructivist position adopted by Mahoney, Arnkoff and others (see Leiman, 1994; Ryle, 1990, 1994b).

Stated in this way, CAT seems to bear a close resemblance to many cognitive therapies. (By 'cognitive therapy' we mean the therapeutic approach first developed by Beck (1970, 1976) which has stimulated a great deal of research and practice over the past 20 years.) Like CAT, cognitive therapy (CT) is a structured and generally brief therapeutic approach. The therapy entails identifying the way problems are maintained by maladaptive or ineffective patterns of thinking and behaviour such as negative automatic thoughts, vicious circles or dysfunctional beliefs. Through guided discovery and collaborative empiricism, patients learn alternative ways of thinking and behaving with the result that they gain greater understanding of and control over their emotional problems (e.g. Beck et al., 1979; Hawton et al., 1989).

One of the main questions asked in this chapter is whether there is something unique or different about CAT which sets it apart from other cognitive therapies. Or, to put it slightly differently, is CAT one version of the generic set of 'cognitive therapies' or is it something else altogether? As its name implies CAT incorporates ideas and techniques that stem from the psychoanalytic tradition. Ryle (1990, p. 208) declared: 'Largely despite themselves, and maybe without knowing it, cognitive psychotherapists' preoccupations are beginning to converge with the agenda of psychoanalysis. In CAT and the PSM can be found the matchmaker capable, I believe, of encouraging this desirable union.' Theoretical developments in CAT over the last decade have resulted in a more explicit incorporation of object relations theory into the procedural model, resulting in its extension and a change of name to Procedural Sequence Object Relations Model (PSORM) (Leiman, 1994; Ryle, 1985, 1992, 1994a). Certain basic procedures, which are captured in the psychoanalytic notion of object relations, take the form of *reciprocal role procedures* (RRPs). That is, they entail the capacity to understand, predict and adapt to the actions and behaviour of others, thus emphasising the *relational* and *reciprocal* nature of human experience. RRPs are acquired from early experience, in particular parental and other family relationships, and from the basic culture in which people live. They operate primarily at an unconscious level and embody the essential rules that govern reciprocal human relations.

This leads us to the second question in this chapter, which is to do with the part played by psychoanalytic theory in CAT. For, to some, the unholy alliance of object relations theory and cognitive theory causes eyebrows to raise and leads to some intriguing questions. For example, what role is given to unconscious motivation? Or, to what extent would CAT endorse the Kleinian view of phantasy in infants? Or, how does the PSORM fit with the idea of primary process? These issues are discussed in detail elsewhere (Leiman, 1994; Ryle, 1994a, b and in this book). From our point of view we ask a simpler and more specific question: to what extent does CAT's incorporation of object relations theory take it outside the pale of modern cognitive therapies? Are there aspects of CAT that would preclude it from being considered a cognitive therapy?

This chapter is primarily concerned with theoretical issues. However, we have chosen to illustrate our analysis using a clinical case. The patient we describe was treated by the senior author using CAT. In presenting this case we ask the question: what would a cognitive therapist do differently and why? To some extent this is an artificial exercise since the therapeutic approach determines what clinical material is seen as relevant and so one can never truly know what another approach may have revealed. Nevertheless, the clinical case provides a good opportunity to see how apparent theoretical differences translate into actual practice. It has long been recognised that what may seem to be substantial theoretical differences often evaporate when practice is examined.

Meanings, conscious and unconscious

In recent years there has been a shift within cognitive therapy towards accepting ideas that seem to be more at home within psychoanalysis. For example, there is a growing acceptance that much of behaviour is governed by unconscious processes (e.g. Bowers and Meichenbaum, 1984; Horowitz, 1994; Mahoney and Freeman, 1985; Safran and Segal, 1991). There is a difference, of course, between what is sometimes known as 'the dynamic unconscious' and the recognition, long known to cognitive psychologists and indeed everybody else, that people do many things unawares. Within psychoanalysis unconscious processes seem to operate as subversive and powerful agents whose aim is to distort the truth and defend against unpalatable feelings or memories, although this Freudian heritage is not the only nor the most balanced account of the dynamic unconscious (see Gordon, 1993). The simple notion that we are unaware of most things that we do is not seriously debated. As Erdelyi (1988, p. 82) put it: 'The notion of unconscious processes, in the sense of psychological processes unfolding outside consciousness, is about as uncontroversial in experimental psychology today as it is in psychoanalysis.' But, as he went on to say, it is at 'finer-grained levels' that problems arise.

One 'fine-grained' problem is to do with *meaning*. Within CT, meaning was originally equated with appraisal: so the quotation from Epictetus, much-loved by cognitive therapists, points to our being moved not by things themselves but by the meanings we give to them. That this originally referred to *conscious* meaning is clear in the following extract from Beck (1976, pp. 53–54):

> The behavioral and psychoanalytic models are similar in that they minimize the importance of meanings that are accessible to introspective observation and report. The behaviorists reject meaning totally and the psychoanalysts emphasize unconscious meanings. . . . The psychoanalytic and behavioral models skirt the common conception of why a person becomes sad, glad, afraid, or angry. The cognitive approach, however, *brings the whole matter of arousal of emotion back within the range of common-sense observation* (our italics).

Through 'common-sense observation', people can come to know the meaning of their emotional experiences, at least at one level. This is different from the psychoanalytic understanding of meaning in which unconscious processes play such a powerful role. It was, and still is, a hallmark of CT that meaning should not be arbitrarily assumed or inferred, but that all meanings should be seen as hypotheses which may be verified or not through observation, empirical testing and reflection. If someone were depressed because he thought that others looked down on him, for example, he might be encouraged to test the meaning of his belief and hopefully disconfirm it. If a therapist believed that a woman's panic attacks were an expression of her feeling trapped in an unhappy relationship, then the therapist would need to find evidence to support this interpretation and be prepared to discard it if that evidence were not forthcoming.

CAT also gives particular importance to enlarging conscious understanding by self-reflection. As Ryle (1990) put it: 'Reformulation, with the development of new tools of self-reflection, offers in most cases, the possibility of rapid change, mediated by practice and sustained by self-observation at a conscious level' (pp. 214–215). CAT therefore aligns itself with other cognitive therapies in drawing on meanings that are open to introspection and empirical testing. However, unconscious meanings are not rejected outright. In fact, they play a central role in the formulation and explanation of problems. In the Sequential Diagrammatic Reformulation (SDR) it is common to portray one or more 'core states' which contain inferences about possible unconscious feelings (e.g. envy, rage). The procedural loops that emerge from such states can have unconscious as well as conscious elements. For example, a placatory trap can be understood in conscious terms as seeking to please others in order to be accepted because one has learned not to value oneself; but it also may signify an unconscious defence against the expression of anger because of a fear that this may unleash a murderous rage.

We now turn to the clinical case to illustrate how CT and CAT deal with the possibility of unconscious meaning. (All names used in this case example are fictional and some details have been changed in order to ensure confidentiality.)

Melanie was a 33-year-old woman who worked as a director of a small company. Following the break-up of a relationship with a work colleague she became anxious and depressed and sought help from her family doctor who referred her on for psychotherapy. She was an attractive, youngish looking women, dressed with studied casualness in a light blue shirt and denim jeans. She related very easily but rather superficially to the therapist (male) and poured out her story, interrupted by frequent bouts of sobbing. She reported a history of repeated failure in relationships with men and thought that there was something fundamentally wrong with her. She expressed feelings of despair and hopelessness. She was moderately depressed though not suicidal and scored 23 on the Beck Depression Inventory (Beck et al., 1961), ticking items such as 'nothing to look forward to', 'a lot of failures in my life', 'expect to be punished', 'self-critical' and 'guilty'.

Melanie said that all her relationships with men had ended badly. At college she had had a long and stormy affair with a tutor who abused her physically and emotionally. Despite her distress she had felt unable to end the relationship and did so only after several attempts. She had had a series of relationships with men over the years, some casual and some more sustained, but found that on each occasion she was let down in some way. Once she had become pregnant and had the pregnancy terminated; she still felt considerable grief when she thought of the abortion. The relationship that precipitated her referral had been an intense and difficult one with Richard, a colleague at work. Eventually, he had broken it off with her. She had subsequently discovered that he had also been seeing a previous girlfriend for almost a year. Melanie was mortified: she felt abused and betrayed.

Melanie was the younger child of older parents. Her father, now retired, had worked as a manager of a shop. Melanie described him as a difficult and rather distant figure whose views dominated the family household. She was acutely aware of his preference for boys over girls; for example, he refused to countenance paying for his daughters' education because they were mere girls. Melanie described her mother as anxious and protective. There was considerable tension at home with frequent rows between her parents. Her mother withdrew from the family, seeking solace in drink and, later, spiritual healing. Melanie had an older sister, Christine, who was married with two young children. Melanie had shared a bedroom with Christine and said she had always felt in her shadow. She saw her as the successful child, academically bright, well organised, hard-working and her father's favourite. In contrast, Melanie saw herself as scatty and unsuccessful despite the fact that she had a high status and well-paid job.

Melanie hoped that therapy might somehow magically transform her and make it possible for her to have a successful relationship with a man. She was convinced that there must be some deficiency in her that had led to all her relationships with men breaking down: if this could be found and put right then perhaps there was a chance that she could be happy. 'I know,' she said, 'I *should* be happy now. I have a job which I enjoy, and am good at, and is well paid. I have my own flat and lots of friends. I travel a lot. But why is it that whenever I get interested in a man, it always goes wrong? It must be something in me, something that I do. But I don't know what. That's what gets me so down.'

For Melanie her repeated difficulties in relationships with men led her to believe that she was deficient in some way. This was the *meaning* that she gave to those experiences. Understandably this made her feel depressed, for in addition to believing herself to be deficient she also felt unable to change her way of behaving. From a CT perspective, this would lead to an exploration of meaning starting from identifying negative thoughts (e.g. 'I am stuck', 'there is nothing I can do', 'I am useless', 'nobody likes me'). Then examples of irrational or maladaptive thinking and assumptions would be elicited (e.g. 'Relationships always go wrong', 'If a man does not like me, then there must be something wrong with me', 'If I care about someone, I have to give in to them'). Finally, the underlying dysfunctional beliefs and schemas would be identified (e.g. 'I don't deserve to be happy', 'I am unlikeable', 'I am a stupid person'). Thus, the *conscious meaning* would be the starting point, but the exploration of meaning would extend further. In this case we might end up with ideas about underlying meanings which Melanie might not, initially at least, be conscious of. For example, a hypothesis might be that she had a 'defectiveness schema'—that is, one which encapsulated a fundamental belief that she was flawed as a person. Thus, while the original emphasis in CT had been on conscious meaning and commonsense observation, this has not precluded making assumptions about possible unconscious meanings: schemas, for example, describe processes that occur mainly unconsciously.

In CAT the process is very similar although the language is different. The client is given the Psychotherapy File where the basic assumptions of the approach are outlined and expressed in CAT language (Traps, Snags, Dilemmas, States of Mind). Melanie rated two of the Traps as particularly significant to her: depressive thinking and trying to please (placatory trap). She also pinpointed the Dilemma, 'If I care about someone, then I have to give in to them', as this seemed to epitomise her difficulties in relationships with men. She also reported experiencing intense emotions such as guilt and anger which she felt she switched into extremely quickly. At other times, she felt a sense of blankness and confusion. This material, together with the information from interviews, led the therapist to make the following preliminary formulation:

At the heart of Melanie's problems lay a doubt about her capacity to sustain a close and intimate relationship particularly with a man. The seeds of this were sown in her experiences as a child when she felt unloved and unwanted (if only she had been the boy her father wanted . . .). Because she felt fundamentally undeserving. Melanie had failed to set appropriate boundaries or assert her own needs in relationships with others. She had been drawn to exciting but untrustworthy men who had exploited her, sometimes abused her, and eventually discarded her. Despite being a successful career woman she felt unfulfilled. Her sister was married and had a family and Melanie felt inadequate and miserable when she met her, comparing herself unfavourably to her. Her conflicted feelings towards her father indicated a persistent and unresolved problem which is broadly Oedipal in nature. In her relationship to the therapist, Melanie also epitomised these problems to some degree. From the beginning she poured out her troubles, letting the tears flow. Her distress, while real, also had a superficial quality about it and the therapist felt 'appealed to' as though he would have to sort her out (but eventually let her down). Her sexuality came into subsequent sessions in the form of wearing sexy clothes and mild flirtation. This suggested that transferential aspects would be an important component of the therapy.

How does the CAT formulation differ from one that a cognitive therapist might have arrived at? Firstly, we should point out that there is likely to be considerable similarity. The focus on Melanie believing herself to be undeserving could, in CT terms, be seen as an 'undeserving schema' underlying her depression and her relationship difficulties. Further, both therapies seek to describe *patterns* that serve to maintain the problem: Traps and Dilemmas in CAT, negative thinking and vicious circles in CT.

The CAT formulation has also gone beyond the conscious meaning in two other ways. Firstly, there is the interpretation that Melanie's problems with men may have stemmed from an unresolved Oedipal problem with her father; that is, in her adult relationships with men she is in part unconsciously re-enacting an earlier, sexualised relationship to her father. Secondly, there is the interpretation that, in her relationship with the male therapist, Melanie replays transferentially some aspects of her general relationship to men. These interpretations come from a psychodynamic perspective and point to possible wider meanings which to the patient are unconscious. Would such unconscious meanings be acceptable within CT?

In CT there has always been the recognition that problems such as depression or anxiety are the product of earlier experiences. This is explicitly contained within the notion of *schema* which describes 'an extremely stable and enduring pattern that develops during childhood and is elaborated throughout an individual's life' (Bricker and Young, 1993). When an emotional problem arises this may be seen as the reactivation of a schema or schemas that have been dormant for many years. An important part of CT concerns the identification and modification of such schemas (see Beck et al., 1979; Kovacs and Beck, 1978). In some problems, for example personality disorders, CT is predominantly concerned with schema identification and modification (Beck and Freeman, 1990; Young, 1990).

It is perfectly possible to infer that in Melanie's case her relationships with her father, which she reported as difficult and distant, could have been a significant factor in the development of an 'undeserving' schema. This is not exactly the same as the Oedipal interpretation, but in both cases an inference is made to events in the patient's childhood and to experiences that are seen to be particularly significant in understanding her presenting problems. In CT there is nothing in principle that would outlaw such interpretations, including the Oedipal one, provided they were couched as hypotheses that would be tested. The cognitive therapist would not too readily jump to such interpretations without having good evidence and would be prepared to modify or discard them if they failed to be supported. Such caution would commonly be found in CAT too.

A similar point can be made with respect to the second interpretation. Transference is not a concept that features in the theory of CT. Nevertheless, the therapeutic relationship may be used as a source of information and hypotheses derived from the relationship about processes that may be operating elsewhere in the patient's life. Generally, patient and therapist seek to work together in a collaborative alliance. But where difficulties arise, these can be seen as due to the activation of particular schemas and the cognitive therapist would be attuned to these and seek to understand them. A cognitive therapist would not be surprised to discover that Melanie might seek to please her therapist even to her own detriment, nor that she might react to the older, male therapist in ways that echoed the way she related to her father.

In conclusion, it is clear that, in both CAT and CT, understanding and clarifying the meaning of the patient's problems is central and in both therapies this entails attention to both conscious and unconscious meanings. Although each approach has an interest in particular and sometimes different meanings, and different ways of going about exploring meanings, both recognise that problems can be understood at various levels of meaning. In CAT the influence of psychodynamic ideas is more obvious than it is within CT. However, in the development of schema-focused cognitive therapy and the work with personality-disordered patients, psychodynamic ideas have begun to appear more frequently in CT (Young, 1990).

Core states, schemas and unconscious motivation

The Sequential Diagrammatic Reformulation (SDR) is the key or blueprint to the CAT treatment. In Figure 7.1 the SDR that was drawn up for Melanie is shown. The central part is a 'core state' in which powerful feelings of emptiness, being lost, in a mess, uncared for and angry are experienced. All bar one of these feelings were directly reported by Melanie as occurring at

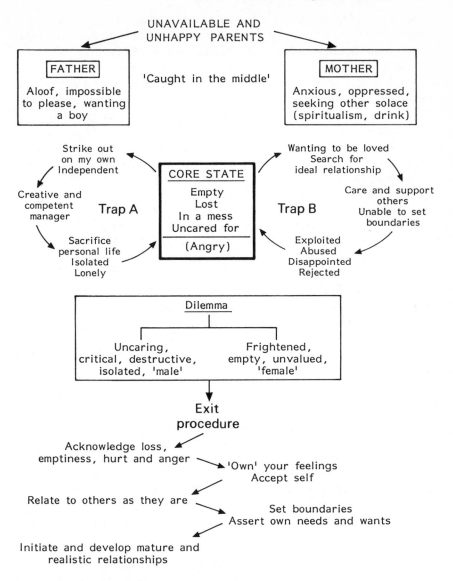

Figure 7.1: Melanie's SDR

times when she experienced this state of mind. The exception is anger which is hypothesised by the therapist as a feeling that was experienced unconsciously. As an indication of its hypothetical nature, it is placed in brackets and separated from the other feelings.

Melanie's SDR was constructed after several assessment sessions. It is a simplification of what may happen when Melanie seeks an intimate relationship with a man. Because of her experience as a child, Melanie was left with a powerful core state in which she felt unhappy, unfulfilled, unloved and (unconsciously) angry. To escape from this state she has three strategies in particular, although there are undoubtedly more, which are portrayed as two Traps and one Dilemma. In one Trap she strives to be independent of others in order to avoid being let down. But this leaves her lonely. In the second Trap she seeks an idealised relationship with a man and in doing so fails to set appropriate boundaries, ending up by being hurt, let down or abused. Both Traps bring her back to the very state she is seeking to avoid. The Dilemma illustrates how Melanie acts as if there were only two extreme choices in relationships: either she is uncaring, critical and destructive or she is dependent, fearful, empty and unvalued. Because she tended to see men as predominantly critical, destructive and uncaring and women as anxious, dependent and unvalued, the poles of the Dilemma were labelled 'male' and 'female'. Caught in these Traps and by the false extremes of the Dilemma, Melanie was unable to find a way that did not take her back to her core state. The way out was shown on the SDR as an exit route that began with accepting rather than seeking to escape from her core state. Therapeutically, this entailed identifying and exploring her core feelings and identifying and changing the ineffective procedures that always brought her back to the core state.

In CT the concept of *schema* is probably closest to the CAT notion of 'core state', although not identical to it. Schemas are essentially frameworks with which we process incoming information and so construct our reality. Schemas may always be in operation but only sometimes is the emotion associated with them activated. In Melanie's case a 'defectiveness schema' could be said to exist which became activated when she experienced strong, negative emotions such as when her boyfriend rejected her. The 'defectiveness schema', when activated, coloured Melanie's experiences so that, for example, her boyfriend's deceit and eventual rejection of her was seen as exemplifying *her* lack of worth, not as *his* untrustworthiness.

Recent developments in CT have seen a greater interest in describing particular schemas or constellations of schemas. Thus, Safran and Segal (1991) have stressed the interpersonal nature and origins of such schemas. Young (1990) has identified 16 different 'early maladaptive schemas' and developed a questionnaire to aid the identification of those that may be relevant to the presenting problem. There is also increasing recognition that schemas, like core states, cannot be easily changed. To quote Bricker and Young:

Schemas are important beliefs and feelings about oneself and the environment which the individual accepts without question. They are self-perpetuating, and are very resistant to change. For instance, children who develop a schema that they are incompetent rarely challenge this belief, even as adults. The schema does not usually go away without therapy. Overwhelming success in people's lives is often still not enough to change the schema. The schema fights for its own survival, and, usually, quite successfully. Even though schemas persist once they are formed, they are not always in our awareness. Usually they operate in subtle ways, out of our awareness. (1993, p. 2)

People may have a schema that they are unaware of, that will resist attempts to change it and that will 'fight for its own survival' often successfully. Such a description would not be out of place in an account of the unconscious processes in psychoanalysis. It is also similar to and consistent with the notion of a 'core state' in CAT which also motivates behaviour, is resistant to change and parts of which at least are presumed to be unconscious.

Another common feature is the recognition that schemas and core states are the product of an individual's developmental history; it is through early experiences, usually emotionally significant ones, that schemas are formed. So the schema of 'emotional deprivation' often arises when parents have been emotionally depriving to the child. The 'failure to achieve' schema may develop if children are put down and treated as if they are a failure at school with parents failing to give good support, discipline and encouragement. Very critical parents may make their children feel unworthy of love and so create a 'defectiveness/shame' schema. In Melanie's case the failure of her parents to pay attention to her led her to believe that she was not worthy regardless of what she might achieve, resulting in a 'defectiveness' schema.

The greater focus on schemas in CT brings with it the recognition that individual behaviour can have meaning which the individual is unconscious of and resistant to accepting. This view is endorsed in the idea of *schema compensation*, described by Bricker & Young (1993) as one of the three ways schemas work (along with *schema maintenance* and *schema avoidance*). In *schema compensation* a person behaves in a manner which appears to be the opposite of what the schema suggests. For example, someone with a 'subjugation' schema behaves in a very controlling way towards other people so that no one will get the better of her; that is, she compensates for her basic sense of weakness by seeking to be strong. This is in effect Adler's notion of 'the inferiority complex'. Another person may present himself as someone who does not need people in order to avoid feeling dependent, which is part of a 'functional dependence' schema. Melanie would seek the attention of others, men in particular, by making herself appear really attractive. In that way she hid her feelings of defectiveness beneath a veneer of sexual attractiveness.

Schema compensation is another way of describing unconscious motivation:

it is presumed that the schema motivates behaviour in a way of which the individual is unaware. CAT also incorporates the idea that people behave in ways that are unconsciously motivated in the sense that people may be driven by a desire to avoid or escape from a core state. For example, a man who has been hurt by a brutalising childhood has a core state in which there are deep feelings of hurt, fear and loneliness. His behaviour towards others is either to avoid intimacy altogether and exploit people for his own ends, or to control those he is close to in order to ensure that they will not be able to hurt him. In doing this he is quite unaware that his behaviour is motivated by the need to avoid such a core state; his motivation is primarily unconscious. In CT terms this would exemplify all three processes of schema compensation, maintenance and avoidance, the schema being either 'mistrust/abuse', 'emotional deprivation' or 'entitlement/self-centredness' or a combination of the three.

In both CAT and CT, therefore, there is an acceptance of the part played by motives of which people are unconscious. The PSORM admits of the role played by unconscious motivation in the incorporation of psychoanalytic notions such as defence mechanisms as examples of procedural sequences (Ryle, 1990, 1991, 1992). Also the hierarchical nature of the procedural sequences is such that conscious intentions and actions are the end results of largely unconscious mental processes. Theoretical models within CT have similarly moved towards the view that people's thoughts, behaviour and feelings are governed by processes of which they are quite unaware. This is apparent in the revised role given to emotional experience.

Emotion

In the early cognitive models of emotional responding it was believed that the cognitive process of appraisal determined the nature of the emotional response in a more-or-less linear relationship. Hearing a sound in the middle of the night will give rise to fear if it is appraised as the presence of a burglar; it might give rise to relief, however, if it is appraised as one's teenager daughter returning late from a party. The appraisal determines the emotional response. However, following Zajonc's (1980) critique, this simple linear notion has been called to question. Emotions are not simply the product of cognitive appraisal. Apart from the evidence that shows that emotions and cognitions are on the whole reciprocally interrelated (Teasdale, 1983), there is also a growing recognition that some forms of emotional experience are processed directly without any conscious appraisal process intervening. Further, the nature of the relationship between affect and cognition is more complex than any linear, causal relationship would suggest.

There are two important implications of this theoretical shift. Firstly, it allows a more significant and powerful role to emotion than hitherto in cognitive theory. Secondly, it opens the door to the incorporation of unconscious processes into the theoretical explanation of emotional disorders. The Interacting Cognitive Subsystems model, or ICS, is a recent example of a theoretical framework in which such ideas have been developed (Barnard and Teasdale, 1991; Teasdale and Barnard, 1993). The basic assumption in the ICS model is that mental activity reflects the collective action of several *specific* processes, each with a particular function to perform. This produces a dynamically interacting system with a range of subsystems, some peripheral and some central. In the ICS model nine subsystems are proposed of which four are central. Cognitive processing depends upon the interactions between subsystems, each of which is specialised in the way it handles specific information. For example, the acoustic subsystem encodes dimensions such as sound frequency, timbre, intensity etc.; the body state subsystem encodes information in relation to bodily sensations of pressure or pain, positions of parts of the body etc.; the object subsystem encodes information that relates to the attributes and identity of visual objects, their spatial positions and their dynamic characteristics.

In the ICS model, emotion is the result of system-wide activity. Each of the nine different types of information can contribute, directly or indirectly, to the experience of emotion. Human emotion, at the adult level, is a distributed phenomenon although the *implicational* subsystem has a prime importance in its production. In this subsystem, sensory and propositional meanings are integrated and high-level regularities, or schematic models of experience, are captured. This is associated with an holistic sense of knowing things about the world which is neither rational nor logical. An important distinction is drawn between different forms of knowledge which reflect the operation of different subsystems. This corresponds to what people say when confronted with the irrational nature of their beliefs: they can recognise their irrationality at an intellectual level, but still believe them 'emotionally'. For example, Melanie might be able to see that she is not in fact worthless or undeserving, that she has a job which she does well, good friends who seem to value her company etc., but such facts do not shake the emotional strength of her conviction in her undeservingness. Within ICS, the 'intellectual' and 'emotional' belief correspond, respectively, to meanings at the Propositional and Implicational levels. The former corresponds to the sense of knowing something 'with the head' while the latter corresponds to a more holistic, intuitive, or implicit sense of knowing something 'with the heart'. It is quite possible for those meanings to be discrepant.

Further details of the ICS model are beyond the scope of this chapter and readers are referred to the original sources. It is an exciting advance in cognitive theory particularly in the way the complexity of emotional production is recognised. One of the nagging problems with the early models underlying CT concerned their over-reliance on the notion of rational and irrational thinking. If someone were depressed and believed that no-one held him in any esteem, liked him or wanted to spend any time with him, then a therapeutic tack might be to show him that these beliefs are untrue. He could come to recognise that there were people who clearly valued him and liked his company etc. But, not surprisingly, while the irrationality of the belief could be recognised intellectually, it often made little difference to the felt conviction. ICS suggests that this is because the focus on irrationality, on what they call the propositional meaning, is not enough. Attention is needed to meaning at the implicational level. What does this mean?

According to Barnard and Teasdale (1991) the implicational subsystem integrates information from a variety of sources (sensory, proprioceptive, propositional). The knowledge that one is underserving is a product of sensory information (one's own bodily feelings for example), the proprioceptive feedback from others such as tone of voice or facial expression, as well as propositions about the world around (e.g. that men abuse and exploit one). Thus a purely rational demonstration that other, important people do in fact value one would have little impact without sensory and proprioceptive information: it would have 'intellectual' value only. This opens the way to the use of therapeutic procedures that are only indirectly related to cognitive appraisals. For example, changes in body state can have a powerful effect on mood. Physical exercise, Gestalt techniques or the use of emotive imagery all have an impact at the implicational level of meaning. Emotional focusing, a technique developed by Gendlin (1981), entails attending to the bodily feelings that seem to come spontaneously resulting in what is called a 'body shift'. This shift is experienced physically and can be accompanied by a powerful emotional change. Within the ICS model important sources of information are being tapped by the use of such techniques.

The ICS model recognises explicitly that emotions are often the product of sources of which the individual may be unconscious. As Barnard and Teasdale (1991) put it: 'Because the information processed by one set of subsystems will not necessarily be propagated to all subsystems, it is quite possible for a person to experience emotion subjectively without having any clear conscious awareness of the source of the emotion.' It is not necessary for subjects to have conscious awareness of the reasons why they are experiencing certain feeling states. In this way the ICS model encompasses the experience of emotions whose origins are, at least in part, unconscious. The parallel with psychodynamic theories of emotional responding is striking.

Aims and methods of therapy

In CAT the aims of therapy are conceptualised within the SDR and actualised as Target Problem Procedures (TPPs). The TPPs provide the formal focus of therapy, and summaries are recorded on a Rating Chart and monitored at the end of each session. The TPP combines description and hypothesis. For example, Melanie's Target Problem was the difficulties she experienced in maintaining an intimate relationship with a man. The TPP that most clearly related to this was summarised as the 'search for an idealised caregiver'. This involved a trap in which she failed to set appropriate boundaries or to assert her own needs because, it was hypothesised, she felt fundamentally unworthy. The consequence was that she often selected men who, superficially, gave her a good time but then treated her badly. While this made her unhappy and angry, she felt unable to express these feelings or blame the men in question. Her unhappiness confirmed her belief in her unworthiness as she felt she was to blame. This also made it difficult to express how angry she felt to the extent that her feelings of anger were predominantly unconscious. To escape from this procedure Melanie needed to be able to accept and then express her true feelings, including negative feelings, in the context of a close relationship and discover that she was not rejected as worthless. In other words, she needed to begin to value herself and be valued for herself. This process could take place both in therapy and in her relationships outside of therapy. The therapist's role is part educational (using the SDR and the TPPs to help Melanie see how to change), part supportive and affirmative (giving her the unconditional support that she normally did not get), and part interpretative (encouraging her to understand the patterns of behaviour, their origins and the way they operate in her current life).

The 'work' of therapy can take place both in terms of material arising out of the therapeutic process (e.g. transference material) and in terms of relationships and other experiences outside therapy. For example, early on in therapy Melanie reported how she had approached Richard, her ex-boyfriend, who had then made it clear that he did not want to live with her. As she told the therapist about the experience, she became overwhelmed by feelings of hopelessness and despair. Her whole body was racked with sobs to the extent that she was unable to speak. The therapist sat and listened, giving support and encouragement. Then as she calmed down, he drew attention to the SDR and pointed out how she seemed to be experiencing her core state in the session and, that in acknowledging and sharing her true feelings, she was beginning the process of change. This then led on to Melanie talking about the therapy. She worried that coming for treatment confirmed her own weakness and unworthiness. She was also worried about what would happen when it ended: would she be able to cope? The therapist was able to acknowledge her fears about therapy ending as genuine and understandable. He suggested that far from being weak in seeking therapy, Melanie was being courageous, and that this was evident in the way she had had to confront very painful feelings. In this way Melanie's experiences in therapy and outside could be brought together and through the structure of the SDR and TPP given a different, more hopeful meaning.

From a CT perspective these therapeutic strategies would not seem odd or unusual although they might not be used in exactly that way. As in CAT there is a concern to organise the therapy around a formulation and to work in a structured and focused way. The patient's experiences become the material for the work of therapy. In addition, specific tasks would be agreed for the patient to attempt outside the sessions and to report back on. The therapeutic work might have centred on helping Melanie identify how her experience with Richard had triggered off certain beliefs and how these beliefs might then have resulted in her selectively attending to certain information. However, change is possible once this process was recognised and understood. Melanie could have learned to behave differently, for example, and to attend to other sources of information, thereby beginning a process of changing her belief in herself as defective or inadequate. In a very similar way to the CAT therapist, the CT therapist would strive to be educational, supportive and interpretative in order to promote beneficial change.

Recent developments in CT have seen greater emphasis given to the understanding and interpretation of the therapeutic relationship. This is particularly the case in schema-focused therapy where maladaptive schemas are examined as they are expressed in the context of the therapeutic relationship. According to Bricker and Young:

> Interpersonal techniques highlight the client's interactions with other people so that the role of the schemas can be exposed. One way is by focusing on the relationship with the therapist. Frequently, clients with a *Subjugation* schema go along with everything the therapist wants, even when they do not consider the assignment or activity relevant. They then feel resentment towards the therapist which they display indirectly. The pattern of compliance and indirect expression of resentment can be explored to the client's benefit. This may lead to a useful exploration of other instances in which the client complies with others and later resents it, and how they might better cope at those times. (1993, p. 5)

An increasing range of therapeutic techniques has been used in CT. In addition to behavioural methods (e.g. goal setting, social skills training) and cognitive change methods (e.g. cognitive restructuring, the Socratic dialogue), emotive techniques such as guided imagery and Gestalt methods have become more common. The use of methods that generate emotions and bodily reactions is consistent with the theoretical analysis we described earlier (the ICS model). In order to access schemas and ultimately to change them, there should be more than Socratic dialogue or rational restructuring. The patient should actually experience the physical concomitants of the emotional response. The success of behavioural methods in the treatment of phobias and anxiety states, for example, may in part due to their ability to gain swift access to emotional experiences.

Conclusions

We have considered how two therapeutic approaches CT and CAT, have several points of convergence both in theory and in practice, CAT is, as its name clearly indicates, a *cognitive* therapy. Ideas from other therapeutic orientations have also been incorporated into CAT, notably from the psychodynamic tradition. Theoretical analyses have been elaborated and extended to take into account the integrative nature of CAT. We asked two questions at the outset of this chapter: is there something unique or different about CAT that sets it apart from other cognitive therapies? Does the inclusion of psychodynamic ideas make CAT less acceptable as a cognitive therapy? From our analysis we would tend towards answering No to both these questions. However, we are very aware that it is all too easy to 'translate' techniques from one school into the language of another and claim that there is no difference between them. This can mask significant theoretical differences and lead to a wishy-washy eclecticism where 'anything goes'. We are absolutely against any such development. It is significant that in both CAT and CT there is a strong emphasis on *theoretical analysis* and that technical advances are considered within broad but distinct theoretical frameworks which are elaborated over time. The fact that there are significant similarities between CAT and CT should not make us lose sight of the value of theoretical differences, nor of the need for theoretical advances in our understanding of complex clinical phenomena.

References

Barnard, P.J. and Teasdale, J.D. (1991). Interacting Cognitive Subsystems: a systemic approach to cognitive–affective interaction and change, *Cognition and Emotion*, **5**, 1–39.

Beck, A.T. (1970). Cognitive therapy: nature and relation to behavior therapy, *Behavior Therapy*, **1**, 184–200.

Beck, A.T. (1976). *Cognitive Therapy and the Emotional Disorders*. New York, International Universities Press.

Beck, A.T. and Freeman, A. (1990). *Cognitive Therapy of Personality Disorders*. New York, Guilford Press.

Beck, A.T., Rush, A.J., Shaw, B.F. and Emery, G. (1979). *Cognitive Therapy of Depression*. New York, Guilford Press.

Beck, A.T., Ward, C.H., Mendelson, M., Mock, J. and Erbaugh, J. (1961). An inventory for measuring depression, *Archives of General Psychiatry*, **4**, 561–571.

Bowers, K.S. and Meichenbaum, D. (Eds) (1984). *The Unconscious Reconsidered.* New York, John Wiley.

Bricker, D.C. and Young, J.E. (1993). *A Client's Guide to Schema-Focussed Cognitive Therapy.* New York, Cognitive Therapy Center of New York.

Erdelyi, M.H. (1988). Issues in the study of unconscious defense processes: discussion of Horowitz's comments with some elaborations. In: Horowitz, M.J. (Ed), *Psychodynamics and Cognition.* Chicago, University of Chicago Press.

Gendlin, E.T. (1981). *Focusing.* New York, Bantam.

Gordon, R. (1993). *Bridges: Metaphor for Psychic Processes.* London, Karnac.

Hawton, K., Salkovskis, P., Kirk, J. and Clark, D. (1989). *Cognitive Behavioural Therapy for Psychiatric Problems: a Practical Guide.* Oxford, Oxford University Press.

Horowitz, M.J. (1994). States, schemas, and control: general theories for psychotherapy integration, *Clinical Psychology and Psychotherapy*, **1**, 143–152.

Kovacs, M. and Beck, A.T. (1978). Maladaptive cognitive structures in depression, *American Journal of Psychiatry*, **135**, 525–533.

Leiman, M. (1994). The development of Cognitive Analytic Therapy, *International Journal of Short-Term Psychotherapy*, **9**, 67–81.

Mahoney, M.J. and Freeman, A.T. (Eds) (1985). *Cognition and Psychotherapy.* New York, Plenum.

Ryle, A. (1985). Cognitive theory, object relations and the self. *British Journal of Medical Psychology*, **58**, 1–7.

Ryle, A. (1990). *Cognitive–Analytic Therapy: Active Participation in Change. A New Integration in Brief Psychotherapy.* Chichester, John Wiley.

Ryle, A. (1991). Object relations theory and activity theory: a proposed link by way of the procedural sequence model, *British Journal of Medical Psychology*, **64**, 307–316.

Ryle, A. (1992). Critique of a Kleinian case presentation, *British Journal of Medical Psychology*, **65**, 309–317.

Ryle, A. (1994a). Introduction to cognitive analytic therapy, *International Journal of Short-Term Psychotherapy*, **9**, 93–109.

Ryle, A. (1994b). Persuasion or education? The role of reformulation in cognitive analytic therapy, *International Journal of Short-Term Psychotherapy*, **9**, 111–117.

Safran, J.D. and Segal, Z.V. (1991). *Interpersonal Processes in Cognitive Therapy.* New York, Basic Books.

Teasdale, J.D. (1983). Negative thinking in depression: cause, effect or reciprocal relationship? *Advances in Behaviour Research and Therapy*, **5**, 3–5.

Teasdale, J.D. and Barnard, P.J. (1993). *Affect, Cognition and Change in Remodelling Depressive Thought.* Hove, Lawrence Erlbaum.

Young, J.E. (1990). *Cognitive Therapy for Personality Disorders: A Schema-Focused Approach.* Sarasota, Florida: Professional Resource Exchange Inc.

Zajonc, R.B. (1980). Thinking and feeling: preferences need no inferences, *American Psychologist*, **35**, 151–175.

8 How analytic is CAT?

A discussion between
Tim Leighton and Anthony Ryle

Cognitive Analytic Therapy has always been concerned to acknowledge its debt to, and to differentiate itself from, psychoanalysis. An essay by Tim Leighton challenging the right of CAT to call itself analytic was the provocation for a discussion between A.R. and T.L. The latter has been working mainly in the field of addiction and is one of the first generation of CAT qualified psychotherapists. The following is an edited record of the conversation.

T.L.   When I first came across CAT, I was interested in the integration. At the time I was very interested in psychoanalysis (and still am) and I saw CAT through psychoanalytic lenses. As I found out more about how CAT actually worked it began to look very cognitive and not particularly analytic. It seemed to me that most of what would be characteristic of psychoanalysis had been eliminated or attenuated—there wasn't any interpretation in the analytic sense, or any theory of drive, and there wasn't the layering that happens in psychoanalysis where over a length of time the analysis uncovers more and more strata of symbolisation and displacement, so that the pictures that emerge during the early part of the therapy can change to very different ones later. I wasn't wanting to insist on all these features, but there did seem to be very significant differences. Also, the CAT model struck me as very much a 'top-down' theory rather than a 'bottom-up' theory.

A.R.   That's 17 points there! First of all I should say that I never had any experience of cognitive therapy as such; my experience was analytically based therapy. But working with Kelly's grids and, later, reading the

Cognitive Analytic Therapy: Developments in Theory and Practice, Edited by A. Ryle
© 1995 John Wiley & Sons Ltd

cognitive authors, I felt they suggested additions to what I was do-ing—important ones. But I would perceive CAT as having always been rooted in psychoanalysis insofar as it has taken a developmental theory very much out of the analytical world. Although I have objections to parts of analytic theory, the influence of development on personality structure seems to me to be a very important issue, and the whole understanding of the transference and its use-which is very central to CAT (and which recently even got into the footnotes of CBT)—is the other major analytic contribution. In that sense the 'A' in CAT has always had its place. Since CAT's early stages, the argument has not been with the cognitive element, which is fairly straightforward, but more to clarify the similarities and differences between CAT and Psychoanalysis.

T.L.   What particularly interests me is to try to sort out what the model owes to psychoanalysis and in what ways it differentiates itself. There are two aspects to this question: one is 'What is analytic about CAT theory?' and the other is 'What is analytic about CAT practice?' CAT is clearly a cognitive therapy, insofar as it is concerned with information processing, and the connection between appraisal, beliefs and action. It understands emotional and behavioural problems in terms of repeated procedural sequences which are self-maintaining in various ways. It differs from, say, Beck's model of cognitive therapy, not so much in including emotion, or by paying attention to the childhood origin of self-defeating beliefs (the accusation that cognitive therapists ignore emotion is unfair), but in positing a richer and more complete account of cognitive processing and in placing a much greater emphasis on the relationship between the therapist and the patient.

As far as the 'analytic' elements in CAT theory are concerned, a main concern is about the accessibility and nature of unconscious material. Other issues which seem important are: in the development of personality, what comes from outside and what is innate, and what drives behaviour? In classical psychoanalysis there is great stress laid on repression: the way in which wishes are prevented from reaching consciousness. as regards practice, the special conditions of psychoanalytic treatment are supposed to be able to wear down the resistances and bring forbidden material into the light. This takes some time, and it is clear from psychoanalytic case studies that, because of the complexity of symbol formation, through mechanisms such as condensation and displacement, much unconscious material carries multiple meanings, so that what emerges in the early part of the analysis may be quite different from the deeper layers which are reached later on. This is one reason why some analyses are so protracted.

Of course CAT proceeds quite differently. You seem to me to have a different view of unconscious mental activity and therefore a different view of repression.

A.R. That's absolutely true. As regards the 'Unconscious', I think the polarisation of the conscious and unconscious systems is unhelpful. Consciousness is the surprising thing. Most mental activity is not open to introspection for various reasons. I would see the dynamic unconscious as a kind of (partially silenced) alternative voice, not unlike the aspects of internal dialogue which *are* available to one, but only deduced from the slips and omissions and the motivated acts we don't accept conscious responsibility for. The emphasis in CAT is on *procedures*, which as you know are complex sequences of mental, behavioural and environmental events, of which we are only partially aware. Some procedures are evidently expressing or serving the interests of this silenced part. But all enacted procedures can be described. How often, and how far, the problems patients needs to deal with are concealed behind false or over-condensed or over-determined clues, rather than being only too clearly manifest in how they treat themselves and others, including their therapists, I am uncertain. What is in the *depths* of *depth* psychology may be *deeply* irrelevant. What is revealed there seems uncannily dependent on the theory espoused by the analyst. But sometimes, of course, that process offers a unique understanding. Sometimes!

T.L. The idea of a structure of personality developed in interaction with others seems both to link CAT with analytic theory and to show up differences. Psychoanalysis theorises about the nature of internal object representations at this stage, the Kleinians in particular claiming that an internal object world is established by introjection, and that the infant's struggles are chiefly about the experience of privation as phantasies of attack by hostile forces (persecutory anxiety). The most important internal object in this battle is the 'bad breast' onto which the infant projects the aggression and greed he or she feels towards it. This escalating scenario is to some extent counteracted by the hallucinatory gratification provided by an idealised 'good breast'. The theory is quite complex but it is primarily an account of an internal drama. Klein does not, of course, claim that external events have no impact at all: she says that they may serve to upset the balance between libidinal and aggressive impulses. However, the clear implication in Kleinian theory is that damage in personality development at this stage is due to innate destructive impulses being 'too strong', or alternatively to an insufficient capacity for the secure cathexis of the 'good breast'. Splitting is seen as a defensive strategy to keep the good object safe from the intrapsychic warfare going on. The need for mother-love in the Kleinian account is driven by a need to reduce primary anxiety. This is the exact opposite of the position taken by the Attachment theorists, who claim that the bonding with the mother is primary, and anxiety follows too much frustration of the needed bond. As I understand it, CAT is closer to attachment theory, and indeed you and John Bowlby both emphasised that very many of your disturbed patients had suffered a history of neglect, deprivation and abuse, which you connected clearly with their difficulties as adults, and you have expressed anger at the way some analytic theory helps to maintain denial of this connection.

A.R.   Yes. I don't accept the model of the internal world of childhood as being dominated by anxiety and innate destructiveness. The work derived from attachment theory, especially that concerned with the transmission of 'working models of relationships', seems very close to CAT ideas.

T.L.   There still remains the question of how object relationships are represented in the mind, and the nature of phantasy. You have explicitly rejected the 'demonology' aspect of object relations theory, but it is central to the development of the reciprocal role repertoire that identifications are made with the object-derived pole of the relationship. Identifications in psychoanalytic theory are accounted for in various ways, from incorporative introjections at the most primitive level, to the little boy's identification with the potentially castrating father to resolve the Oedipus complex, thus forming the superego, to Anna Freud's ego defence of 'identification with the aggressor'.

A.R.   Identification, incorporation, introjection are all covered in the idea that one primarily learns *patterns of reciprocal roles*. Either pole can be enacted, and identification with the aggressor is an example of that. In fact, Joseph Sandler said more or less the same thing years ago.

*   *   *   *   *

T.L.   You have offered Vygotsky's statement that 'what a child does with an adult today, she will do by herself tomorrow' as a starting point for a CAT answer to this question. But Vygotsky was, I believe, referring to the acquisition of skills and competences. In combination with his idea that thought in childhood begins with dialogue with another person, then becomes a conversation with the self, and then 'goes underground' as internalised thinking, Vygotsky's statement could provide a basis for a theory of identification.

   You have extended Vygotsky's statement by saying 'what an adult does not allow a child to know today, she will not allow herself to know tomorrow'. As I understand you, you are not saying that a person is limited by what is given culturally. What the child needs are adults who are concerned to help her reflect on her experience and create meaning. Lack or insufficiency of this leads to procedural restriction. The idea of not being allowed to know links very clearly to psychoanalysis. Parental prohibitions are often unconscious, and are maintained as unconscious by the fear of some catastrophe.

A.R.   I *am* saying that a person is both formed and limited by the particular culture of their early years. One can be not allowed to know or not allowed to reflect on one's experience, by not being given the attention or the words. Not being given these will be the result of the parent's own procedures, which may be similarly restricted. In the end it is the meanings conveyed through pre-verbal exchanges and through language that determine the range of our experiences and actions.

*   *   *   *

T.L.   I would like to look at what goes right. Do we have a concept of optimal development? Freudian theory in its classical form is a theory of the organism and its drives. Consciousness arises as part of the formation of the ego in order to mediate between the demands for drive-gratification and those of reality. Transference is explained as the redistribution of libidinal cathexes. In CAT, innate drives are acknowledged, but it is held that there is a potential for the individual conscious subject to manage these, particularly if he or she has experienced certain kinds of relationships with other people. In my view this is one of the justifications for seeing CAT as analytic rather than simply cognitive. It seems to me to be a development of the line of psychoanalysis exemplified by Fairbairn, Guntrip, Winnicott, and on a rather different tack, John Bowlby. Of course you explicitly relate CAT to object relations theory; I think there is a link not just theoretically but also ethically to these analysts.

A.R.   I'd happily go along with those resemblances, and I would certainly ditch concepts like 'redistributing libidinal cathexes'. But I would put still more emphasis on the sociocultural and less on the biological elements.

T.L.   That sounds closer to Winnicott than to Bowlby. Winnicott was not at all keen on Bowlby's stress on biological factors. He felt ethology was a dead-end in terms of explaining human behaviour. But perhaps we can come back to biology later. One of the things I wanted to talk about is aim-directed action, which is the central focus of CAT. Classical psychoanalysis developed the idea that the real meaning of activity was that it was attempting to gratify instinctual drives, which is in one sense as pure aim-directed action as you can get. The aims are unconscious and usually heavily disguised. But post-war psychoanalysis has taken more and more interest in the role of language, and also in the mother/baby relationship as opposed to the Oedipal triangle.

A.R.   To me, *meaningful* means invested with human, culturally based, personally felt significance, which is very different from instinct. Why the procedural sequence model emphasised intentional action was partly as a protest *against* drive theory, which has always seemed to me to be a very inadequate account of human behaviour. Obviously we all have drives: that is taken for granted in a sense; but they don't explain very much about the differences between human beings, because they are so culturally transformed and transmuted and expressed in so many different ways. It is those expressions which are so interesting and complex rather than the drives themselves.

T.L.   In my opinion Freud would not argue with what you have just said, but this is an area of vital difference between CAT and analysis, I think. Psychoanalytic theory holds that the complexity you have described *can* be reduced to drives: the therapy is aimed at making conscious the wishes that are the drive representatives, and it generally takes a long time because of the labyrinthine vicissitudes of the instincts. Freud even felt the complexities of civilisation could be accounted for in this way. CAT rejects this, but does it have anything to say about the nature of the drives at all?

A.R.   It depends how you put it. Of course human beings have a capacity for destruction. If you say everything we are must be innate, then we are innately destructive, but that doesn't explain the interesting things like why there have been cultures and why there are people in whom aggression has been transformed into non-damaging forms, and there are others in whom it is glorified. It is the effect of those cultural differences and the differences in personal history in patients that we need to understand. Cultural shaping both permits, creases, enlarges, complexities and also limits the expression of our nature.

T.L.   It has been pointed out, by Chomsky for example, that the similarities in cultural expression seem much more striking than the differences, and it is suggested that culture is shaped and constrained by parameters such as innate linguistic structures. It is certainly astonishing how human beings across cultures and across historical time seem to think, feel and act in broadly similar and comprehensible ways.

A.R.   Broadly similar, but also very different. The human race has evolved biologically for 5 million years people think that language has been around for 200 000 years; written language appeared about 5000 years ago. The differences between me and someone born 200 000 years ago or 5000 years ago or 100 years ago are not biological, they are cultural. I don't say we have necessarily improved, but we have certainly become more complicated, which I regard as a virtue. I am, you are, and the people around us are creations of this particular corner of the world with its Judeo-Christian culture and all that stuff: we are all quite similar because we have basically had the same input.

T.L.   I agree with that, but what is striking to me is how similar the cultures are despite large superficial differences, especially in terms of basic human motivations. A lot of work has been going on this century to understand cultural differences, so I find it quite hard to get this point across. I feel as though I could wake up in classical Athens or even ancient Sumeria and fairly quickly come to understand how people ticked. People are not that different. Family structure varies within quite narrow limits. The literature of other cultures is usually surprisingly comprehensible.

A.R. I think we tend to read what is accessible. You could say that once we became social animals all societies had to deal with the same issues, such as the prolonged dependency of the infant, and the differentiation of sexual roles. So we all have similar issues growing up, whether it is in ancient Sumeria or in Hackney. It is not just that the package of genes you get is so similar. But our patient's problems are fundamentally explicable in terms of their detailed personal experience, and it seems to me that how well or badly they navigate the complexities of the world is a measure of how their early experiences have shaped them.

T.L. I don't want to pursue this too far, as I don't think I am very far away from you. For me psychoanalysis does rather well in providing a way of thinking about how people behave with each other and how they work and play; but where it doesn't do so well is when it tries to address historical issues. A clear example of this is where Freud starts speculating about the primal horde and the first father being killed by the sons. I realise he got this from Darwin, but it seems a classic piece of romantic nineteenth-century myth-making. I think the same problems sometimes arise when psychoanalysis reconstructs the events of infancy. A point you have made, with reference to Melanie Klein, is that there is really no evidence that what she claims actually occurs.

A.R. I think a lot of the work of the last decade, and the critical writing of, for example, Drew Westen and others does throw considerable doubt upon the official Freudian account of the order of events in childhood.

T.L. Does that matter?

A.R. Yes, I think it does. What is it that id discovered in the course of a prolonged analysis? Is this slowly peeling back the layers and getting to the depths contacting the early stages of development, or is it creating a very peculiar relationship into which the analyst puts certain kinds of interpretations and understandings? Where does the belief that everybody is helped by contacting this capsule of unremembered experience come from? I don't think you ever do get it, and in the course of trying to, you may actually be creating a new myth which may or may not be particularly helpful. But the theory demands that nothing short of that journey can do whatever it is supposed to do. Others things can make you feel better, take away symptoms or whatever, but that is considered a peripheral concern! The idea that everybody has to have this very peculiar relationship in order to understand themselves is very opposed to my view of culture in general. Education on the whole is not about going back, it is about going on.

T.L.   That makes me think of the development of Freud's theory itself: proto-psychoanalysis was all about getting back to the traumatic memory and producing abreaction. That was more or less abandoned, or at least sidelined, when he discovered wishes and the need to interpret wishes, the redistribution of bound-up libido. Later on he developed a great interest in the transference, and I think that at this point psychoanalysis begins to look much more like CAT.

A.R.   The other way round of course!

T.L.   But it is much more interesting from our point of view when psychoanalysis is understood as the repetition of a particular kind of relationship which is worked through in some way.

A.R.   That, I think, was the most profound contribution in many ways. But being related to a theory of necessary regression to the earlier stages, and those stages being pushed back from the 3 to 5 of the Oedipus complex to the 0 to 1 of the Kleinian clashes of phantasy, has produced this totally impracticable therapy of seven years on the couch, which seems to me to have very little to do with people's needs to be helped with their problems. I has produced some quite fascinating stuff but a lot of the stuff is about that peculiar process rather than about human life as she is lived. The developmental theory as it has evolved has been linked with the requirement for a more and more impractical treatment. My irritation with that was a major impetus towards the development of CAT. I believe that if psychotherapy is good for people it should be available to those who need it. It never has been, but it is more likely to be if it is economically feasible.

*   *   *   *   *

T.L.   Can we get back to CAT theory. What does object relations mean in terms of the PSM? The original PSM didn't seem to me particularly psychoanalytic; it was a straightforward cognitive model.

A.R.   The PSM, with its emphasis on intentional acts, was a way-station. In fact, to defend it, the stage of appraisal and evaluation can bring in your whole life experience, you different values, conflict between aims and so on. Potentially you could incorporate the whole of psychoanalysis within that cycle. But it does read a bit too much like a guided tour through action.

T.L.   There have sometimes been people either in psychoanalysis or on its periphery, who have had similar objections to those you have had, and who have developed powerful psychotherapies. I am thinking of Sulllivan and Suttie, Ferenczi, Fairbairn, Franz Alexander, but they all stand in the shadow of Freud. Suttie perhaps doesn't . . .

A.R. Many of them didn't stand in the shadow, they were buried by the establishment.

T.L. The reason I mention them is to discuss the relationship between object relations theory and the PSORM. If you look at Fairbairn's models of the inner world, for example, you still find a psychic economy theory with aggressive forces and repression. There seems a compulsion to retain a metapsychology which I believe I have heard you say you don't think is very useful.

A.R. I don't think that *that* metapsychology is helpful, but I do think theory *is* useful and necessary, but theory ought to be compatible with what is known. The trouble with all those theories is that they are only checked out against the utterances of analysands, which is not a very good set of data on which to construct a whole developmental theory. I think many psycho-analysts realise that now, and are becoming more open to observational data just in the last few years.

T.L. That does seem an advance. But I still have some difficulty with what CAT leaves out, even though it may not be supported by data of the kind we're talking about. Psychoanalysis from Freud onwards does stress that internal structures are developed in interaction with the environment, but the emphasis is on the intrapsychic, because analysis is concerned with conflict and the mechanisms of managing the conflict. In the Kleinian tradition the mother plays a big role as the container of projections and is acting very much as a psychic extension of the baby. Here the ideas of phantasy and reverie and so on seem not only useful but vital.

A.R. I think the emphasis needs to be on *linking* the interpersonal and the intrapsychic. In an odd way Klein, though bringing object relations into the centre, rarely showed an interest in actual relations.

T.L. Well, maybe not, but those influenced by her, especially Winnicott, certainly did. He developed the concept of 'object use' to get to the point where the object survives the phantasy attacks and becomes real and available for relationship. His ideas about transitional space and the ability to play seem very important to me. My point is that this is a different kind of account of how a baby develops into a person. If a phrase like 'average expectable environment' is used, then we have to understand 'expected by what?'

A.R.   Well, as you know, Mikael Leiman places Winnicott closer to CAT than other analysts because he saw the transitional object as mediating the space between people and internal space, which is where the role of the sign is located. Most of us would also prefer Winnicott's human style of talking about his patients, which has none of the hysterically black flavour one finds in Kleinian interpretations. 'Average expectable environments' and 'good-enough mothers' were ways of locating the normal and ordinary.

T.L.   Is it fair to say 'object relations' in CAT terms means something close to Stern's 'representations of interactions that have been generalised'?

A.R.   Stern's RIGs are clearly similar to CAT's RRPs. In CAT's version of object relations theory, attention is centred on the acquisition of these patterns of interaction. The world, the self and the other are learned about in the context of early relationships, where thought, feeling, desire, action and communication are inseparable. We do not apply a relationship pattern to an object representation: in my view, we experience others in terms of the spectrum of responses united in the RRP. The divisions are those of psychologists, not of the subject.

T.L.   If we return to Vygotsky for a moment, his idea was that the child and the parent do things together, with the adult providing a commentary. The child takes over the commentary and uses it to guide her activity when she is on her own. At first the commentary is spoken out loud, but then it goes inside and becomes silent, or even unconscious. This is thought.

A.R.   It is not just a commentary, it is the shaping and structuring of activity through time, context and communications which the adult provides. We are dependent on our caretakers for the provision of these early tools/words, signs, although children quite quickly begin to invent signs too, to use with their caretakers. Signs are first *between* people, and then *in* people's minds.

T.L.   There is to my mind something innate about this sign-producing capacity. In the pre-verbal relationship between baby and mother the exchange of signs is quite considerable . . .

A.R.   What is innate *becomes* a sign by being invested with meaning. Mikael Leiman's paper on Vygotsky discusses infant pointing: when the child reaches to grasp something it is a simple physical act, which is responded to as if it were an intention. In this sense intention comes to be formed by acts being shaped and named between the parent and the child.

*   *   *   *   *

T.L.   Well, it seems to me as though the juxtaposition of Winnicott with Vygotsky in our conversation points up a contrast between an emphasis on being and an emphasis on doing. The link is perhaps creativity. There seems room in the theory of signs for the creation of individual difference as well as learning to be a participant in the pre-existing culture.

A.R. Creativity is a dangerous word: we are all in favour of it, like virtue, but we like it to be mysterious. I am not clear where you place it in relation to the 'doing' versus 'being' contrast. Being is about self-awareness while not pursuing goals or chasing one's tail too actively, perhaps. Or casting off placatory false selves? But creativity—making something new—comes from activity. It involves a transformation or recombination of existing forms or meanings, or, rarely, the invention of new ones. But even new ones are closely related to pre-existing ones: they have to be intelligible. Insofar as creativity often seems to emerge 'from the unconscious', this would support my view that the unconscious is as socially determined as the conscious mind. The theory of signs allows for individual difference: the wider the cultural inheritance an individual has, the great his or her possibility of rich new insights. And provided that the childhood was enabling.

T.L. Well, I am in two minds about this. I agree with much of what you say, but I don't go along with you entirely. I think there is a sense in which the social matrix hinders a special kind of relation to reality, and that it is possible to get beyond that to an emotional space of direct, personal, living experience. I imagine you think this is a socially constructed illusion, but I am not sure that the aesthetic and the spiritual reduce entirely to a social semiotic. I would also like to say that creativity in the external world, which is of course 'activity', is dependent on, or substitutes for, an internal creativity. And I think this creative function arises pre-conceptually, although of course it involves thinking of a kind. It's quite close to Bion's idea of 'alpha function', which enables 'beta elements'—which include ideas, impressions, feelings, stimuli of various kinds—to be processed into something personal. It is possible to transmit ideas without making them personal in this way. But I would like to move on to something perhaps more directly connected to CAT theory.

I believe that a person's successful navigation in the world requires a kind of fourfold relationship with the self. First there is a self-soothing function, a relationship based on a feeling of safety in which one feels held and able to relax and go to sleep. Secondly there is a self-monitoring function—'where am I?' 'what is the situation?' 'how do I feel?' 'what can I do?' Thirdly there is a self-advocacy or self-encouraging function which will say 'go on and do it'. And finally there is intentionality: 'why am I doing what I am doing?' 'what am I hoping to achieve in doing it?' All of these seem important and different. There is also the ability to have a workable relationship, not necessarily one of compliance, with the culture in which one lives. If we want a more complete theory of why people do things, how they relate, and how they feel about things, we have to hold on to all these aspects.

A.R.   Yes, that's right, but I would add a self-reflective capacity which enables us to examine all of the above. In this respect we are quite unlike animals. A lot of cognitive and analytic writers like to think of us as being on a biological continuum, but I think there is a radical difference between humans and animals in that we are living almost entirely within a culturally shaped symbolic world.

T.L.   This links with an idea in psychoanalysis, particularly in the Lacanian tradition, that the entry into the symbolic order creates a radical and irreparable split. Lacan would not see the development of the self in relationship with others as a benign and creative process but one based on a story of lack and loss. The child's relationship with the parent consists of a set of alienating identifications as the child responds to the desire of the other. The feeling of wholeness is based on an illusion, an image in the mirror.

A.R.   My immediate response is that if that were not the case what would we become? Are we just seeds that want to flower, but that are over-cultivated and pruned and distorted? I don't think we are. It seems to me that we cannot but acknowledge that we are formed by our biology and by our caretakers, and that the self we end up with was shaped in the mirror of the other. Only 'mirror' is misleading. Parents both acknowledge and reflect the child's experience, *and* communicate a response which can include both an indication of meaning and a strategy of coping. This is a clearer account than Bion's 'metabolism', I think. Without this kind of reflection the child cannot become reflective. From the time when we acquire speech we are engaged in dialogue internally. We can't say 'what a pity it is that we are formed and have to be formed by experience'. The one thing we can say is that once we have a sufficiently complicated conversation going on in our head we can begin to consider the terms of the conversation. So that consciousness is the only tool which allows us to make a choice other than that which we were given. But it is complicated because the way in which we reflect and the way we make our choice is also structured for us. I have to wonder if the arguments I am making are just those of the culture in which I was brought up. Intellectual life at the edge is all about questioning those structures, and there is always a process of conformity and oppression entering in, but also of protest. But you can't deal with it by saying it shouldn't have happened. You deal with it by seeing how quickly and how far we can advance in getting some independence of it.

T.L.   I have some objections to this line of argument. I fully accept that the development of the self is a dialogic process. But you are at great pains to say that it is culture, not biology, that is important. If you admit biological givens they are bracketed off as being irrelevant. But this is like a sculptor ignoring the nature of her material. The form gives significance, but only in relationship with the material. I believe that the developmental processes are crucial, and that they include a great deal more than the attainment of the intellectual capacities you have described. In fact I am worried that one of the things that can go wrong, both in childhood and in psychotherapy, is the precocious achievement of these capacities. There is an increasing interest in the emotional deprivation of the precocious child. It can be as though mothering functions are provided by the child's own mind. Winnicott would certainly say that if a child is forced to perform at this level, what is happening is the creation of a false self, and that buried underneath is a deprived true self who perhaps doesn't want to be stimulated in this way. There does seem to be some kind of desirable developmental timetable, and I don't think it is entirely cultural, except in the sense that child-rearing practices are presumably modified, in the manner of natural selection, to produce the kind of adults needed by a particular society. We are dealing with the individual distress resulting from this. I think there is a danger that a brief therapy like CAT might produce a repetition of the push to precocious intellectual management of the world.

A.R.   I don't think I have only discussed the attainment of intellectual capacities. The attainment of self-reflection demands access to the self *and* a way of knowing and thinking about the self. That's not a false-self development. I 'bracket off' biology because it contributes little to our understanding of the differences therapy is concerned with. The procedural repertoire one gets ought to match the world one is living in well enough to enable one to manage it all right. If you are living in a very structured society in which you know your place (e.g. if you were born a serf on a feudal estate) it is fairly clear what is expected of you, and you probably don't require much self-reflection to live your life through to the end. One of the features of the modern world is that very few people live a life that is externally defined for them in that way, so the requirement for flexibility and reflection is much greater that it was, and the strain on the integrity of the personality is also much greater. That is a cultural change, and probably history has been in that direction. To sum up, my emphasis on culture is (a) because I think it deserves it, and (b) because it is left out of both cognitive and psychoanalytic accounts. People still write as if we are the sum of our biological evolution. Of course we *are* animals—and thank God for that! But we are *human* animals: even our bodies are known to us through what we have learned culturally.

*   *   *   *   *

T.L.   It is not general human ability and whether it is innate or not that interests me either, although I would say that the range of human competence is simply amazing and is not explained by learning theory or any other theory that psychology has produced. I am interested in what we have to take into account in order to produce reliable change in a therapeutic encounter. Unfortunately there is a tendency, and psychoanalysis has it in large measure, to move away from therapeutic procedures, finding out what works, towards creating a huge global psychology of the human person, which might not be so important.

A.R.   But I think it *is* important, and haven't big global issues figured in our conversation? But I feel psychoanalysis has got it upside down. Psychoanalysts talk as if history was the creation of psychology. I would say that the order is: history, anthropology, sociology, psychology. The last cannot explain its antecedents. The emphasis on the innate and the individual, and the emphasis on biology, is a kind of cop-out. Voloshinov said that quite clearly in his Critique of Freudianism. He saw the popularity of psychoanalysis in the 1920s as a cultural movement; it took you off the hook of being responsible for what was going on in the world.

T.L.   Voloshinov was only the first of many both inside and outside psychoanalysis who have said something similar. Psychoanalytic thinking doesn't have to be used to avoid social issues. There have been many valiant attempts made to use psychoanalysis to catalyse social change, from Marcuse to Michael Rustin. It is also possible to start with psychoanalysis as an enemy, and then to make it into a friend. For example, Juliet Mitchell showed that the feminists cannot afford to ignore psychoanalysis.

A.R.   Well, I have to agree that psychoanalysts *can* be socially responsible, and that psychoanalysis *cannot* be ignored. But there is a conservatism and a complacency towards the world in evidence too, in psychoanalytic institutions.

*   *   *   *   *

T.L.   There are two big areas I would like to move on to, which are relevant to any discussion of a therapy that is related to or descended from analysis. These are sexuality and the mythical. Despite Freud's propensity for philosophical speculation, I think he tended to be a non-mystical kind of character, and there is something quite hard-nosed about the way psychoanalysis looks at, say, dreams. He is interested in dreams and in myth, because of what he thinks they reveal about primary process, about disguised representations of psychic truth. The dissenters, such as Jung and Adler, differ from Freud mainly in their attitude to these big areas. Jung rejected the emphasis on sexuality, as did Adler, for whom power relations were more interesting. Jung's interest in myth and symbol is of a much more mystical kind than Freud's. Where does CAT stand on these issues? In CAT, when one creases a story with the patient of his or her life, is this the creation of a helpful myth? One or two people who have made contributions to CAT have come from a background of transpersonal psychology. Do their contributions belong to the 'A' part of CAT or is this something else? Is it just a humanistic environment in which the psychotherapy exists?

A.R. I am personally resistant to mystical elements, but favourable to humanistic ones. It is time somebody explored the relation of CAT to these, but it won't be me. As regards the broader question about myth, a brief reply would be that anything which human beings say, do, believe or experience is relevant to psychotherapy, whether it is systematised into a religious cult or belief system or an individual dream. They are all human productions; what we have made we have made. With a dream, however you understand it, you know that it is invented, and that is the interesting part to me. I would say the same with the myths of civilisation. But you're right to suggest some distortion or neglect of this area in CAT. The teaching of CAT has tended to emphasise the logical choice-making kinds of behaviour. On the whole we live our lives using a package of procedures which aren't very logical and which often incorporate personal myths, but we use them. But in therapy it is useful to look at them and trace them, because then you can stop doing the things you don't want. But that is not really a model of how we normally proceed.

T.L. Absolutely. The critiques of the information-processing models of the human mind are very important. I really don't think that we dream, feel, think in the ways they describe.

A.R. No, we don't usually, but we *can* do For example, scientific thought is a very peculiar, very structured, rule-bound way of trying to avoid certain forms of error. It is not know we think about our ordinary lives.

T.L. That is important. Logical constructions are *post hoc* structures which are imposed on the chaos of being.

A.R. Not only! The theory of CAT was not imposed on the practice of CAT, it evolved from it. We didn't have a theory and then invent CAT. We started doing it, and that made us think about what we were doing and so on in a 'to-and-fro' programme. The evaluation of the consequences of what we do is not just a *post hoc* exercise giving a magical sense of control, it can steer us through the chaos.

*   *   *   *   *

T.L. I am struck by your stress on the words 'AS IF' in the Psychotherapy

File. It suggests that a patient is in difficulties because he or she lives 'as if' such and such were true. They seem to me to be the most important words in the Psychotherapy File.

A.R. I'd like to explore this area of logic, meaning and experience rather more fully. We do use logical modelling in CAT, in the form of TPPs and SDRs, to show people how they produce the results they procude. The 'AS IFs' are part of that, implying a different assumption or perception, and this is an important bit of 'science' to be tested against experience. The reformulation letter takes us into the other field of how we might interpret the meaning of our experience differently. What we are doing there is enabling people to look at what they know through a different 'feeling lens', so it is an interpretation of meaning which has nothing to do with logic at all. Once you are into that, patients vary in the modes they can use to explore meaning. Some are wonderfully creative with words, some draw pictures. In the end people need every route they can find to make sense of their experience. I don't think we are the only experts on that, and we should not claim to be. But if you want to understand an individual, you need to take on board whatever makes sense to them, insofar as you can understand it.

*　　*　　*　　*　　*

T.L. Can we now explore the area of sexuality, as it is clear that the primacy of the sexual drive and its effects on object relations is a fundamental tenet of psychoanalysis. Character formation and symptoms are explained in terms of psychosexual development, and unconscious sexual wishes are a major target of analytic interpretation.

A.R. Well, we know sexuality exists from early on, and I think Freud was very helpful in making that common knowledge. Aggression is also a part of our basic make-up, a necessary and a dangerous part. There are also quite positive parts of us that are equally innate. Obviously the control of aggression and the shaping of sexuality were major parental and social enterprises in Vienna at the turn of the century, and there was a fair amount of hypocrisy and harshness. Freud's contribution was to make sexuality less frightening and less taboo-ridden, so that it could be thought about. Now we don't see so many classical Oedipal neuroses, and when we do it is because there has been a particularly seductive mother or a particularly threatening father or whatever.

T.L. Well, I certainly believe that changes in society must produce different character structure in individuals. Some changes, particularly those affecting paternal authority and society's support for that authority, will affect the Oedipal situation. However I also think the focus on sexuality is very important and relevant today: sex and relationships are primary problem areas for many people. It's as though in a more fluid, uncertain society, hysterical symptoms are less common but problems that have to do with a more primitive pre-Oedipal situation come to the fore. The Oedipus complex is about fixing a social structure in the individual's psyche.

Another vital area concerning modern psychotherapy is the sexual abuse of children by adults, and its damaging effects. As we know, Freud discovered early on that in therapy his female patients would recall forgotten sexual abuse by the father, and at first he thought this was the cause of hysteria. Later he rejected this theory on the following grounds: that there was reasonable doubt that the abuse had actually occurred in all the cases; that the unconscious does not operate by the logical rules of secondary process, and so it is impossible to distinguish between a memory of an external event and an emotionally charged fiction; and that therapies based on the seduction theory didn't reach a satisfactory resolution. We have a much better knowledge now of childhood sexual abuse: we know it is not uncommon, and I see no reason at all to disbelieve someone when they describe the abuse they have experienced. However the sudden arrival of a memory of this kind in therapy does worry me somewhat. This is because today there is a big revival of the idea that the trauma of abuse in childhood is at the root of most emotional disturbance. The revival is not just in professional circles but has a popular dimension. The whole area is a very emotional one, and in such a climate mistakes are made. I myself do not want to rule out the possibility that some memories of this kind are created artificially, and that they might be created out of incestuous wishes and phantasy as psychoanalysis has maintained. While I want to recognise that the dogmatic application of Freud's theory has often led to more abuse when the experiences of patients were disbelieved, I also think we all have unconscious incestuous wishes as children. The major variable is the behaviour of the adults in the situation.

A.R.   This brings us to what I think of the dangers of psychodynamic therapy. If you interpret events from early enough in life, before words or clear understanding, patients may start to think that what you say is the truth. I think there is much less danger in brief therapy, where we don't have time to implant memories! To go back to the general question of sexuality, I am perhaps more Adlerian than Freudian, because I think that the primary issues are ones of power and control, and that sexuality is one of the main arenas in which those issues are fought out. The model of human need seems to me to be around the issue of closeness-or-not—we all seek closeness to a certain extent though we also like to be separate— and around control and submission, where if power is more or less balanced, and not cruel, we can feel safe. Inevitably for a large part of our childhood we are in the relatively powerless position. So the way in which closeness and control get linked together is a central issue. One of the most profoundly controlling experiences is to be beaten up or sexually abused. The body which is intruded upon and hurt is going to get a strong message of powerlessness.

Whether every male child wants to have intercourse with his mother and kill his father I rather doubt, though some clearly do. I don't argue against the power of sexual phantasy or the power of desire of various sorts, but I also think that of every 100 referrals it is a *very* small percentage where that is the therapy issue. Most patients are dealing with the consequences of things that happened in childhood and are remembered by them. In short, I don't think Oedipal conflict is the universal problem without the analysis of which you can't be all right.

T.L.   You say that abuse reinforces a sense of powerlessness, and I agree. I have also found that it sometimes produces a feeling of power and control. The child seems to have felt 'There is something about me which causes adults to behave in this way'. This can produce feelings of responsibility and guilt around the abuse, especially if the child enjoyed the contact or the attention. I have known abused patients who felt there was something powerful about them which caused other to lose control.

A.R.   The reality of the relationship was one of powerlessness. But the sexualised child may indeed learn to use the power of sex to control others, or to revenge themselves, or as the *only* coin they know how to use.

T.L.   We've briefly discussed sexuality. I could pursue this because I really think there is something special, something primal, about sex in the human psyche; but I'd like to ask you about something else. So many people seem to have a deep sense of badness within, and I wouldn't find that so odd considering the climate of criticism and/or neglect that many children grow up in. But what really does seem extraordinary, and which analysis provides an explanation for, is that a two- or three-year-old child should think of herself as 'bad'. In Winnicott's account of the analytic treatment of a little girl, the Piggle, she talks about herself as 'bad' and 'black', and she is persecuted by a phantasy object called 'black mummy' who rides in a 'babacar'. It is clear that what has happened is that another baby has arrived, and she has been pushed out. She expresses that as 'I am a bad person' even at the age of three. The mother writes to Winnicott to say that her daughter has never been told she is a bad girl. She had certainly not experienced the contemptuous, dismissive treatment some children get; on the contrary, the parents are concerned and attentive.

A.R.   I think that children have quite clear conceptual limitations and don't get things quite right. They are more egocentric and take more responsibility for what happens. By three or four a child is perfectly capable of having a murderous thought, and of knowing it ought not to have such thoughts. It doesn't have to have been actually punished for the thought; it is taking responsibility for something it didn't actually do and doesn't distinguish between the desire and the act. Once you accept that that can happen, then we are all liable to feel guilty, because we are all going to have unforgivable desires to varying degrees. If you have been threatened with castration as a punishment then you are going to have such thoughts in a harsher form. I think the false attributions and the limitations of the child's ability to understand causality and responsibility are sufficient explanation for guilt which seems, alas, universal.

T.L.   It appears that you are accepting half of the analytic account and rejecting half. A child's misunderstanding of things and drawing false conclusions is a major part of analytic theory—for example when the girl's lack of a penis implies to the child that it has been cut off. What you don't like is the idea that we are predisposed to misunderstand things in a particular way, or that we come into the world ready to create a world of unconscious phantasy in which there are 'natural' equivalences, such as penis ≡ faeces ≡ babies and so on.

A.R.   You're absolutely right—I reject most of that.

T.L.   This brings us to a very central activity of psychoanalysis, that of *interpretation*. After all, psychoanalytic treatment consists in making careful interpretations of the patient's unconscious material, based on the free associations, and working through the resistance which is going to be there if the interpretation is correct.

A.R.   Or if it is *incorrect!* My own view is that interpretation is a dangerous act, because interpreted subjects are being told something about themselves which they can't know about. Even if it is tentative, and the patient is given a chance to comment, it is still a very persuasive act to give an interpretation which is supposedly related to one's problems. If a person is given an interpretation five times a week for several years, the acceptance of it probably has very little to do with its truth. I think my critiques of the Steiner and Joseph papers are really about my anger at the way theory seemed to me to generate interpretations which were profoundly negative and implicitly collusive. I think you can say the same thing about a lot of Freud's cases; he was clearly a persuasive interpreter. I think it is a dangerous act, and if we do it at all we should say 'It *could* be that this is explained in this way, but this is a hypothesis'. We should *not* say directly 'We have here your unconscious destructive impulses at work' or 'In phantasy you have incorporated your father's omnipotent penis'.

The offering of a description and a joint reformulation is actually containing and not too disturbing, because we don't insist on knowing what the patient doesn't know. We do give patients a language to think about what they know, and that often leads on to them knowing new things. I am not saying that we don't influence them, and that there is not some persuasiveness at work. But I think that to sit out of sight of a reclining person and to occasionally drop into the pool a distillation or interpretation is a very powerful thing to be doing. To sit next to a diagram and say 'Do you think that makes sense of what you do?' or 'Have we been around that loop today?' is very different, and to me it is nearer the ordinary way in which humans learn. It is by joint work and tools, which is the Vygotskian model and which is respectful. Now I'm not saying that it always works, and there are some people who may have to go into forms of regression. I am not sure what percentage that is.

T.L.   It seems to me that there are different kinds of interpretation. Perhaps some kinds of interpretation can happen safely in CAT. What about transference interpretations, which are made very frequently in psychodynamic therapy?

A.R.   They are central to CAT, like when you describe a loop as happening in the room.

T.L.   But that's different from a patient telling a story of something that has happened outside of therapy, and his being told that it is about what is going on between him and the therapist, rather than what it seems to be about in the world outside.

A.R.   It can be both. Not everything that happens is transference. But a lot of what you are told by patients is, or is a metaphor for, or an example of, something that is happening in the therapy. But procedures can be revised in daily life as well as in the transference. I had a lovely example of a metaphoric story in the last session with a borderline patient, who came in and said he was feeling pretty good. He had been re-tiling his bathroom, and when he had pulled off a little patch at the top he had found that they all had to come down because the whole wall was sodden. He had to strip the wall down and reproof it, and he had been very proud because he hadn't lost his temper. 'But', he added, 'there is still some more work to do after this session'. I didn't interpret it because I didn't think I needed to.

T.L.   It is sometimes better to talk about reality through an unconsciously understood metaphor, rather than to interpret unnecessarily. It reminds me of Bruno Bettelheim's belief that the vital role of fairy tales was to communicate understanding of children's concerns and problems in a symbolic form, when a talk directly would be far too anxiety provoking.

Also, in that way the child can choose what needs to be talked about, by insisting on a favourite tale.

A.R.   'Unconsciously understood' means to me 'that is an illustration of, an example of, an important issue or procedure'. Kleinians, however, do go quickly and directly into interpretation in child analysis.

T.L.   Yes, and Melanie Klein maintains that good interpretation of this kind is followed by a reduction in the child's anxiety and an ability to play more freely.

A.R.   Klein's bodily metaphors are probably quite accessible to children, without that meaning they represent the child's unmediated experience. There is no objection to metaphor in CAT, but also none to direct description.

T.L.   Is it the interpretation of unconscious wishes that you object to as being dangerous?

A.R.   No, I don't object to them, though I find unconscious motivation a slippery concept. I think that how you go about it is important. I quite like putting the idea of 'unmanageable feelings' in brackets in the SDR rather than saying 'Murderous envy'. Then you could say 'There is clearly something which you find hard to get into, probably for the reasons that we have gathered from childhood, so you seem to be doing this to get away from it'. That is a sort of permission for those feelings to be there. We can guess what they are, but we shouldn't be too quick to concretise them. But to accept that the patient feels that there is a dangerous, fierce, damaging, destructive, unmanageable core can be very important. I agree with the Kleinians here; it is very reassuring to be told that one's therapist understands how destructive one is. So in the end the SDR is quite a Kleinian instrument! It is a direct statement of all that is there.

T.L.   I agree about the importance of accepting core destructiveness. I remember a patient who told me at the beginning of therapy that she feared she was going to be in complete control during our sessions. She made a lot of attempts at sabotaging and destroying the effects of the therapy, and it was pretty clear that quite a lot of her behaviour was connected to a destructive rage. I thought is was important to keep acknowledging the destructive part, and she seemed to be saying that she needed that too. I asked her to draw her states of mind, and they were all as bad as could be. There was nothing good, and I think she couldn't draw anything good because I might have picked up on that and been deflected from the bad. And eventually she began to take responsibility for this part of her, but it had to be fully accepted first.

So, I am wondering, is it the intrusive and punitive aspects of interpretation that you object to, or the fact that a lot of interpretations come from a dogmatic adherence to theory?

A.R. Well both. And of course it is easy for interpretations of hostility to generate a paranoid response which seems to prove that the interpretations were right.

T.L. Do you think that can happen in CAT with descriptions of procedures? For example, I am wondering whether there is developing in CAT a kind of orthodoxy of 'split egg' diagrams where you immediately recognise the splitting between the idealisation and the denigration.

A.R. The history of the egg diagrams is a good example of how, without a concept, you don't recognise phenomena so easily. Until the egg diagram was formulated, therapists often didn't notice that there was a split. But having the concept it becomes a limit on what you can recognise, which is why continuous theoretical development is so important. I am now emphasising the need to look for multiple negative states.

I think CAT has taken the best out of object relations theory, and the SDR offers a much clearer picture of fragmentation and splitting than can be given verbally, and it gets away from the idea of motivated resistance and defence. I think the provision of accurate description and the image of the different self-states offers the first chance many patients have had to be *outside* the states. The combination of working together to get that description and of having a map of the self is, I think, our most interesting contribution.

*   *   *   *   *

T.L. Perhaps it is now time to try to answer the question 'How analytic is CAT'?

A.R. Why don't you give your answer?

T.L. Well, it is clear that CAT does owe a great deal to psychoanalysis, especially to those developments that stress the interpersonal. I would not want to say that it *is* a kind of psychoanalysis, but I do believe that the thoughts of those of us involved in CAT are not too far away from some of the British Independents. I think Christopher Bollas has said that most of his patients are consciously aware of and troubled by their destructive impulses, and that it is the love and creativity of the patient which is often missing and which needs to be acknowledged in the therapy. He also typifies a new kind of open-mindedness in psychoanalysis when he says that Freudian analysts ought also to be Kohutian, Kleinian, Lacanian, Winnicottian etc., because each of these approaches covers only a limited perspective. I think the CAT understanding of Projective Identification as a reciprocal role procedure would be acceptable to analysts in this tradition.

My own view is that psychoanalytic thinking is vital to CAT in two main areas. The first is that mysterious emergence into selfhood in infancy which I feel has a real bearing on our expectations of relationship in adulthood. Psychoanalysis is prepared to venture into the prelinguistic, and to acknowledge the effect of preverbal experience. I agree with you that it is not so much about recovering encapsulated memories, but I think it is about understanding how early experiences combine with phantasy and how that might continue to have an impact on interpersonal relations. The analytic literature is full of good ideas about this—for example, Bollas's concept of the transformational object, in which the other is experienced as the *process* of transformation. He contrasts the object of desire with the object identified as metamorphosis of being, and points out how the remembering of this object relation is not cognitive but existential, based on intense affective experience. Now I find this idea very illuminating and helpful in understanding patient's expectations of the psychotherapist. In a lengthy psychoanalysis it might be possible to remember early experiences; In CAT this is less important than providing a description of the effects of such expectations on a patient's life.

The other area in which I believe CAT needs to clarify its theory in relation to analytic theory is its account of how revising cognitions actually produces change. There has been a chasm of incomprehension between the analysts and the cognitive therapists about this, with the analysts rather looking down on 'symptom removal', and the cognitive therapists saying 'Well, if the targeted negative thoughts are gone or improved, what's the problem?' I think CAT has a real opportunity to bridge the gap. I think it is most important to distinguish between cognitive/perceptual processes that produce affect, which are very often not accessible to consciousness, and those that attempt to make sense of the affective state after it has been produced. The assumption, often made in cognitive therapy, that a person's theories about the cause of his emotions are the same as the actual causes, is not justified. Again, if someone who is depressed is selectively attending to negative cognitions, which have an unpleasant affective tone, then it must be an affective selection process which is admitting these thoughts to consciousness. It is also unclear that if one helps someone construct a new series of associations that the old ones will go away. In fact there is evidence that latent associational networks do influence behaviour and conscious thoughts and feelings. It has been widely found that people tend to develop self-serving attributions about the self, and if negative automatic thoughts were simple cognitive errors, they would surely extinguish. These attributions must have been adopted as a strategy; at some point it must have seemed less painful than an alternative course. They continue to operate, with the original reasons for the strategy remaining unconscious, and probably with new 'explanations' in place. If we postulate that these strategies were adopted in the intense and sometimes overwhelming milieu of childhood object relationships, then we have a profoundly psychodynamic theory. CAT does indeed address these issues with its concept of 'core pain' derived from Mann, and which is now often referred to in the reformulation as 'unmanageable feelings', and in its assumption that procedures which do not work have an historical explanation, and that the explanation is important therapeutically. The SDR is, for me, an important symbol of the permanence of a person's history. The old associational networks do not get erased like magnetic tape and get replaced by other 'better' programmes, but the picture can be modified, parts that were dissociated can be linked and so on. How these changes take place is a complicated question, I think.

It has been interesting having this conversation with you because we are not 'adversaries' defending positions. I have found over the five years in which I have been using CAT as a therapy model that it has been very helpful, even with people who might be excluded from, or would have difficulty using, analytic psychotherapy. I have learned how CAT works from my relationships with them. I value the flexibility, the potential for growth in CAT, and the importance placed on not knowing everything. I do think that a coherent theory to guide practice is essential, even though psychotherapy theories, especially with regard to how they deal with transference and countertransference, can be seen as defence mechanisms. Or as you put it, theory contains and holds the therapist. Which is a very psychoanalytic idea.

A.R.   I think we both agree that the issues raised in trying to answer the question are not done with, and I hope the discussion will provoke continuing dialogue. But I think I would distance myself from psychoanalysis more than you do.

I would say that the theory of CAT shares with psychoanalysis the notion of the developmental origins of personality, and of the link between the inter- and the intrapersonal, and that as regards practice, CAT shares the understanding of transference and its use. In many other respects, CAT offers major differences and can be seen to constitute a form of critique of established psychoanalysis. So if being analytic implies agreement with and acceptance by the practitioners and institutions of psychoanalysis, then CAT clearly does not qualify. I personally do not regret this. I think the time has come for psychoanalytic ideas to be part of general psychology and exposed to the intellectual challenge of other workers in the field. And the time has also come—indeed it is long overdue— for psychoanalytic practice to be evaluated alongside other therapies. The particular ways in which the ideas and institutions of psychoanalysis have evolved deserve study as part of the history of ideas, and through the methods of sociology and anthropology, but there is nothing sacred about them, and they may have served their purpose.

One could argue, of course, that CAT is a true bearer of the analytic tradition, maintaining the capacity for innovation and revision which was characteristic of Freud.

9 Auditing CAT

Francesca Denman

This chapter discusses the experience of setting up an audit of activity and outcome in two units which specialised in treating patients with Cognitive Analytic Therapy (CAT). The chapter focuses on the practical difficulties of auditing CAT and tries to draw out general implications for audit in psychotherapy.

General considerations

Increasingly audit is recognised as a vital part of medical practice. Its aim is to improve or maintain high standards of practice and to improve the targeting of limited resources. This is as true for psychotherapy services as for any others; Parry's (1992) path-breaking review of audit in psychotherapy ends with the trenchant remark that unaudited practice of psychotherapy is now indefensible. Indeed a number of features of psychotherapy make the use of audit especially vital. Psychotherapy is different from drug treatment in that the active elements are not prepackaged and quality-assured by a drug company before supply. Rather, the active elements are delivered as a skill by health professionals as they also are in surgery.

Maintaining the quality of the 'active ingredient' provided is therefore an important function of audit. In both surgery and psychotherapy new techniques are pioneered in specialist centres and then are spread more generally throughout the community of practitioners. In differently experienced

Cognitive Analytic Therapy: Developments in Theory and Practice, Edited by A. Ryle
© 1995 John Wiley & Sons Ltd

hands these new techniques may be expected to have differing outcomes. Quality audit is therefore vital to maintain uniformly high standards.

But psychotherapy differs from surgery in the nature of the kind of contact involved with the patient. In psychotherapy the involvement of the therapist in the therapeutic process (countertransference) is both important to therapy and problematic for it. The therapist's therapeutically relevant and emotionally laden involvements do not end with the patient; they may also extend to an organisational level (as it were 'organisational' countertransference) and investments in the organisation may bias or affect therapy. The starkest example of this process is seen in the tensions which develop in departments that are conducting research into different modalities of therapy. Audit in psychotherapy has a function in such situations because it can unearth unconscious counter-transferences and challenge received or entrenched ways of doing things. One example of an audit which surprisingly went some way towards achieving this aim is given in Denman (1993). I recounted the experience of doing an audit (in that case of audiotapes) which fortunately turned out to be detached from the emotional embroilments of individual cases but stayed close to the in-session concerns of the therapists. This feature allowed the audit to identify and address certain difficulties that therapists were having in a way which was immediate but which did not seem persecutory and which had not been picked up by supervision. As a result the organisation responded with considerable changes despite a number of glaring structural inadequacies in the audit process.

Psychotherapy also differs from surgery in another way. In psychotherapy a wide variety of conditions are treated with what seems superficially a similar technique. Worse still, the superficial similarity of the treatments offered gives way on closer inspection to considerable individualisation of formulations and therapeutic techniques. Personal factors in the patient and in the therapist take on an importance considerably greater than they have in other treatments. Because of this a further function of audit in psychotherapy lies in the hope that techniques derived from audit will assist the community of psychotherapists to improve practice and to 'prescribe therapy' more rationally. More abstract research than audit, and most particularly the use of randomised controlled trials to probe issues of differential efficacy, has resulted in a confusing and disappointing lack of clear results. Furthermore, and politically more significantly, research has had rather little effect on the actual practice of therapists. Several authors have discussed the inadequacy of the randomised controlled trial paradigm for research in psychotherapy (e.g. Fonagy and Higgitt, 1989) and particularly for research in psychotherapy which is intended to have clear practical application to the practice of psychotherapy in the real world. Audit, with its circular process of examination, organisational change/adjustment and re-examination might work to raise standards and outcomes where the more linear model of the randomised controlled trial had failed. This hopeful view of audit is taken by Parry (1992), but it may also hold dangers. Audit is not cheap science and good audit is more, not less, organisationally exacting to carry out than good science.

Auditing CAT

Despite the value of audit and the general esteem in which it is held, very considerable difficulties face the auditor in relation to documenting and evaluating the functioning of a department of psychotherapy. In order to illustrate the practical problems, I now turn to the description of aspects of the audit of two departments offering CAT at two central London teaching hospitals—Guy's and St Thomas's.

Three parameters define a comprehensive audit (Donabedian, 1988): *input*, which refers to the delineation of the resources available and their organisation; *activity*, which describes the activities of the organisation in delivering care; and *output*, which denotes the effects of the care on the patients' well-being and satisfaction.

Input data

The input data of the two organisations, which differed slightly, were described easily in terms of their salient features without formal survey. St Thomas's and Guy's both had departments of Cognitive Analytic Therapy under the direction of the same consultant psychotherapist who, along with other senior Cognitive Analytic Therapists, provided supervision to trainee therapists from a range of backgrounds. Most of these therapists each took on a few patients at a time without pay, in return for tuition; they performed the greatest proportion of the work of the departments. Some attempt was made to send more difficult patients to more experienced therapists. At that time one department (Guy's) took referrals directly (that is, without intervening psychotherapeutic assessment) from a general psychiatric clinic. A closer description of this service and its philosophy can be found in Watson and Ryle (1992), but in essence any patient referred as a psychiatric outpatient who was not judged in need of a specific disposal (admission, pills or systematic desensitisation for example) was offered CAT. St Thomas's took patients referred specifically for psychotherapy more generally from general practitioners and psychiatrists and screened those referrals at intake with an interview by a consultant psychotherapist. However, this interview did not constitute a barrier preventing access to treatment as the consultant involved rarely turned down patients for therapy and mainly offered CAT as a first intervention.

Activity data

Activity data, which included diagnostic, demographic and disposal data, were already being collected routinely at St Thomas's. At Guy's such data were collected using a computer system (CATsys) which had been developed by a member of the auditing team (C.D.).

In addition, a review was carried out of the quality of therapy. This was attempted by conducting a semi-formal assessment of the quality of the therapist's notes in a run of consecutive patients at each centre. CAT, unlike other therapies, lays great stress on the joint production by therapist and patients of documents (usually language-based) which constitute tools for new learning. These documents (the reformulation and the SDR) are meant to encapsulate a procedural understanding of the patients' difficulties. Therapy is focused on the procedures which have been jointly delineated and is reviewed at termination in a further document, the goodbye letter. As a result of the stress on these documents, their formal adequacy was thought to give some guide to the competence of the therapist in doing CAT and so, it was hoped, indicate the quality of therapy achieved.

The documents were inspected by five senior CAT therapists and were rated for a number of different features, including emotional impact, communicative appropriateness, cognitive clarity, and procedural adequacy. (See Ryle (1990) for a further discussion of these features in relation to reformulation.) Without knowledge of a case it is difficult to assess the accuracy of a reformulation in terms of its fit with the patient's story, so we looked for fit with the theoretical requirements of CAT and for internal consistency with other materials in the documents. Clearly, even if a reformulation possessed these features it might still be inadequate for the individual patient, so our criteria represented necessary but *not* necessarily sufficient standards for adequacy.

Output data

Data on outcomes were routinely collected at one centre (Guy's) in the form of a standard battery of tests which were administered at initial interview and at the three-month follow-up visit which is built into the format of CAT. The measures collected were: the Beck Depression Inventory (BDI) (Beck et al., 1961); the Symptom Check List 94 (SCL-94) (Derogatis, Lipman and Covi, 1973); the Inventory of Interpersonal Problems (IIP) (Horowitz et al., 1988); and a social circumstances questionnaire (SAS) (Weissman and Bothwell, 1976). In addition a record was kept of those patients who dropped out of therapy, including the number of the last session which they attended.

Results of the audit

Demographic data

Demographic data were gathered on 153 patients, which allowed some delineation of the demographic characteristics of the patients attending at the two departments. The centres operated different filtering systems before taking on a patient for CAT, and it was of interest to see whether the resulting case mixes would differ. In the event the centres did not differ with regard to the average ages, sex ratio and proportion of single people attending. Both centres had an equally high proportion of white British patients (75%), which contrasted unfavourably with the high proportions of other ethnic groups in the local areas and featuring as users of other parts of the mental health services. However, there were differences between the centres in relation both to the educational attainments of referred patients and to their socioeconomic status. The centre which took referrals direct from a psychiatric clinic (Guy's) had more patients with low socioeconomic class, and the centre which took referrals more generally (St Thomas's) had strikingly more patients with graduate status.

Waiting times

An attempt was made to collect data on waiting times for assessment and for treatment at the two centres, as an important parameter of quality of activity. However, we could not gather this information because a considerable proportion of the notes (or entries on the computer system) lacked accurate dates.

Quality of therapy

An audit of notes was carried out to look at the quality of therapy offered at the centres. Comparisons between the two centres were not possible because we could not complete interrater reliability studies to prove the uniformity of ratings. Raters noted a number of typical failings which were common to both sites. The most frequent failing identified in the notes was of a reformulation letter which embodied an empathic and seemingly accurate account of the patient's life and current target problems but which then failed to give an accurate procedural formulation either in the form of a set of target problem procedures or of an adequate SDR. In such cases the goodbye letter often had a sugary tone and failed to mention ambivalent or negative feelings about termination.

Outcome data on the patients at one centre (Guy's) existed for those patients who completed therapy ($n = 32$) and there was good evidence for improvement in this group. Follow-up measures were taken at three months post-therapy (at which time the patient also saw the therapist again for a further interview).

Pre- and post-therapy scores for the 32 patients completing therapy were analysed. The mean 'pre' (mean 1.61; SD 0.62) and 'post' (mean 1.31; SD 0.78) scores on the IIP were significantly different ($t = 2.27$; sig 0.025) as were the mean 'pre' (mean 1.40; SD 0.72) and 'post' (mean 1.04; SD 0.78) scores on the SCL-94 ($t = 2.67$; sig 0.008). The scores on the BDI were also significantly reduced (pre-therapy mean 19, SD 10; post-therapy mean 14, SD 10; $t = 2.77$; sig 0.006). However, the scores on the SAS were not significantly changed (pre-therapy mean 19, SD 9; post-therapy mean 18; SD 10; $t = 0.82$; sig 0.415).

In the absence of a control group, the falls in scores which signal immediate psychological distress (the BDI and the SCL-90) are perhaps less impressive than the fall in the scores on the IIP. This is because one might expect general distress to decline with time in any case but the IIP seems to measure long-term interpersonal difficulties. The social adjustment scale measured things like housing circumstances which would be unlikely to have changed in the timescale of the study.

There was some evidence that there was a link between outcome and quality of treatment offered. Drops in the SCL-90 and BDI scores were correlated significantly with the rated emotional impactfulness of the reformulation (0.46, $p < 0.05$ for the SCL-90; 0.41, $p < 0.01$ for the BDI). Procedural adequacy of the reformulation was correlated with drop in the SCL-90 (0.47, $p < 0.05$) and procedural adequacy of the goodbye letter was correlated with the drop in the IIP score (0.37, $p < 0.05$). Finally there was a correlation between a global rating given by the auditor to the overall quality of the notes and drops in the SCL-90 (0.51, $p < 0.01$) and the BDI (0.38, $p < 0.05$).

These five correlations between outcome and quality are encouraging but they need to be interpreted with considerable caution, given that a total of 21 correlations were calculated. Also it is always possible, especially with psychological variables, that, even if valid, the correlations do not represent cause and effect but instead are the result of a common relationship between the variables and a third unmeasured variable.

No demographic features predicted the outcomes of those patients who completed therapy.

Study of those who completed therapy did not exhaust the audit. One-fifth of patients who were booked in for therapy failed to attend their first session with the therapist and a further third attended the first session but dropped out later on. No audited feature predicted who would drop out from therapy.

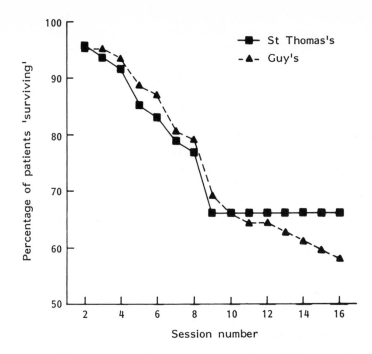

Figure 9.1: Survival curves showing attrition of CAT patients at Guy's and St Thomas's Hospitals

There were trends in relation to low socioeconomic class and severity of the initial condition, but these did not reach statistical significance. There were differences in the dropout rate between the two centres. At St Thomas's the rate of 'no-shows' to session 1 was 16% and of subsequent dropout 29%. At Guy's the rate of 'no-shows' to session 1 was quite a bit higher at 23% and the rate of subsequent dropout was marginally greater at 33%.

Although the data are marginal it is instructive to ponder the survival curves of patients at the two centres, shown in Figure 9.1. The graphs show percentage survival for those patients at Guy's and St Thomas's who started therapy (i.e. attended the first session). The increased attrition at Guy's can be seen to have resulted from continuing attrition after session nine.

The data on dropouts lent slight support to an impression which was prevalent at the two centres, that therapy was in some ways better conducted at St Thomas's and that there were fewer dropouts there. Certainly, in general, the therapists at St Thomas's were more experienced CAT therapists. However, the better results in relation to dropouts may relate only to differences in the sociodemography between the two centres.

Difficulties in conducting the audit

Therapist hostility to the process of audit, both passive and active, represented the single most important difficulty. Therapists as a group dislike filling in forms and tend to be lax about storing notes. Although, feedback to therapists generated enthusiasm for the audit process and less overt hostility to the auditors; sadly, this did not improve compliance significantly.

It should be noted that both centres were already under-resourced and there was no recognition of the fact that new resources were needed to conduct a successful audit. Secretarial and research time was grudgingly made available, and when it had been found it was often 'poached' for other activities. All too frequently the introduction of computers was seen as a way to solve administrative difficulties without there being a corresponding appreciation that computers needed operators and that data must be recorded in an appropriate format before it is entered.

While computers have more generally been seen as vital to the enterprise of audit, there are difficulties in retrieving from computers, in a useful form, the kind of unstructured text data which therapists feel is necessary. Computers also require specialised skills (fortunately now becoming more widely available) and in consequence many audit systems (including CATsys) expire with the departure of their enthusiastic but secretive creators. Furthermore computers rarely make the gathering of data easier than it had been by hand; rather they make the gathering of more data easier than it would be by two hands. So, while installing computers increases the potential level of output of a department, it does not make existing tasks easier to perform.

Audit is primarily a political and social enterprise rather than a scientific one. Its principal aim is to change practice for the better. In the pursuit of this aim it may be necessary to do things which would not be the best policy during a scientific research project—for example feeding back initial results to workers early in the process. The kind of data which needs to be gathered is local and not necessarily of general interest to the scientific community. These unglamorous features of audit are often minimised in departments of psychotherapy where the production of scientific papers is a chief aim but one which can turn out to be at variance with the needs of the audit process.

Lessons learned from the audit

The value of comparing services   The two-site model allowed audit to be conducted in the form of a natural experiment. The similarities of approach and leadership at the two centres allowed comparisons to be made between differences in organisation of the sort which had major service implications. Taking all patients not thought suitable for other treatments (e.g. admission or pills) from a general psychiatric clinic, which was the model at Guy's, and taking only those patients referred specifically for psychotherapy by psychiatrists and general practitioners, the model at St Thomas's, represent appreciably different models of service. That the results of the two services should be so similar suggests that the barriers to entry operated consciously and unconsciously by many psychotherapy services may be unnecessary and may deny treatment to a group who, in practice, could benefit. Chiesa (1992) researched the introduction of an initial barrier before assessment at a psychotherapy service. The barrier took the form of a request to fill in and return a questionnaire. Chiesa found that while the rate of failure to attend first assessment was diminished when the questionnaire was introduced, there was no evidence that the suitability for psychotherapy of the attenders was thereby increased and the rate of early dropout from therapy was also unaffected.

The importance of involving therapists in audit   The auditors and the audited must, if not already one and the same, at least stay in close touch. In the audit described here, therapists were heartened by the positive outcome results. Feedback of these results at a variety of formal and informal meetings diminished hostility to audit considerably. Sadly this did not in general stimulate an interest in the mechanics of audit amongst the therapists. Rather an 'expert syndrome' developed, with one member of the team (C.D.) becoming identified as the resident audit expert to whom all questions could be referred and then (all to often) forgotten. This meant that audit took some while to take off again after C.D.'s departure.

Conclusions

A 'warts and all' audit of Cognitive Analytic Therapy has been described. Many of the problems and limitations of the audit exercise will be similar for other departments of psychotherapy not practising CAT. However, some of the features of CAT should make it especially easy to audit. The use of measurement and monitoring is built into the structure and philosophy of the therapy, making compliance with auditing by both patient and therapist more likely. In CAT, specific documents are generated whose formats are to some extent defined by the requirements of an explicit theory, and this allows quality assurance monitoring to be attempted on the documents.

These audit-friendly features of CAT are perhaps not present entirely by accident. There are obvious links between the concept of procedural change in CAT and the idea of the audit cycle; if therapy is to some extent 'psychic audit', then audit can be seen (albeit fancifully) as therapy for therapy. Therapies need to be able to self-monitor and improve themselves and the audit-friendliness of CAT should be a positive advantage to both auditors and therapists.

The audit described here also shows how a relatively simple exercise of defining quality standards for the documents of CAT and the use of a simple and fairly standard battery of outcome measures can constitute the core of an achievable rolling audit for CAT. It would be valuable now for the community of CAT therapists as a group to define a basic audit package which should ideally be incorporated into the practice of CAT as a general rule. This might include the use of quality standards applied to audiotapes of therapy (which would clearly have advantages over audit of notes), but equally such an endeavour might be too time-consuming for routine audit. Naturally it will be vital to introduce regular reviews of the results of such auditing and to make sure that practice does change as a result. CAT therapists ought to be good at this; it is, after all, what they are meant to be doing in therapy.

Editor's note

A computerised audit system was established after Dr Denman's departure from Guy's, and therapist cooperation has been achieved. Therapist training and supervision have improved. Audit of the 1993 cohort of patients shows that the attrition rate of patients who attended their first session was only 17%, and that despite markedly higher psychometric scores at intake the scores on discharge were only marginally higher than before.

References

Beck, A.T., Ward, C.E., Mendelson, M., Mock, J.E. and Erbaugh, J.K. (1961). An inventory for measuring depression, *Archives of General Psychiatry*, 4, 561–571.

Chiesa (1992). A Comparative Study of Psychotherapy Referals. *British Journal of Medical Psychology*, 65, 5–8.

Denman, F. (1993). Quality in a psychotherapy service: a review of audiotapes of sessions, *Psychiatric Bulletin*, 18 (2), 80–82.

Derogatis, L.R., Lipman, R.S. and Covi, M.D. (1973). SCL-90: an outpatient rating scale: preliminary report, *Psychopharmacology Bulletin*, 9, 13–29.

Donabedian, A. (1988). The quality of care: how can it be assessed?, *Journal of the American Medical Association*, 260, 1743–1748.

Fonagy, P. and Higgitt, A. (1989). Evaluating the performance of departments of psychotherapy, *Psychoanalytic Psychotherapy*, 4 (2), 121–153.

Horowitz, L.M., Rosenberg, S.E., Baer, B.A., Ureno, G. and Villasenor, V.S. (1988). Inventory of interpersonal problems: psychometric properties and clinical applications, *Journal of Consulting and Clinical Psychology*, 56, 885–892.

Parry, G. (1992). Improving psychotherapy services: applications of research, audit and evaluation, *British Journal of Clinical Psychology*, 31, 3–19.

Ryle, A. (1990). *Cognitive Analytic Therapy: Active Participation in Change. A New Integration in Brief Psychotherapy*. Chichester, John Wiley.

Watson, J.P. and Ryle, A. (1992). Providing a psychotherapy service to an inner London catchment area, *Journal of Mental Health*, 1, 176–196.

Weissman, M.M. and Bothwell, S. (1976). Assessment of social adjustment by patient self-support, *Archives of General Psychiatry*, 33, 1111–1115.

10 Research relating to CAT

Anthony Ryle

The relation of psychotherapy research to theory and practice is a complex one. We are a very long way from being able to enunciate a theory of human nature and change which could generate hypotheses capable of elegant disproof through experimental designs. The attempt to emulate such designs has generated some distressingly simple models, but the pressure to demonstrate and measure what psychotherapy can achieve has nonetheless been a healthy one, providing some safeguards against the bias generated by enthusiasm for particular models (which is not to deny that such enthusiasm is probably a potent therapeutic factor).

The first presentation of a new therapy is usually in the form of individual case histories. When well observed, these can be as valuable as were the contributions of natural history to biology, providing the starting point for more critically designed studies of a number of cases through which some idea of the general effects of, and specific indications for, the approach may be gained. Traditionally the next step is a controlled trial comparing the approach with an alternative. While the placebo effect which confounds drug trials should not be a problem—for maximising the effect is a legitimate aim of psychotherapy—the standardisation of input (the same dose of the same substance) cannot be reproduced, each patient–therapist pair being necessarily unique. The matching or homogeneity of populations on the basis of psychometric and clinical data, already somewhat dubious in drug trials, is a real problem when one considers, to take one example, how many different human experiences and personalities may contribute to the development of

Cognitive Analytic Therapy: Developments in Theory and Practice, Edited by A. Ryle
© 1995 John Wiley & Sons Ltd

depression. The bulk of the research carried out in past decades on this model has failed to demonstrate clear advantages for any one approach over any other, although intervention is more effective than no intervention, and in a few cases particular treatments are shown to be better for particular conditions.

In the face of this, two trends have become dominant in psychotherapy research. The first is to standardise input by careful, detailed manualisation of procedures and by checking their delivery from audio or video tapes of sessions. Despite the risk of damaging the normal joint evolution of a working alliance by patient and therapist, this has led to a welcome clarity about the guiding assumptions behind different approaches. Associated with this has been an increasing concern with the microanalysis of the therapeutic process, through which the short-term effects of particular interventions can be assessed for their impact on, for example, the therapeutic alliance or the patient's reports of the session. The quality of small-scale interventions can, in turn, be related to outcome. The use of individually focused measures related to each patient's problems and designed to identify the specific kinds of change which the particular approach seeks to achieve can further strengthen such approaches (e.g. Curtis and Silberschatz, 1986; Goldfried, Greenberg and Marmar, 1990; Orlinsky and Howard, 1986).

In the present chapter, CAT-related research (not including individual case histories) is presented and reviewed. With hindsight, of course, (and with more funds) much of it would have been differently designed, but it can at least be claimed that the evolution of CAT theory and practice has occurred in a context where research has always been a factor. Rather than present the research in historical order, the following structure is employed: research influencing the model; descriptive, uncontrolled studies; controlled trials and studies of process and its relation to outcome.

Research influencing the development of CAT

A major influence in the emergence of CAT as an integrated approach was the work carried out over many years in which patients in weekly dynamic psychotherapy were studied simultaneously with repertory grid techniques. Grid methods offer patients a way of describing themselves and others, or, in the dyad grid (Ryle and Lunghi, 1970), their relationships with others. The analysis of grids generates mathematical or graphic representations of associations between the elements (people or relationships) and constructs (terms of comparison and contrast) and between elements and constructs. Much of this work was summarised in Ryle (1975), in which preliminary attempts to link psychoanalytic and cognitive descriptions were made. The main indirect effect of this work was that it showed me how much patients and others could learn from the act of completing a grid and from discussing the results after analysis. Patterns and generalisations which emerged from the systematic completion and analysis of the grid gave new and useful understandings to the person, understandings which were at once accessible and usable, and had nothing to do with the 'dismantling of defences'. And the dyad grid, in giving access to the patterns determining self-care and relationship with others, offered a new way of describing some of the ideas of object relations theory (Ryle and Breen, 1972; Ryle and Lipschitz, 1975).

Indirectly, therefore, repertory grid techniques, applied in this way, were both a source of integrative understandings and an example of how patients could be actively involved in self-observation, while the results of grid techniques represented a jointly created tool of value in the process of therapy. More directly, the initially descriptive uses to which grid results were put suggested ways in which, in outcome research, specific changes relating to the individual problems of the patient could be defined in advance so that the grid changes which should occur could be predicted. This opened up the possibility of matching the behaviourist's measures of changes in visible symptoms or actions with measures of cognitive or 'dynamic' change. To do this, however, an agreed definition of desirable change had to be arrived at, at the start of therapy.

A study of a set of notes of completed therapies yielded the three patterns of Traps, Dilemmas and Snags which were the basis of what became the reformulation process. Of these, Dilemmas can be seen to derive from grid techniques, in which the options open to an individual can be seen in polarised, graphic form (in the graph of the first two components) or mathematically in the form of unusually high or low correlations between constructs which suggest 'if-then' or ' either-or' Dilemmas.

The first paper based on these descriptions, linking patients' ratings of change in relation to them to predicted changes in construct correlations in the grids, showed that the changes were in the predicted direction in 27 out of 36 instances (Ryle, 1979). This paper, based on six patients, and a further outcome study (Ryle, 1980) established many of the defining features of what later became CAT.

Descriptive studies

Five studies describing the application of CAT to defined populations and reporting measures of change, but not offering controls, are summarised here.

A community mental health centre in Greece

Garyfallos and his colleagues (1993) reported a series of cases attending a community health centre in Thessalonika. The aim of the study was to measure change using a standard post-therapy interview, and pre- and post-therapy testing with the MMPI. At the post-therapy interview patients were also asked how well they remembered their TP and TPP descriptions, and how helpful they had found various aspects of CAT practice such as the Psychotherapy File, self-monitoring and diary keeping, rating sheets, the relationship with the therapist and the time-limit. The patients were diagnosed using DSM-III(R) criteria; they showed a predominance of anxiety and depressive disorders and a high proportion received Axis 2 diagnosis. Of 56 cases in whom Axis 2 diagnoses were reported, 17 met borderline personality disorder criteria. Patients were assessed two and 12 months after termination. Of 85 patients recruited, 10 dropped out of therapy and 11 remained in therapy at the time of writing. Of 64 completers, 56 attended the 2-month follow-up, and 33 of the 39 eligible attended at 12 months. Six patients at two months and none at 12 months requested further therapy, and recall of their reformulations was high at both follow-up occasions. The MMPI repeated at two months showed significant mean changes on nearly all scales and this was still true at 12 months. Patients' recall of the reformulation was good and the average response concerning the helpfulness of the various CAT elements was positive on both occasions.

Comment This study provides information about the patients treated and about the impact of therapy, and reports some data on patients' reactions to the therapy. It offers, therefore a (cross-cultural) 'yardstick' against which other services can measure their effectiveness, or in relation to which other approaches serving similar populations can be assessed.

Cases of deliberate self-harm

The application of CAT to patients admitted to hospital after episodes of deliberate self-harm is reported and case material described in Cowmeadow (1994). It was considered that CAT was helpful in its flexibility, early focus, rapid engagement and inclusion of problem-solving techniques. The fact that assessment and the brief or very brief interventions were carried out by the same person was important in this population of people who are characteristically very sensitive to rejection. The brevity and time-limit, however, may not have been helpful for some patients. Further material from this study is presented in Chapter 3.

Comment   This is a valuable clinical study of a poorly served patient group, in which the early focus on describing the long-term antecedents of deliberate self-harm seems to have been of particular value.

Childhood sexual abuse survivors

Clarke and Llewelyn (1994) report the treatment of seven female survivors of childhood sexual abuse with 8–16 sessions of CAT. Six patients completed therapy and measures of symptoms and of self-abuse showed improvement in the completers. Patients completed single-element and dyad grids before and after therapy. From these it was apparent that, while two of the women revised how they construed the relations of men to them, the view of how women related to men (as victims) was little altered. The authors suggest that some of these patients might have benefited from longer therapies, and that transference work with a male therapist might have been of benefit.

Comment   The use of multiple outcome measures in this study was important, in that the limited evidence of dynamic change from the grid prevented over-estimation of the effects of therapy. The grid data was not used in the reformulation process; its value in identifying the complex implications of victimisation is illustrated in the next paper.

Two women who stabbed their partners

Pollock and Kear-Colwell (1994) report the detailed grid analysis and the treatment along CAT lines of two women seen in a forensic setting who had stabbed their male partners. It provides an interesting extension of some of the issues raised by Clarke and Llewelyn (above). Both women experienced serious and prolonged abuse and both had experienced re-victimisation. The patients both completed role construct repertory grids with supplied role titles, including a number of versions of the self. Both patients saw themselves primarily as guilty offenders and, following their offences, were unable to see themselves as victims. Therapy focusing on the 'abusing–abused' reciprocal role procedure and on related procedures, and making use of Sequential Diagrammatic Reformulation, was effective in both cases. One ceased self-mutilation and was made an informal patient, and the other was discharged into the community. Both entered into new relationships with men, evidently on different terms.

Comment   This is a model presentation of the use of grids in the reformulation process of two very disturbed offenders. It suggests that the use made of grid techniques (as in the early stages of the development of CAT) as an aid to reformulation, and not only as a measure of change, should be more widely employed.

A CAT group

Duignan and Mitzman (1994) and Mitzman and Duignan (1993) report the first use of CAT techniques in group therapy. Each author was involved in one to three of four individual pre-therapy sessions, during which a psychiatric diagnosis was made, psychometric tests and grid testing was carried out and a reformulation letter and an SDR were agreed. Duignan and Mitzman report that three of the eight patients met borderline personality disorder criteria and one narcissistic personality disorder. Seven of eight patients completed the 12 group sessions, of whom only two requested further therapy. Psychometric scores fell significantly and changes in grid measures were of the same order as those reported for individual therapy in the study of Brockman and colleagues reported below. In the paper by Mitzman and Duignan the specific use made of SDRs in the group was demonstrated by following one patient through the group and showing how key interactions with others were explicable in terms of matching the two SDRs.

Comment   This study combines process and outcome measures and describes a new application of CAT methods. It has clear implications for practice. The audiotaped records of interactions in the group provided strong evidence for the relevance and value of SDRs.

Controlled trials

A hospital outpatient service

Brockman et al. (1987) report the outcome of treatment in 48 outpatient randomly assigned to either 12 sessions of CAT or 12 sessions of treatment following the model of Mann (Mann and Goldman, 1982). The therapists, trainees from various professional backgrounds, treated patients in both conditions under common supervision. Mann's model was chosen as it resembled CAT in the time-limit and the explicit sharing with the patient of a focal issue. Measures of change were psychometric (Beck Depression Inventory, General Health Questionnaire, Crown Crisp Inventory) and grid measures. The latter were based on a standard dyad grid and included nomothetic measures, namely Positive and Negative Self Attitude scores (PSA and NSA), based on the sum of the angular distances between the element self-to-self and three positive and three negative constructs respectively. Ideographic measures were (a) the Grid Prediction Score (GPS) based on the mean predicted angular distance change in construct correlations identified as related to the patients dilemmas pre-therapy, and (b) patient ratings post-therapy on Target Problems Procedures agreed at a pre-therapy assessment meeting.

There were significantly better outcomes for the CAT sample on the TP and TPP ratings, but these disappeared when initial score levels were allowed for. CAT produced significantly larger changes in the grid measures. Effect size calculations for CAT over the Mann condition were calculated as 0.53 for the PSA, 0.38 for the NSA and a little under 0.5 for the GPS.

Comment   While the design was intended to minimise the chance of showing a difference in outcome, it would have been stronger had it been possible to have the two conditions separately supervised by supervisors committed to their model. It is a pity that no dynamic therapists have used the grid as a means of measuring change. It seems likely that this study has demonstrated a real effect; CAT, with its explicit focus on aspects of 'cognitive structure', seems to produce more cognitive restructuring than a purely dynamic approach.

No formal replication of this study has been carried out, but in unpublished studies many patients have been assessed on similar lines. As in this study, the Grids Prediction Score was based on the analysis of self-to-other elements only, as in some cases the values of this differ markedly from those for other-to-self (an observation awaiting systematic investigation). Changes in the grid measures were in the same range, with the Grid Prediction Score usually being around 20° of angular distance, a figure is close to the standard deviation for construct angular distances in the populations studied. TP and TPP ratings are not now considered as research measures, as those devised by patient and therapist are better regarded as part of the therapeutic process. Intercorrelations between difference outcome measures seldom reach significance, especially those between grid measures and self-report questionnaire scores. It remains my view that grid techniques continue to give access to psychological variables of central interest to psychotherapists, and the failure of researchers in the field to utilise them or devise other methods of measuring 'dynamic change' is regrettable.

Poor self-management in insulin-dependent diabetic subjects

A sizeable proportion of insulin-dependent diabetic subjects have poor control over their blood sugar levels and are at greatly increased risk for serious medical complications. This results from their failure to carry out blood tests, follow diets and take insulin in appropriate dosage. The provision of specialist nurse education and other interventions, mostly behaviour therapy, have had little sustained impact on this patient group (Surwit, Scovern and Feinglos, 1982; Leventhal and Cameron, 1987; Bloomgarten, Karmally and Metzger, 1987). Measurement of haemoglobin A1 fraction gives a reliable indication of mean level of blood sugar over the previous three months and can be used to identify subjects at risk and the effect of intervention.

The causes of poor self-care are complex. Psychiatric illness is not a common factor, although depressive self-neglect may be one cause and neuroticism scores are moderately associated with poor control.

This problem has been studied over many years at St Thomas's Hospital in cooperation with Professor Sönksen and his colleagues, initially by Milton and subsequently by Fosbury. Milton (1989) described, through case vignettes, the many ways in which emotional and psychological factors can influence self-care. In an unpublished study of 32 patients selected on the basis of HbA1 levels of over 11% and randomised between CAT, intensive nurse education, neither or both, she showed that CAT, with or without education, produced a significantly greater fall in HbA1 levels at a 9-month follow-up. In an associated grid study she showed that poor self-management was associated with a negative construal of clinic staff.

Fosbury has followed this pilot study with a further randomised trial comparing nurse education and CAT (up to 16 sessions). Recruitment of patients who are, by definition, non-compliant, many of whom were secondary or tertiary referrals and lived far from the hospital, was not easy. Of those recruited, 50% showed medical complications and the mean duration of their diabetes was 16 years (range 3–30); their mean HbA1 level was 11.9% (normal range 5-7%). In this study particular use was made of SDRs, and the various non-compliant acts such as omitting insulin, over-eating and drinking were located on the procedural loops and hence linked with other aspects of self-care and relationship patterns. Case examples are reported in Ryle, Boa and Fosbury (1993).

Preliminary results of this study show that, while education is associated with a drop in HbA1 levels at the end of the intervention, this is not sustained, whereas CAT produces a significantly greater drop at the 9-month follow-up ($p < 0.02$) (Fosbury, 1994a).

In a linked study, Fosbury (1994b) has assessed 28 newly diagnosed cases of insulin-dependent diabetic subjects, with the aim of establishing how far it may be possible to identify those likely to have future problems in self-care. In view of the high personal and service costs of poorly controlled diabetes, this study is particularly important as it could open the way to intervention before negative procedures in relation to clinical staff and self-care become entrenched.

Comment   It is unusual to have biochemical outcome measures for psychotherapy, and it is gratifying that CAT seems to be the first treatment to
produce sustained alterations in patient self-care. If the full results confirm
this, this research could be influential in supporting funding for therapy in
medical settings. While diabetes is particularly demanding on the sufferer,
other conditions in which poor self-care is a serious problem might also benefit
from this kind of intervention. One such condition, asthma, is considered below.

Poor compliance with treatment for asthma

Bosley (Bosley et al., 1992; Bosley, Fosbury and Cochrane, submitted) has
carried out an investigation into the impact of CAT on treatment compliance
in asthmatic subjects, as part of a larger study of psychological problems and
compliance carried out with Dr. G.M. Cochrane (UMDS at Guy's Hospital).
Subjects' compliance was measured through the use of Turbohaler inhalation
computers, which recorded the time and date of each inhalation, without the
subjects being aware. Half of all patients omitted one-quarter or more of their
prescribed dosage. Non-compliant patients were offered counselling, without
the fact that their non-compliance was known being declared. The intervention
was focused on general issues of self-care, but including asthma management.
This was linked to the appropriate procedures described in the SDRs.
Compliance, measured in the Turbohaler computers, was significantly improved
by the intervention over a 12-week follow-up.

Comment   While its treatment is less complex to carry out than that for
diabetes, poor compliance is common in asthma and is associated with higher
rates of morbidity and mortality. This research reinforces the suggestion that
rational education needs to be combined with therapeutic approaches in many
medical conditions, and demonstrates that time-limited CAT can be an
effective intervention.

*Outpatient treatment of anorexia nervosa: a comparison of educational
behaviour therapy and CAT*

Thirty patients aged over 18 and suffering from anorexia nervosa were
assigned randomly to outpatient treatment with either educational behaviour
therapy or CAT, for 20 weekly sessions. Therapists were experienced in the
former but had only brief introduction and ongoing supervision in CAT. The
study supported the idea that outpatient treatment is suitable so long as
severely ill patients are excluded. The outcome at one year was similar for the

two groups on objective measures. CAT patients reported subjective improvement as significantly greater, and there was a non-significant tendency for fewer CAT patients to stay in the poor-outcome category.

Comment   This pilot study serves to demonstrate that CAT is at least as safe and effective as a more educational approach. The small size of the sample and the relative inexperience in CAT of the therapists are likely to have reduced the chance of demonstrating differences; it is to be hoped that further studies will be carried out.

Process studies

Self-state sequential diagrams and the self-states grid

Ryle and Marlowe (1995) describe five patients with borderline personality disorder in whom identified separate self-states were the elements in repertory grids completed by the patients. The descriptive features of the self-state, as recorded in the grids, were compared with SDRs constructed in the early sessions. The study showed that patients can discriminate between self-states in terms of constructs referring to mood, access to emotion, sense of self and sense of other. These descriptions, in most details, were consistent with those recorded in the SDRs, suggesting that the reformulation process was satisfactory; but the routine use of self-state grids during reformulation is recommended. The value of conceptualising borderline patients in terms of self-states and state shifts is supported by this study.

Comment   The SDR and self-states grid are not, of course, arrived at totally independently, as both emerge from the work of recognition and reformulation. The grid, in this sense, is a means of actively involving the patient in the process through a method which can clarify the discriminations made.

Impact of reformulation

Evans and Parry (in press) report a study of four patients with borderline personality disorder treated with CAT. The aim was to investigate the impact of reformulation of these 'hard to treat' patients. Three questionnaires were administered after each session (Personal Questionnaire, Penn helping alliance and perceived helpfulness of therapy ratings). In addition, 3–4 sessions after the reformulation letter was read out, subjects were given a semi-structured interview at which the impact of the reformulation was explored. The interview suggested a major positive impact from the reformulation, but none of the questionnaires recorded significant short-term impact. The authors consider how far this reflects the focus of the instruments used, and how far the impact of reformulation may be spread over the prior joint collaborative work and subsequent use of the reformulation.

Comment   This paper suggests an interesting area for further research.

The relation of SDR self-states to variations in transference and countertransference

Two of the five patients described in Ryle and Marlowe (1995; see also Ryle, 1995) rated their attitude to the therapist after each session on the Therapy Experience Questionnaire. Therapists similarly recorded their sense of each session on the Sessional Grid. Variations in scores derived from these instruments were related to the sequential diagrams. It was considered that the self-states and procedures described in the SDR served to predict and explain the interactions implied by the TEQ and Sessional Grid.

Comment   These papers offer further evidence for the accuracy and value of self-state SDRs.

The accuracy of reformulation in CAT: a comparison of methods for identifying recurrent relationship themes

Bennett (personal communication) and Bennett and Parry (in preparation) describe studies in which audiotape records of sessions 1 and 2 were scored using two established methods, namely the Core Conflict Relationship Theme method and the Structural Analysis of Social-Behaviour-Cycle Maladaptive Pattern. Comparison of the themes identified by these methods with those recorded in the SDR showed very high levels of agreement, indicating that it is possible for therapists and patients to arrive at descriptions of the patients' core interpersonal and intrapersonal patterns.

Comment   This work is part of an ongoing study of process from which a clear picture of CAT practice and clear criteria for measuring therapists compliance with the model should emerge. Incidentally, the standardised methods of identifying relationship themes are considerably more time-consuming than the reformulation process.

Current research

Three of the studies described above (those by Ryle and Marlowe, Ryle, and Bennett and Parry) are part of a long-term cumulative study of patients with borderline personality disorder (BPD), in which the overall impact of CAT will be assessed and related to process measures.

There are very few outcome studies of borderline personality disorder in the literature. The view generally held is that these patients have a tendency to drop out of therapy and that successful psychotherapy needs to be prolonged and intensive; three times weekly for at least four years is indicated according to Gunderson and Sabo (1993), although these authors report some slight support for time-limited work. Recent reports include that concerning the impact of 'dialectical behaviour therapy' (Shearin and Linehan, 1993), a model involving individual and group work (total about two-and-a-half hours weekly), usually for two years. They report positive effects over the first 31 weeks of therapy, associated with the patient's perception of the therapist as supportive and not critical. This behavioural approach pays considerable attention to the therapist's countertransference. Stevenson and Meares (1992) report on a series of patients treated twice-weekly for one year in a model derived from a range of self psychologies, in which therapists received supervision on audiotapes of their sessions. The subjects showed improvements on a range of measures and 30% no longer fulfilled BPD criteria at follow-up. CAT shares features from each of these two approaches, and comparison with the further work of the two teams, in terms of clinical method and outcome, will be important.

In the present study, patients presenting with BPD are recruited from outpatient referrals on the basis of a standard diagnostic interview. They are psychiatrically assessed and medication, if prescribed, is managed independently of the project. Routine psychometry is carried out. Up to 24 sessions are offered, the number being negotiated at around session 10, and follow-up sessions are offered at one, two, three and six months. The post-therapy research assessment takes place after three months, with a repeat of the diagnostic interview and psychometry and with a tape-recorded post-therapy interview covering all the issues identified at assessment or reformulation, on the basis of which both patient and therapist rate symptomatic and dynamic (procedural) change. All sessions are audiotaped and used for self-supervision; therapists each get 30 minutes of supervision weekly, in groups of three. Sessional audiotapes and the routine therapy documents and the questionnaires described in the papers reviewed above are also assessed as part of the process analysis.

Of 22 patients recruited to the project and attending the first session, two were referred out as unsuitable, two attended once only, one moved away and two dropped out, one of whom re-presented and completed therapy in the next year. Thirteen of the fifteen patients who have completed therapy have been assessed around four months after termination. Eight of these no longer met borderline diagnostic criteria. Two of these and the five with persistant borderline status were referred on for a variety of treatments. Five patients have been assessed one year later; all showed further reductions in psychometric scores and only one remained in treatment.

Comment   This is very much a work-in-progress report. The speed and detail with which the process and outcome studies can be accumulated will depend on whether research support is acquired, and long-term follow-up will be attempted. It does seem, even on what has been done, that CAT has a claim to be considered as an appropriate part of any comprehensive psychiatric service. Its ability to produce profound change in at least some patients in a six-month intervention reflects, I would believe, the powerful impact of reformulation in terms of the self-state SDR, but clearly this claim needs more research backing.

Future research

Despite its research origins, the momentum of research activity in CAT has been slow to gather speed. This can be attributed to the demands of service provision and of training and, of course, to resource limitations, but it is to be hoped that these excuses will have decreasing influence. The inclusion of a research component in the Advanced CAT training has already indicated that active curiosity can be combined with clinical skills, and some of these student projects may well develop into formal research enterprises. It may also be the case that, having achieved recognition as a defined therapy making claims which some see as outrageous, CAT will attract the interest of academic researchers with commitments to different approaches.

References

Bennett, D. and Parry, G. (in preparation). The accuracy of reformulation in cognitive analytic therapy: a comparison of two methods for the identification of recurrent relationship patterns.

Bloomgarten, Z.T., Karmally, W. and Metzger, R.N. et al. (1987). Randomised controlled trial of diabetic patient education: improved knowledge without improved metabolic status, *Diabetes Care*, **10** (3), 263–272.

Bosley, C.M., Fosbury, J., Parry, D.T. and Higgins, A.J. (1992). Psychological aspects of patient compliance in Asthma, *European Respiratory Journal*, **5** (suppl. 15).

Bosley, C.M., Fosbury, J.A. and Cochraine, G.M. (submitted). The psychological problems associated with poor compliance with treatment in asthma.

Brockman, B., Poynton, A., Ryle, A. and Watson, J.P. (1987). Effectiveness of time-limited therapy carried out by trainees: comparison of two methods, *British Journal of Psychiatry*, **151**, 602–609.

Clarke, S. and Llewelyn, S. (1994). Personal constructs of survivors of childhood sexual abuse receiving cognitive analytic therapy, *British Journal of Medical Psychology*, **67**, 273–189.

Curtis, J.T. and Silberschatz, G. (1986). Clinical implications of research on brief dynamic therapy: formulating the patient's problems and goals, *Psychoanalytic Psychology*, **3** (1), 13–25.

Cowmeadow, P. (1994). Deliberate self-harm and cognitive analytic therapy, *International Journal of Short-Term Psychotherapy*, **9** (2/3), 135–150.

Duignan, I. and Mitzman, S.F. (1994). Measuring individual change in patients receiving time-limited cognitive analytic therapy, *International Journal of Time-Limited Psychotherapy*, **9** (2/3), 151–160.

Evans, J. and Parry, G. (in press). The impact of 'reformulation' in cognitive analytic therapy with difficult-to-help clients, *Clinical Psychology and Psychotherapy*.

Fosbury, J.A. (1994a). Cognitive Analytic Therapy with poorly controlled type 1 diabetic patients. European Association for the study of diabetes, Conference Abstract, 27 September–1 October 1994, p. A175.

Fosbury, J.A. (1994b). Cognitive Analytic Therapy with poorly controlled insulin-dependent diabetic patients. In: Coles, C. (Ed), *Psychology and Diabetes Care*. Chichester, PMH Production.

Garyfallos, G., Adampoulou, M., Saitis, M., Sotiriou, M., Zlatanos, D. and Alektoridis, P. (1993). Evaluation of cognitive analytic therapy (CAT) outcome, *Neurologia et Psychiatra*, **12** (3), 121–125.

Goldfried, M.R., Greenberg, L.S. and Marmar, C. (1990). Individual psychotherapy: process and outcome, *Annual Review of Psychology*, **41**, 659–688.

Gunderson, J. and Sabo, A.N. (1993). Treatment of borderline personality disorder: a critical review. In: Paris, J. (Ed), *Borderline Personality Disorder: Etiology and Treatment*. Washington, American Psychiatric Press.

Leventhal, H. and Cameron, L. (1987). Behavioural theories and the problem of compliance, *Patient Education and Counselling*, **1**, O. 117–138.

Mann, J. and Goldman, R. (1982). *A Casebook in Time-Limited Psychotherapy*. New York, McGraw-Hill.

Milton, J. (1989). Brief psychotherapy with poorly controlled diabetics. *British Journal of Psychotherapy*, **5** (4), 532–543.

Milton, J. (unpublished). Brief psychotherapy compared with nurse education for improving diabetic control in insulin-dependent patients showing poor self-care: a pilot study.

Mitzman, S. and Duignan, I. (1993). One man's group: brief cognitive analytic group therapy and the use of sequential diagrammatic reformulation, *Counselling Psychology Quarterly*, **6** (3), 183–192.

Orlinsky, D.E. and Howard, K.I. (1986). Process and outcome in psychotherapy. In: Garfield, S.L. and Bergin, A.E. (Eds), *Handbook of Psychotherapy and Behaviour Change*. New York, John Wiley.

Pollock, P.H. and Kear-Colwell, J.J. (1994). Women who stab: a personal construct analysis of sexual victimisation and offending behaviour, *British Journal of Medical Psychology*, **67**, 13–22.

Ryle, A. (1975). *Frames and Cages*. London, Chatto and Windus.

Ryle, A. (1979). Defining goals and assessing change in brief psychotherapy: a pilot study using target ratings and the dyad grid, *British Journal of Medical Psychology*, **52**, 223–233.

Ryle, A. (1980). Some measures of goal attainment in focussed, integrated, active psychotherapy: a study of fifteen cases, *British Journal of Psychiatry*, **137**, 474–486.

Ryle, A. (1995). Transference and countertransference variation in the course of cognitive analytic therapy of two borderline patients: the relation to the diagrammatic reformulation of self states, *British Journal of Medical Psychology*, in press.

Ryle, A., Boa, C. and Fosbury, J. (1993). Identifying the causes of poor self-management in insulin-dependent diabetics: the use of cognitive analytic techniques. In: Hodes, M. and Moorey, S. (Eds), *Psychological Treatment in Disease and Illness*. London, Gaskell (Society for Psychsomatic Research).

Ryle, A. and Breen, D. (1972). The use of the double dyad grid in the clinical setting, *British Journal of Medical Psychology*, **45**, 483–489.

Ryle, A. and Lipschitz, S. (1975). Recording change in marital therapy with the reconstruction grid, *British Journal of Medical Psychology*, **48**, 39–48.

Ryle, A. and Lunghi, M. (1970). The dyad grid: a modification of the repertory grid technique, *British Journal of Psychiatry*, **117**, 323–327.

Ryle, A. and Marlowe, M.J. (1995). Cognitive analytic therapy of borderline personality disorder: theory and practice and the clinical and research uses of the self states sequential diagram. *International Journal of Short Term Psychotherapy*, **10** (1), in press.

Shearin, E.N. and Linehan, M.M. (1993). Dialectical behaviour therapy for borderline personality disorder: treatment goals, strategies and empirical support. In: Paris, J. (Ed), *Borderline Personality Disorder: Etiology and Treatment*. Washington, American Psychiatric Press.

Stevenson, J. and Meares, R. (1992). An outcome study of psychotherapy for patients with borderline personality disorder, *American Journal of Psychiatry*, **149** (3), 358–362.

Surwit, R.S., Scovern, A.W. and Feinglos, M.N. (1982). The role of behaviour in diabetes care, *Diabetes Care*, **5** (3), 337–342.

Treasure, J., Todd, G., Brolly, M., Tiller, J. and Denman, F. (1994). A randomised trial of cognitive analytical therapy versus educational behavioral therapy for adult anorexia nervosa, *Behaviour Research and Therapy* (in press).

11 Future developments

Anthony Ryle

Most of the work described in this book was accomplished during the past five years. During this period the demand for training in CAT continued to increase, putting considerable strain on the small band of teachers and supervisors, despite which time and energy were found to replace the old informal arrangements with a national organisation, the Association of Cognitive Analytic Therapists (ACAT). This body is now a fully professional organisation, responsible for representing CAT and maintaining standards of practice and teaching. This change was not without its costs and pains, both for the 'old guard' who saw cheerful discussions over dinner replaced by stern committees, and by trainees who experienced moving goalposts as training was increasingly formalised and its academic content increased.

There are now scores of CAT practitioners in various primary professions who have treated at least eight CAT cases under supervision and attended a variety of training occasions, and such training is now available in an increasing number of centres around Britain. The training programmes set up in Finland and Greece are now firmly established, and individuals in other European countries are arranging, in various ways, to get themselves trained. 1994 saw the graduation of the first students to complete an Advanced Training in CAT (a total of four years training). Their graduation allows them to register as psychotherapists with the United Kingdom Council for Psychotherapy.

Despite the arbitrary and unpredictable ways in which service planning in the altered National Health Service takes place, it seems likely that the

Cognitive Analytic Therapy: Developments in Theory and Practice, Edited by A. Ryle
© 1995 John Wiley & Sons Ltd

time-limited nature of CAT and the slowly accumulating evidence for its effectiveness will ensure it a place, probably a growing one, in the psychological services of the future.

In terms of practice, the distinguishing feature of CAT will continue to be the central role accorded to joint descriptive reformulation, and the use of this to enhance patients' capacity for self-reflection through its application to daily life and to the therapy relationship. As training continues to expand and as experienced practitioners are recruited, it is likely that both the basic CAT skills associated with reformulation and the component skills derived from cognitive, psychoanalytic and other approaches will be further elaborated and refined.

More work needs to be done on defining the problems of specific diagnostic groups and on the value of combining CAT with other approaches. It seems clear that some patients require a primarily cognitive–behavioural approach initially, before they can use CAT: examples would include serious substance abuse, profoundly limiting obsessional disorders, and some stages of anorexia nervosa or serious bulimia nervosa. Conversely, CAT may make some previously unreachable or unmanageable patients accessible for other treatment modes such as day hospital programmes or group therapy; this would be true, for example, of many cases of narcissistic or borderline personality disorders. Simultaneous treatment in CAT and other modes has not been tried systematically, but I have found the combination of CAT and Art Therapy to be effective in a number of cases. The underlying issues relate to two questions:

- How far can symptomatic disorders be treated by attending to problem procedures underlying the symptoms while not addressing the symptom directly?
- How far can time-limited CAT practice create the conditions in which access to repressed and feared affects become possible?

It seems clear that the CAT therapist should recognise those therapies in which additional strategies are called for, and that CAT research should aim to clarify these decisions.

The use of CAT methods in group therapy has been discussed in this book, and various ways in which this might develop will be explored in the next few years. There has been a fair amount of work with couples, but this has not yet been systematically recorded. Anecdotal evidence suggests that quite young children can use reformulation; it is to be hoped that here too some systematic observations will be made.

All of these future possibilities point to the need for more research, much of it initially at the level of careful observation and measurement in single case studies. The work with patients with medical conditions who fail to manage their illnesses satisfactorily might well extend beyond the important research reported on diabetic and asthmatic subjects. Such work saves personal suffering and resources, and also presents a role for therapy which even traditional, strict 'medical model' doctors can appreciate. Research associated with the ongoing study of borderline patients is yielding reliable ways of measuring process and 'CAT delivery' and will sharpen our capacity to identify specific CAT features and relate their presence to outcome, as well as giving detailed indications of how far CAT is effective in these patients.

As regards theory, the parallel work of other authors concerned to structure therapy around a few defined issues, and the work of others who combine psychoanalytic and cognitive–behavioural methods, will be of particular interest. It is to be hoped that mutual exchanges and challenges will clarify key elements and lead to the eventual integration of the integrationists. For the time being and for some time to come, however, I believe that CAT needs to preserve its own separate identity and to continue its dialogue with itself, strengthening those aspects which are unique to it and continuing to build on its broad and uniquely integrated theoretical base and its particular practical methods.

Index

Play R → Dual Drives — Oral Phase → Weon Breast
Oedipus ② Oral Phase → Vague / Innate Knowledge
Klein → Penis → Dominance of Persecuting Fear
Paranoiac
Frustray → Hates / Rectory → Bad Object
Good Exp → Bad Breast
Split Projecy

Later 'Klein' Envy: Paedet on breast
Proj I.P. Onto objects = (Freud)
Into Objects
Bad Breast
Induced to Act in Phantasy
Tit For Tat (?) Receipt! Empathy Induce
Counter Tx
Container — Container

Satisfying
Frustrate → Furious
(Ideal fantasy)
(Narcissistic)
Ideal? Self
Libido
Attitudes
Promiscuity

Balint — Baby < Harmonious Mix up > Trust
Absence → Basic Fault
(But) Needs Loving Rx Acting In!
Fear of Distancing — Cling
Closeness — Avoid

Weon K
(Repress
D.P.)

RACE Actor Imaging   Dreams Balanced vs Unbalanced
                HERO   UC →   Unconscious

JUNG   ANIMA 'She'/Galahad Animus
            SHADOW   Of Good/Bad Paranoia/Scz Klein

        Types   INTRO/EXTROVERT
                        NEUROSIS To BALANCE

    Last 35 Problems; In Last Resort — Find Religious View

Oxford 7th Ed.

Id Superego Ego → Internal Object Relation

? =

UC Conflicts

CHARACTER Anal
Anal
Syntonic → Disp

(+) Triangulated
3rd Part

vs Act out U.C

Censors

Ego TRANSFER P.S.

In Interactions with Parental figures
Infant internalises relay between
Self & Other — "Object" of fear/desire etc
Representation of Self ⇔ Emotions ⇒ Representation of Parental "Object"

Real & Phantasised Relations

Nurturing Self

Relues for some analysts Freud Anna

Freud p947 Certain Sex Sibling Rival Libido Degree
Incest Narciss

Ego → World

Id

Agency

Repress

True Hate

object

Late Freud
Self & Other L

+ Internalised Parental values in Super Ego

Infant UC Superego

Infant & Introject

Now Ego ID Internalised Self Way & Other

U.C

vs Split

Repress
Negate
Isolate
Project
Introject
Transform to Opposite
Rationalise
Intellectualise
+ Reaction Form → Dep D.

Sublim
D. Denounce
Ma Defender Compromise
Barriers

Current Reality

Defences Censors

Ego

Resist
Free Assoc
Basic Affects Ego Anx

Oppose but and Freud D = Affect

ID
U.C
Please

Repress
vs Super
Eg

D Hide Opposite evidence
2ry to U.C Trauma

True Oedipus
To Opposite Sex

- ve Oedipus (+
To same sex parent
Vs Rival Sex

E Ideal E Bad
Them & Bad ""
Not
Other
Self

Narcissm

Last Freud
: Splitting

Oedipus ⊙ Overome by IPE → Superego
Same Sex Parent